The First American

The Suppressed Story of the People Who Discovered the New World

By Christopher Hardaker

Foreword by Dr. Charles Naeser

New Page Books
A Division of The Career Press, Inc.
Franklin Lakes, N.J.

THE FIRST AMERICAN
EDITED AND TYPESET BY GINA TALUCCI
Cover design by Howard Grossman/12e
Printed in the U.S.A. by Book-mart Press
Photos courtesy of the Denver Museum of Nature and Science are credited as DMNS.
Photos courtesy of Cynthia Irwin-Williams are credited as CIW Collection.

To order this title, please call toll-free 1-800-CAREER-1 (NJ and Canada: 201-848-0310) to order using VISA or MasterCard, or for further information on books from Career Press.

The Career Press, Inc., 3 Tice Road, PO Box 687,
Franklin Lakes, NJ 07417
www.careerpress.com
www.newpagebooks.com

Library of Congress Cataloging-in-Publication Data

Hardaker, Christopher.
    The first American : the suppressed story of the people who discovered the New World / by Christopher Hardaker.
        p. cm.
    Includes bibliographical references and index.
    ISBN-13: 978-156414-942-8
    ISBN-10: 1-56414-942-0
        1. Indians—Origin. 2. Paleo-Indians. 3. Excavations (Archaeology)—Mexico. 4. Mexico—Antiquities. I. Title.

E61.H256 2007
972′01--dc22

2006103013

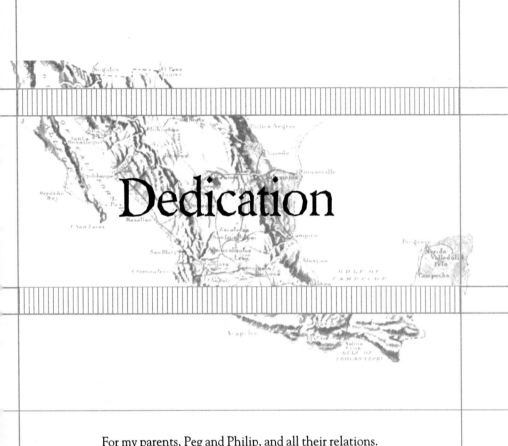

Dedication

For my parents, Peg and Philip, and all their relations.

Juan Armenta Camacho with
America's oldest art.

Acknowledgments

Many people are responsible for this story, and for getting it into print. Juan Armenta Camacho, the eye of the hurricane, passed away in quiet anonymity. Armenta was a loving family man, and the spirited discoverer of America's earliest art and America's earliest cultural region, a true hero who, for his reward, was fired. And to the being and memory of Cynthia Irwin-Williams, one of the finest dirt archaeologist in the Americas who found herself in the middle of the impossibility that just couldn't be; the surviving records of her work that survived nailed the archaeological reality of the discoveries, even though they were difficult to rationalize. Virginia Steen-McIntyre kept the legacy alive by publishing articles whenever she could, and was responsible for making that legacy known to the millions of viewers of NBC's *Mysterious Origins of Man* show in 1996. Without her participation, experience, and commitment to scientific truth, it would have taken another decade to put the puzzle pieces together, including her translations of key Mexican documents. She continues documenting the data on DVDs and at the Website *valsequilloclassic.net*. A profound gratitude goes to Marshall Payn, without his interest and curiosity, the Valsequillo discoveries would still be hidden in the shadows; he gave a damn.

And the dearest appreciation is offered to the late George Carter, for his life and tenacity in the face of great and impassioned resistance, and for the wisdom of asking a tenacious pit bull such as Marshall to look into the Valsequillo affair. Everlasting appreciation goes to Hal Malde, lead geologist, for his patience, knowledge, and wisdom in answering and re-answering questions about the geology of a befuddled mind; also to

Sam VanLandingham, who pushed the envelope by introducing microfossil investigations into the mix; to Robert McKinney, MIT geologist, a good friend and geological guide during and after the work; and to Charles Naeser and Barney Szabo for their knowledge of the affair and clarity provided during the research. Becoming an e-mail pal to legendary paleontologist Charles "Rep" Repenning will always be cherished.

I would also like to thank the INAH personnel that worked on the 2001 project: Mario Pérez-Campa, Patricia Ochoa-Castillo, Adrian Baker, Sabrina Farias, Edgar Nebot, paleontologist Joaquín Arroyo-Cabrales and his assistant was Valeria Cruz-Muñoz. And also the project director, Ana Lillian Martín del Pozzo (UNAM).

Likewise, thanks to historian Cyclone Covey for much-valued discussions at the beginning. Filmmaker Ted Timreck proved a valued ally and anchor while trudging through this unknown realm. I would like to thank Jane Day and R. Paul Firnhaber for their guidance and inspiration. Also, thanks to Edith Lowell for her translation of several important letters by Armenta during a hectic time—you were a real lifesaver. I would like to extend a special mention to the staff of the National Anthropological Archives in Maryland, where most of the historical material used in this book is now stored. Bill Cote produced a smashing private film keying in on the history and the ongoing debates about the sites. And thanks to my agent, the wonderful Maryann Karinch of the Rudy Agency. Also, thanks to Kristen Parkes, Kirsten Dalley, Gina Talucci, Michael Pye, Ron Fry, and the entire production and marketing team at Career Press.

And in general to the pre-Clovis pioneers, such as Calico's Louis and Mary Leakey, and Dee Simpson, who spoke truth to overwhelming power, and to old friends such as Fred Budinger, The Friends of Calico, and Richard Cerutti, who have hung in there under great duress while sitting on top of those very pretty artifacts that just can't be.

Contents

Foreword..9

Part I: America's Earliest Art...12

    Chapter 1.1: Two Old Bones 13

    Chapter 1.2: In a Perfect World..23

    Chapter 1.3: Juan Armenta Camacho and America's Earliest Art...........30

    Chapter 1.4: The INAH Field Trip...41

    Chapter 1.5: Cynthia and Juan Versus the Communists 49

    Chapter 1.6: Valsequillo's First Spearhead..56

Part II: Revolution...59

    Chapter 2.1: The First Peabody Excavations, 1962..............................60

    Chapter 2.2: Hueyatlaco, 1964 and 1966...87

    Chapter 2.3: "He Did What?!": Lorenzo's Vandalism.........................100

    Chapter 2.4: Barranca de Caulapan and the First Dates.....................105

    Chapter 2.5: Lorenzo's Wrath..122

Part III: Impossible...133

    Chapter 3.1: An African in the Mojave..134

    Chapter 3.2: Valsequillo: Coming of Age...147

Chapter 3.3: A Fork in the Road: Archaeology Versus Science.............................156

Chapter 3.4: The Dirt on Archaeology..174

Part IV: Valsequillo Rising...192

Chapter 4.1: Raiders of the Fringe...193

Chapter 4.2: Southern Revelations...203

Chapter 4.3: "Skull? What Skull?"..210

Chapter 4.4: No Big Thing...222

Chapter 4.5: Battleground for a Pleistocene America...............................227

Chapter 4.6: Unbelievable...231

Part V: The Puzzle Palace...241

Chapter 5.1: Negotiating the Impossible..242

Chapter 5.2: I, Species: The Mods...249

Chapter 5.3: What a Piece of Work Is (Pre-Modern) Man.....................254

Chapter 5.4: *Homo erectus popeyensis*..260

Chapter 5.5: The Revolution That Wasn't...270

Chapter 5.6: Dancing With Bison...277

Notes...288

Bibliography...296

Index...310

About the Author..319

Foreword

This is a book about our knowledge of Early Man. There are two subplots: Early Man in the Old World and Early Man in the New World. Much is known about Early Man in the Old World, where new discoveries continue to expand our knowledge base. Unfortunately, in the New World our knowledge is largely limited to Clovis and younger cultures. The study of potential pre-Clovis sites is not encouraged, and those who report a possible pre-Clovis site do so at significant risk to their career. An important part of this book reviews what is known about an Early Man site along the shore of Valsequillo Reservoir south of Puebla in central Mexico. It is a fascinating tale with a lot of data—which are accepted by most geologists and not accepted by most archaeologists.

As a scientist I am embarrassed that it has taken more than 30 years for archaeologists and geologists to revisit the bone and artifact deposits of Valsequillo Reservoir. In the late 1960s and early 1970s, data were presented that suggested Early Man had been in the New World much earlier than anyone had previously thought. Rather than further investigate the discoveries, which is what should have been done, they were buried under the sands of time, in the hope that they would be forgotten. My idea of science is to investigate anomalous data and hopefully learn something new. Unfortunately, the "Clovis First" mentality was so ingrained in North American archaeology that no further work was undertaken.

My first contact with the bone and artifact deposits of the Valsequillo Reservoir came in the early 1970s, when I was asked if I would date zircons from some tephra units (layers of volcanic pumice and ash) that overlay the artifact-bearing beds. I agreed to take on the study as I was aware of the controversy regarding the age of the site. At the time I was sharing an office with Barney Szabo, the geochemist who had provided the uranium series dates that started the controversy. His ages suggested that the artifact beds were in excess of 200,000 years old. This did not sit well with the archeologist in charge of the project. The original paper by Szabo, Malde, and Irwin-Williams (*Earth and Planetary Science Letters*, 1969 v. 6, pp. 237–244) sets the stage for the controversy: geochronology versus archaeology. This is the only paper of which I am aware where one coauthor submits a rebuttal in the midst of an otherwise straightforward scientific paper.

Additional data suggesting an old age for the deposits came shortly after the Szabo paper. Virginia Steen-McIntyre, while studying the characteristics of the overlying tephra units, discovered two things that suggested an old age. Although neither of the techniques she used provides a direct age in years, the results can be compared with similar material of known age and thus an age for the unknown deposits can be inferred. She found that hypersthene crystals in the tephras were deeply etched. Rather than being pristine, well-formed crystals, they resembled a picket fence. Hypersthene crystals from a 24,000-year-old tephra in a similar climatic environment elsewhere in Mexico displayed minimal evidence of etching, suggesting that the age of the Valsequillo tephras is greatly in excess of 24,000 years. Her second piece of evidence is from tephra-hydration dating, based on the amount of water absorbed by the volcanic glass shards in the tephras. When volcanic glass shards form, they typically contain minute gas bubbles. With time the glass gradually absorbs water. The greater the amount of water in the glass, the older is its age. Eventually, the gas bubble cavities begin to fill with water. This is known a superhydration. Bubble cavities in the two Valsequillo tephra layers that could be dated by this method contain water. Comparison of the percentage of water in the bubble cavities to the percentage in tephras of known age suggests an age of about 250,000 years for the Valsequillo tephras. Thus, by the time I got my zircons to date, three lines of evidence suggested that these deposits were greater than 200,000 years old.

I determined fission-track ages on zircons from two of the tephra units overlying the artifact beds. The Hueyatlaco ash yielded a zircon fission-track age of 370,000±200,000 years, and the Tetela brown mud yielded an age of 600,000±340,000 years. There is a 96 percent chance that the true age of these tephras lie within the range defined by the age and the plus or minus value. Now, there were four different geological dating techniques that suggested a far greater antiquity to the artifacts than anyone in the archaeological community wanted to admit.

Virginia Steen-McIntyre presented all of the results on the geology and age of the deposits at a symposium on New World archaeological geology in 1973. The following quote from a summary of the conference (*Geology*, 1974, p. 77) has been on my wall ever since: "C. Irwin-Williams, who did the original archaeologic work, believes that such a great age is virtually impossible, and that sources of error must be sought in the dating methods."

With the exception of a few papers by Virginia Steen-McIntyre in the geological literature, the unique and exciting discovery of an old Early Man site in North America ceased to exist. In my mind this is where the scientific method failed. There were geologic indicators that someone had been here 200,000 or more years ago. Unfortunately, the existing paradigm was that no one preceded the Clovis culture to the Americas, and that it was a waste of time and resources to even look for pre-Clovis sites. Through the scientific method of investigating the world around us, many paradigms have come and gone, being replaced with newer ones, such as the Earth and other planets circle the sun, the Earth is spherical, the continents have drifted, and evolution explains the great diversity of species. The idea of Clovis being the first New World culture needs to be tested, not just accepted.

I was pleasantly surprised a few years ago when I learned that Marshall Payn was going to revisit the Valsequillo deposits. A lot of new and exciting data has come from this renewed interest. Perhaps the most exciting is the data presented by Sam VanLandingham on diatoms (microscopic fossils) from within the artifact beds and overlying (younger) beds. He finds species of diatoms that became extinct about 80,000 years ago. That is another piece of geological evidence that indicates an old age for these deposits.

So, now we have at least five independent geological age estimates that all indicate an old, pre-Clovis age for the Valsequillo site. The factors that affect the accuracy of each of these techniques are so different that it is highly unlikely that all five techniques could significantly overestimate the age. One of my colleagues always tried to interpret geological processes using the principal of "Occam's Razor"—the simplest explanation is usually correct. In this case, we have the choice of accepting the results of five independent geological techniques as correct, and concluding that the artifacts are greater than 200,000 years old or, alternatively, arguing that, for very different reasons, there is something significantly wrong with each of the geological age estimates.

I think that the readers of this book will find that the Clovis First paradigm is listing badly, and quite possibly has sunk against the rocks of renewed scientific inquiry.

C. W. Naeser
Herndon, Virginia

Part I

America's
Earliest Art

The only thing new is the history you don't know.
—President Harry Truman

Chapter 1.1

Two Old
Bones

In 1959, two fossilized bones were discovered on opposite sides of the earth. Each promised to change the way we looked at human evolution. One succeeded; the other did not.

In June, Louis and Mary Leakey discovered "Zinj," a prehuman skull deep within Africa's Olduvai Gorge. Zinj, short for *Zinjanthropus boisei*, belonged to the genus Australopithecines, which immediately preceded our genus *Homo*. A year later, Mary happened across a couple of bones on the side of a road. They were much more human-like, the real tool users. They were knighted *Homo habilis*, Latin for "handy man"—the tool maker. For others, Olduvai George.

For 30 lackluster years, Louis Leakey remained true to his theory that east Africa held the keys that would unlock the evolutionary secrets of the human species; a generation of looking finally paid off. These discoveries established East Africa as the fertile crescent of human beginnings. Age estimates ran anywhere from 300,000 to 500,000y. Dates from a new technique called Potassium/Argon (K/Ar) that dated lava and volcanic ash said it was more like 2,000,000 years ago (2ma).

Africa's role in human evolution, previously considered a backwater, became paramount. It turned the archaeological world upside down. Because of the attention paid to this discovery, the past 50 years have witnessed countless African excavations paying homage to our premodern ancestors and their modernizing progeny. Africa's new fame owed it all to the discovery of a single bone.[1]

Two bones that shook up the world were found months apart in 1959. Top: Tetela 1, America's earliest art piece found by Juan Armenta Camacho, April 1959, Valsequillo River, Puebla, Mexico.

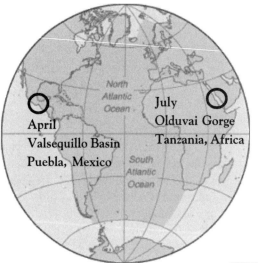

North Atlantic Ocean

July
Olduvai Gorge
Tanzania, Africa

April
Valsequillo Basin
Puebla, Mexico

South Atlantic Ocean

Bottom: "Zinj," a.k.a. *Australopithecus robustus*, found by Mary Leakey, July 1959, Olduvai Gorge, Tanzania. Zinj became a household name, alongside its discoverers, Louis and Mary Leakey. Armenta's engraved bone slipped into the dark. Now lost, missing, or destroyed, it was last photographed in 1978.

Photos:
Zinj: DMNS;
Tetela: David Hiser.

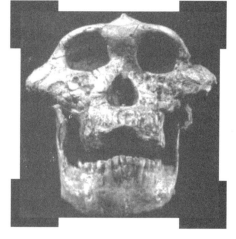

A few months earlier in central Mexico, self-taught fossil hunter Juan Armenta Camacho was prowling around the Valsequillo basin, about 120 kilometers southeast of Mexico City, a favorite haunt of his since the early 1930s. The hardened alluvial deposits of this ancient basin were a world-renowned source of Ice Age fossils: horse, camel, tapir, saber tooth cat, and three kinds of extinct elephants—mammoth, mastodon, and the four-tusked gomphothere (ryncotherium).

During his rounds on that April day in 1959, Armenta found a bone sticking out of the hardened sediments. He pried it free. Just another mineralized pelvis fragment from an old elephant, but he kept it anyway.

That evening he began cleaning the specimen, brushing off the gritty matrix still sticking to the piece. Then he saw them: engravings of extinct animals, such as a feline figure with spears running through its body, a serpent's head, a tapir, a short-faced bear, and several types of elephants.

Taking center stage was the incredibly ancient gomphothere, a four-tusked cousin of the mastodon, and recently given a cameo role in the Lord of the Rings series. It was gone from the States a million years ago, but apparently hung out with the other elephants in central Mexico a lot longer. Nobody knows exactly when it died out.

A year later the engraved bone was on exhibit at the Smithsonian Institution in Washington, D.C. It was given its own spread in *LIFE Magazine*. It was not a hoax. The art had been engraved when the elephant bone was still fresh, still "green." The elephant and the other animals pictured had all died out at least 10,000 years ago, marking the end of the Pleistocene Ice Age. The mineralized art piece had to be at least as old as the last Ice Age, if not older.[2]

Armenta's life of exploring and study had paid off. He always knew there were artifacts among Valsequillo's prehistoric bones, but the pros always snubbed his evidence. Not this time.

In Mexico, it was hard to get any more exposure than Juan Armenta Camacho received. His New World discovery was on par with Leakey's discovery in Africa. Each finding meant an entirely different thing, but each carried a TNT punch that shook the foundations of archaeology. Mexican scientists had judged that the Valsequillo beds could go back several hundred thousand years, perhaps to the beginning of the Pleistocene.

Almost simultaneously, two archaeological revolutions exploded on opposite sides of the world. Leakey and Olduvai Gorge became household words, and Armenta and Valsequillo drifted into nothingness. How come?

In 1961, the engraved bone was hallowed by the prestigious volume, *The American Heritage Book of Indians*. It echoes what many archaeologists and prehistorians were beginning to ponder about the Valsequillo discovery.

In the spring of 1959, at a site known as Tetela, to the southeast of Puebla, Mexico, four bone fragments were discovered, on one of which was engraved heads of a feline, serpent, mastodon, and hunting scenes, all executed with an extraordinary artistic capability, considering its probable age. The find was kept secret for more than a year while Professor Juan Armenta Camacho...invited preeminent specialists to study that which is perhaps a discovery that will mark a new epoch, which will likely be locked in the books of prehistory. The belief at present, based on geology and on fossils found in association with the engravings, is that they can be actually dated to the beginning of the long ice-free period [Sangamon interglacial] previous to the main Wisconsin glaciation. If it is true, they will prove to be of first importance, not only for the ancient history of America, but for the entire world.[3]

By 1967, three archaeological sites had been excavated at the Tetela Peninsula, all in the same geological deposits. One of the sites, Hueyatlaco, was about 100 meters away from the spot where Armenta found the art piece. All sites contained unmistakable stone artifacts, including sophisticated spearheads and flake blades, in direct association with Ice Age fossils. Known as the Valsequillo Gravels, the stratified deposits were composed of alternating channel deposits and related alluvial beds, buried one on top of the other. In turn, these layers were all buried under lake beds, a widespread volcanic mudflows and several beds of volcanic ash.

At the close of 1967, the Valsequillo discoveries threatened the "Clovis First" model—the theory of 12,000y mammoth hunters first excavated at Clovis, New Mexico. The Clovis had arrived with a full blown hi-tech stone technology that included sleek, thin, points with deep basal flakes called flutes. They conquered the hemisphere in about a thousand years. The theory had them arriving in the United States around 12,000 years ago. Initial dates from the Valsequillo Reservoir were 22,000y, almost twice as old.

An artifact found in a nearby arroyo had been shell dated by Carbon 14 to 22,000y. Were the Valsequillo sites on the Tetela Peninsula the same age? Were they even older?

Dating the Valsequillo sites became an unexpected problem. Many quietly disputed the geological link between the arroyo and the Tetela sites. Then they tried an experimental technique called Uranium Series on bone next to the artifacts. The dates: 250,000 years old, roughly; it was 1969. In 1973, a geological study of the archaeological beds demonstrated that the geology was a lot older than anyone imagined, older than anyone *wanted* to imagine, older than most *could* imagine. If the geologists were right, the hunters of Valsequillo were either Neanderthals or *Homo erectus*.

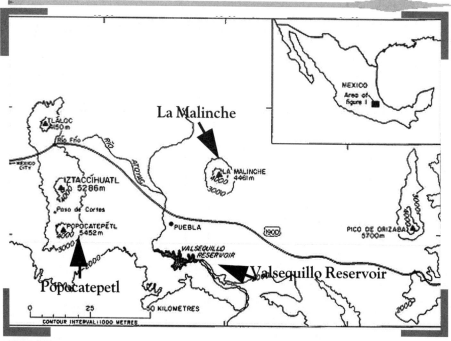

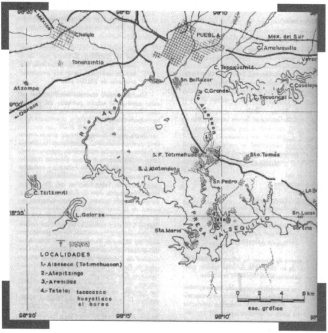

Precarious, but sexy. These are Armenta's maps showing the reservoir surrounded by volcanoes. Valsequillo's drainage system has been at work for hundreds of thousands of years. Luxurious for critters and their hunters, there are also plenty of volcanic features to date.

A Perfect Team for a Perfect Archaeology

Cynthia Irwin-Williams, a Harvard graduate student working on her Ph.D. with an already impressive scholastic and field resume, was chosen as lead archaeologist for the 1962–1966 Valsequillo project. Others affiliated with the project were some of the leading Paleoindian archaeologists, geologists, and paleontologists the United States had to offer.

Archaeologically, everything was in perfect order. The artifacts and features were unquestionable, clear, and self-evident:

❋ The artifacts and bones were buried in place.

❋ They were within a mappable geological formation of stream sediments and volcanic deposits.

❋ They were with artifacts becoming more sophisticated as time passed, from flake tools to retouched blades and then to bifacial spearheads; these were early technological transitions common to the Old World but never before seen in the Americas.

❋ The spearheads were more primitive than the earliest accepted projectile points made by the 12,000y Clovis hunters.

Everything pointed to archaeology older than the Clovis period. Everything pointed to Valsequillo as the paradigm buster, a site that would destroy the primacy of the prevailing Clovis theory. They only had to wait for the dates.

Then, thunder struck—250,000 years, give or take 50,000 years.

Then something stranger happened. The archaeologists walked away; they just went home. For them, the dates were so old that to take them seriously would impugn their own scientific credibility. In a 1968 letter to Dr. Hanna Marie Wormington, archaeologist Cynthia Irwin Williams warned that if the dates were published, "every reputable prehistorian in the country will be rolling in the aisles." So, the archaeologists left and never returned. Valsequillo was ignored totally, and an official report was never written up. The artifacts stored in Mexico, including Armenta's art piece, are now missing. After her death, Dr. Irwin-Williams's 3,000-plus field photos and slides, her daily field notes, and other primary data also disappeared. Plaster casts of a few artifacts, remaining archives, and photos and memories of surviving personnel served to piece this scandal together.

Mexico

For Mexican archaeologists, the word spread that it was all a hoax, that the artifacts were planted by laborers hired to work on the sites. Among U.S. professionals who knew the archaeologists, the planting scenario was not accepted but neither were the geological estimations of 200,000 years! Instead, a dark fog descended on Valsequillo. Scholastically, the region has been treated as a forbidden archaeological zone. Was it a conspiracy of silence among a secret archaeological priesthood, the original Skull and Bones society? Was it a case of institutionalized shock? Amnesia inspired by schizophrenia? Was it a "what will the neighbors say?" sort of thing?

However the situation is characterized, the U.S. community simply rejected the findings of the geologists, preferring to say that such conclusions were erroneous and impossible, and then, similar to dismissive youngsters in a sandbox, they took their toys and went home. According to Charles Naeser, a geologist involved with dating both Olduvai Gorge and Valsequillo: "While I would have thought these [200,000-year-old dates] would have stirred up a lot of interest—and they are very revolutionary concerning the evolution of man in North America—it appears that it just went off into a black hole."[4]

In the end, the archaeological community was willing to let the discoveries ride on the shoulders of the archaeologist in charge, Dr. Cynthia Irwin-Williams. She never published an official report, which is the duty of every archaeologist who digs at a site, and especially because it was these sites. In 1989, she finally resolved to complete it—something had occurred to her that might answer the riddle. A year later she was dead.

This is the story of a remarkable art piece, the folks who excavated the sites near its discovery, the additional artifacts they found, the geological studies that have been done, and the archaeological establishments on both sides of the border who veered away from answering the challenge the discoveries posed. It was not the only discovery in the Americas that questioned the official 12,000y limit for New World archaeology, but, as candidates went, the Valsequillo sites were simply the best, most perfect contenders for the pre-12,000y crown.

It is also a story of a concrete and unresolved breach between the geosciences and anthropology (which includes archaeology). Without overstating, it remains as much a conflict today as those early confrontations between science and the Church, over the concept of evolution itself. At stake is the failure of geology's fundamental premises, principles, and laws—if the archaeologists turn out to be right. If the archaeologists turn out to be wrong, they will have committed a number of academic sins, the greatest of which is hubris—that their theoretical structure for American prehistory, and of human evolution in general, was unassailable. The Valsequillo findings would tear that accepted evolutionary framework to shreds. Their corporate decision to forget about the discoveries—to dismiss the entire affair as "erroneous" and "impossible"—would critically stunt the growth of their own discipline for a generation. Had the archaeologists at least sought to resolve the anomalies presented by the geological sciences, it would have demonstrated the open-mindedness that is key to the practice of any science. Instead, the professional tendency over the years was to ridicule, demonize, and then ignore those who seriously asked: *What ever happened to Valsequillo?*

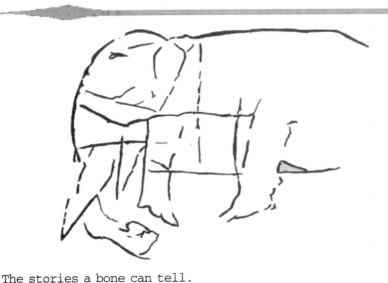

The stories a bone can tell. A Pleistocene bestiary caught Armenta's eye that night when cleaning off the bone. Top: the four-tusked gomphothere. Bottom:Armenta's discovery with carvings from a rubbing superimposed. Photos: Juan Armenta Camacho.

Top: feline figure pierced by spears. Bottom: individual elements from the mineralized art piece. Photos by Juan Armenta Camacho.

Nor was there the faintest professional interest in the discoveries when Irwin-Williams died. Among the many obituaries written for this great archaeologist, only one mentioned the word *Valsequillo*, and still only in passing. Further, no mainstream archaeologists took it upon themselves to continue her work to complete the report. As an archaeologist myself, it was frighteningly apparent that had it been left to the orthodox archaeological authorities—those who determine the proper subjects and limits for research and publications, the proper grant requests, and the proper Ph.D.s to award—*this book would never have been written*. In the decade that followed Irwin-Williams's death, there was every indication that the orthodox community regarded "the controversy" as dead. There even may have been a corporate sigh of relief. If so, it was short-lived.

Besides the fascinating chronicle that unfolds, there were immense implications unleashed from Valsequillo during the 1960s that have been left hanging, ignored, and unanswered by those we entrust with New World antiquity. The fact that it took a private citizen from outside the academic archaeology mainstream to take on the core issues of the discoveries speaks volumes. MIT-degreed engineer Marshall Payn, at the behest of a dear friend, took it upon himself to ask the right questions and seek the services of the right experts to test again the geological conclusions that were ignored a generation ago. By chance, he was able to recover Irwin-Williams's surviving notes, summary reports, letters, and photos before they were transferred to the Smithsonian archives. He also paid for a six-week excavation of Hueyatlaco, the most famous (infamous) of the Valsequillo sites. Beyond the geological information we could gather, perhaps we could also answer the question that was on everyone's mind: *Were there more buried artifacts at Hueyatlaco?*

Atepetzingo 1. A sketch of an engraved bone from a nearby tributary. Similar to everything else, this priceless artifact is also missing. If you look at the piece sideways you can see the head of a horse taking over almost the whole piece, and perhaps even a parrot in the middle. Photo: Juan Armenta Camacho.

Chapter 1.2

In a Perfect World

"Hi, it's Marshall. When can you get to Puebla?"

It was a warm Tucson morning in May 2001 when I answered the phone.

"Uh, about three days. Why? Did McKinney finally liberate the driller?"

"No, they're beginning to dig—trenches I think?" said the low-key voice.

It was hard to breathe. It's not often that things become as good as they can get, but things suddenly were. The first archaeological excavation at Hueyatlaco in 35 years was going to start in less than 72 hours, out of the blue, as far as I knew.

"Excavate?! What?! What? Who? Mario?"

"Yeah, Mario, the usual suspects," he said. "The same folks you met in December from INAH (Instituto Nacional de Antropología e Historia); Pati Ochoa, Adrian Baker, some others, including geologist Ana Lillian del Pozo, the principal investigator from UNAM (*Universidad Nacional Autónoma de México*). Anyhow, get down there as soon as you can. There's already a skeleton crew setting up. Get together with Virginia, she knows the town. See ya."

"Wait. But, but, but..."

"Yeah, what?"

"What about the driller, the, all that..." I stuttered.

"I don't know. Still locked up in Nuevo Laredo, I guess. Give me a call when you meet up with Virginia."

My mind was spinning. *It's on!* Not only was it on, but it was going to be a full-fledged excavation, not just an underground peak with slim cores.

Bob McKinney was a geologist and MIT school chum of Marshall's. I first met Bob and his assistant, Chuck Wilson, in Mexico City five months earlier on a December 2000 recon trip to the Valsequillo Reservoir. It was my first introduction to real Mexico, which for me was anything more than surfing spots up to 40 miles south of Tiajuana. My eight years of K–12 Spanish had essentially evaporated, so it was a relief that Bob was fluent.

The plan had been to use a two-man portable drill to sink a dozen inch-wide cores into the most productive of the Valsequillo Paleoindian sites, Hueyatlaco. I would be there to film the action and to look out for small chips of flaked stone. The idea slipped into the twilight zone when Mexican customs doubted Bob's sincerity. Puebla is famous for its mining, and there was a problem convincing Nuevo Laredo customs agents that the driller was for archaeology. Something akin to "fat chance," or "yeah, sure" kept coming up in spite of written assurances from the INAH archaeologists. During the months-long limbo, we decided to explore Puebla and check potential drilling sites at the reservoir.

Mario Antonio Pérez-Campa, one of the INAH directors of the 2001 expedition, picked us up at the airport, checked us in, and gave us about a half-hour before heading out for dinner with Pati Ochoa, the other INAH director. It's still a blur, but we ended up in a magnificent plaza with delicate hedge work surrounded by outdoor restaurants. It gave everyone a chance to discuss just what it was that happened nearly 40 years ago.

The Mexican take on the discoveries was drastically different than the one circulating in the United States. According to Jose Luis Lorenzo, the INAH archaeologist overseeing prehistoric projects at the time, several of the artifacts had been planted, and he said he had proof. Mario and Pati, students of Lorenzo, were left with this impression as well, but neither had seen any of the raw data collected during the 1960s. Nobody in Mexico had, except for Lorenzo. Nobody had seen any of the artifacts collected from the sites, either. Everything had disappeared. This included the mastodon's hip bone with engraved art—arguably the oldest art in the world, not just the Americas.

In 1995, the retiring Lorenzo decided to write the definitive report on the Valsequillo affair, roughly covering the years of 1960–67. He collected all available data, though not the artifacts, and carted them home to work on there. He died a year later.

It took some digging around at INAH and UNAM just to find this out, and when they did, Mario and the others asked Lorenzo's widow, Lorena Mirambell, if she knew where all the information was. She said she had no idea and did not care. "What do you want with that stuff?" she complained. "It was all a hoax, the stuff was planted! It was nonsense!"

Not really the response they wanted. She was, after all, a diva of Mexican archaeology with a lot of pull, so they left it at that for the time being. Nobody seemed to know where the artifacts ended up. And because the word from above said they had been planted, and part of a hoax, nobody seemed to question or care. In Mexico, the planting scenario was the Rule.

The idea of planting did not sit well with the U.S. community because that would mean several laborers with less-than-grade-school educations were able to pull the wool over the eyes of leading stars of U.S. archaeology and geology. Nobody in the United

States took Lorenzo's planting claims seriously—at first anyhow (and, according to Smithsonian archaeologist Dennis Stanford, many still don't). Lorenzo's fantastic and damaging allegations were filled with contradictions and lies that any second-year archaeology student could easily spot. For U.S. scholars, there were no qualms about the archaeology or the archaeologist in charge. The artifacts were certainly artifacts. There were plenty of photos, notes, and stellar witnesses to support the integrity and authenticity of the finds.

If the planting scenario *was* ever seriously considered in the United States, it was only *after* the impossible dates were announced in 1969. *Then* the planting scenario became plausible—a lot more plausible than the evolutionary implications of the dates reported by the U.S. Geological Survey geologists:

✳   250,000-year-old spearheads and sophisticated art.

✳   In central Mexico.

·   ✳   Made by prehuman Neanderthals or even *Homo erectus*.

It was the USGS's conclusions about the age of the sites that the U.S. archaeologists violently rejected. The artifact beds *could not possibly* be a quarter-million years old. For most U.S. archaeologists, it was a lot easier to believe that the project geologists had it all wrong. So, either the geologists totally blew it, or maybe, just maybe, those rascals on the Mexican labor force did indeed sucker-punch the U.S. archaeologist by planting the artifacts. For more than 30 years, the questions and innuendos quietly lingered until all traces of professional curiosity simply died.

Bob's cores would be a first step in unraveling the mystery. They would tell us if the artifact beds had indeed washed in at the end of the Ice Age (c. 10–20,000y), or if the artifacts really did come out of fossilized creek beds that had been locked up tight underneath a terribly old volcanic deposit.

Field Trip

The next morning we met up with Mario and Adrian at Cuicuilco, at the conical pyramid located next to the Olympic park in southern Mexico City. The pyramid had been covered by a lava flow, and Adrian had been placed in charge of excavation strategies. He had hired one of the best lava flow splitters in the city to help separate the lava from the masonry. Thanks to Marshall's support, they had been finding features that predated the pyramid by at least a thousand years, including the longest and oldest stele known in the New World, dated to about 2200 B.C. Beyond amazing, it is a truly romantic excavation that celebrates the grandeur of an ancient and unique pyramid covered in lava, and the culture that produced it.

Adrian was very hip to the cultural tensions existing between El Norte and Mexico. He did me a favor greater than he will ever know when he corrected my misuse of the word *American* as a reference to people living in the United States. "What you don't understand," he told me one day, "is that all of us in the Western Hemisphere are *Americans*. But you have appropriated the name like it only belongs to you, and that says volumes for the troubles our nations sometimes have with each other." It was at that moment that the separation took root in my mind. The United States no longer meant America, it meant gringo.

Joaquin Arroyo, an INAH paleontologist, arrived after our Cuicuilco tour and treated us to a wild ride from Mexico City to Puebla, pointing out volcanoes and other landmarks along the way. Halfway between, we stopped for an early lunch where I was introduced to *mole poblano*, a chocolate-based sauce invented in Puebla, on top of my turkey. I smiled politely. The restaurant sat on the saddle separating the Valley of Mexico from the Valley of Puebla. Joaquin pointed to the base of a hill south of the toll road. "That's Tlapacoya." Tlapacoya was Sr. Lorenzo's own nominee for the "earliest site in the Americas," dated to about 24,000y. Gringo archaeologists didn't buy it. The Mexicans still did.

When we arrived at Hueyatlaco, the reservoir was full to the brim. The old excavations were about 15 feet underwater. The local population had grown during the last 30 years, and the precious lakeside turf was being threatened by the local building boom. We were glad to hear that INAH recently used this high-level mark to define a new protection zone for the Ice Age bone beds that litter its shores at the lower levels.

After a couple hours figuring out the best places for sinking the core holes, the Mexican team returned to Mexico City. Bob, Chuck, and I stayed the night in Puebla, returning to Mexico City the next day on a first-class express bus that dropped us at the airport (two hours, 75 miles, extreme comfort, 10 bucks, deal). The reservoir work was planned for late spring in 2001, the "low" season.

Back in Tucson I spent the next months untangling a story nobody could have made up. As much a soap opera as scientific revolution, the story was full of archaeological giants, legendary characters from my pre-grad years. These were the cream-of-the-crop experts who specialized in the First Americans. This alone stimulated me because for the last 40 years, some of these same scientists had a penchant for dismissing any and all "early man" claims in the Americas older than 12,000y. How did they handle the news of clear geological evidence for an archaeology that dwarfed Clovis by more than a factor of 10! How did they handle being that far off the mark—as in 200,000 years off?

U.S. Valsequillo Project Personnel 1962–1973

PRINCIPAL INVESTIGATOR
J.O. Brew
Peabody Museum, Harvard

ARCHAEOLOGY
Cynthia Irwin-Williams
Peabody Museum, Harvard

H. Marie Wormington
Denver Museum of Natural
History, Project Advisor

GEOLOGY
Harold E. Malde
U.S. Geological Survey (USGS)

VERTEBRATE PALEONTOLOGY
Clayton E. Ray
Vertebrate Paleontology Division,
Smithsonian Institution

Mario Pichardo del Barrio
Virginia Polytechnic Institute
(Armenta's student; Ray's assistant)

VOLCANIC ASH CHRONOLOGY
Virginia Steen-McIntyre
USGS, Field Geochemistry and Petrology

MOLLUSCAN PALEONTOLOGY
Dwight W. Taylor, USGS

SOIL STRATIGRAPHY
Roald Fryxell
Radioisotopes and Radiation Laboratory,
Washington State University

PALYNOLOGY (Pollen)
Paul S. Martin
University of Arizona
Geochronology Laboratories

14-C DATING
Meyer Rubin
USGS Radiocarbon Laboratories

R.M. Chatters
Radioisotopes and Radiation Laboratory,
Washington State University

U-SERIES DATING
Barney Szabo
USGS Branch of Isotope Geology

ZIRCON FISSION-TRACK DATING
Charles Naeser
USGS Branch of Isotope Geology

NEUTRON ACTIVATION ANALYSIS
Gordon Goles
University of Oregon

PALEOMAGNETIC DATING
Joseph C. Liddicoat, USGS

It also included someone nobody ever heard of outside Puebla city: Juan Armenta Camacho. If every great story has its hero, Armenta definitely fits the bill. Without his discovery, chances are Valsequillo's basin would have remained untested. As the years passed, the newly constructed Valsequillo Reservoir filled up more and more. Until 1962, it was below 2,040 meters above sea level (masl). Later in the 60s, it was as low as 2,049 meters during the dry season. But currently, there is only a window of about a month when even the highest artifact beds at 2,055 meters are exposed above the water level. Armenta would have been the first to admit that it was a chance discovery, but it was his lifelong persistence, patience, and, most of all, love of prehistory that made it happen. He also left behind a monograph of his work and experiences: an edition of 1,000 copies paid for by himself.

Armenta embodied all that is true and good about science, of assuming the forced innocence of an open mind, of examining things and their implications regardless of the social (politically correct) consequences. His was a mind where science determined academic theory, not the other way around. Though an amateur, he was a warrior of knowledge, and would not be denied. I do not know whether to think of him as a victim of class warfare or professional jealousy, or maybe a little of both. He most certainly is a martyr to science. In truth, he was and remains a hero. When Lorenzo and INAH outlawed *this* guy, they not only confiscated all his notes and specimen collections, they stole the life and soul from a very devoted and very capable scientist. When they outlawed this guy, they shot themselves in the foot. His book, *Vestigios De Labor Humana En Huesos De Animales Extintos De Valsequillo, Puebla* (1978), remains a testament to his life's work and situates us decades ahead in Valsequillo research. According to Armenta, there may be more than 80 additional kill and butchery sites just beneath the water's edge.[5]

Valsequillo project geologist, Hal Malde, provides a glimpse of this extraordinary man.

> Juan, I believe, grew up in Puebla, and I suppose he completed his education at the University of Puebla, although I understand he never earned an advanced degree. Still, he apparently had the honorary title of "professor," and I think he must have taught some classes at the University. Juan was a good walker, and he loved to explore the countryside, which he would reach by taking the local buses. Of average height, with a trim build, he favored somewhat dapper attire. When going to the field he dressed as if on a safari, with brown broad-brimmed hat, bush jacket, and a musette bag over the shoulder. He sported a neat mustache and smoked a pipe (Mapleton blend, as I recall). Anything that entered the musette bag was taken at the end of the day to the regional museum where it was carefully cataloged and stored.
>
> Juan was very proud of his family. When I first met him in 1964, he lived with his family in the center of Puebla, near the University, in a second-floor apartment. This domicile consisted of rather small rooms crowded with keepsakes, as is typical of most Mexican homes, some of which were emblems of the family's Catholic faith. The children, from oldest to youngest, were Celine, Maricarmen, and Juan Manuel—all bright and well-mannered. Juan was kindly and humorous, and he liked to tell jokes, which he did with flair. He spoke good, hardly accented, English, and several letters from him show a good command of English vocabulary and grammar.

> As an assistant, he trained a much younger man, Juanito Hernandez, who looked like a direct descendant of the Mayans. Sadly, Juanito later defected and allied himself with Jose Luis Lorenzo at about the same time that Lorenzo brought his charges that artifacts at Hueyatlaco had been planted. I don't recall what Armenta did for assistance after that, but that was a time when he had been banned from Valsequillo in any case.[6]

Another hero of the story is the indispensable Dr. Virginia Steen-McIntyre, who kept the memory of the discoveries alive in a series of publications and television appearances during the 1990s. She was lead author in the second of two peer-reviewed geological papers written about the discoveries. She also translated Juan Armenta Camacho's monograph. She remains a potent advocate of the use of science to resolve the controversy.

To the distress and annoyance of many archaeologists, she was the only scientist who would just not go away. The feeling was mutual. The way archaeologists did science left her distraught. They never answered her questions, such as, "You're not going back?!" Worse, this geologist was an insider who worked on the project in the later years. She knew where the bodies were buried. UNAM Vulcanologist Dr. Ana Lillian Martin del Pozzo, 2001 principle investigator (PI), specifically requested her presence to identify the old trenches and artifact layers. In the final analysis, Virginia's articles, including her contribution to Michael Cremo and Richard L. Thompson's *Forbidden Archaeology*, and her TV appearances on Mexico's version of *60 Minutes* and NBC's 1996 "shock" science special, *The Mysterious Origins of Man*, introduced a new generation of Americans, on both sides of the border, to the unsolved mystery that is Valsequillo.[7]

The more I read, the more the Valsequillo Affair resembled a murder mystery. The true victim was not a person, but the principles and worldview of an entire academic discipline. When the ages for the sites were announced, either geology or archaeology died. The key principles and working frameworks shared by archaeology and human evolution disagreed to such a degree with the geological conclusions that both could not be true; 20,000 years can never equal 200,000 years—reality permits only one.

Today, both geology and archaeology remain viable and thriving disciplines, meaning one of them remains in a state of serious denial.

Thirty years ago, a science died. It was time to figure out which one. At first my loyalties were divided between my traditional roots in archaeology versus science, because, if true, Valsequillo science would leave those roots in ruins. If true, it would mean that the intelligence of our prehuman ancestors was greater than anyone wanted to believe or could believe. The more I found out, the more I understood that the Valsequillo sites were actually a crime scene—the crime of omission—and my loyalties shifted to the ancestors. At stake was a fundamental discovery revealing the last phases of human evolution, and the birth of those highly fissionable commodities: consciousness, intelligence, and language.

Chapter 1.3

Juan Armenta Camacho and America's Earliest Art

It was just another fossil-hunting day at the Reservoir. Riding home on the Puebla-bound microbus, Juan Armenta Camacho had no idea that the bone in his knapsack would shake the world. Later, he would say that it resembled any other fragment of an extinct elephant pelvis.

Every time he went exploring there was the hope that artifacts would turn up with the bones he found. Things he thought were artifacts had been shown to Mexico City scientists, but they were never good enough. He had found a piece of flint driven into a mammoth leg bone back in 1935, but that wasn't good enough, either. Now, on April 15, 1959, that was about to change. Puebla, the flashpoint of the Mexican Revolution, was about to host another.

"Who You Gonna Call?"

The 1940s and 1950s witnessed an expansion of the city of Puebla. When construction projects unearthed Pleistocene fossils, which was often, there was only one person to call: Juan Armenta Camacho. An accountant by trade, he was trained neither as an archaeologist nor a paleontologist, but he had done his homework, and did his best to keep up with both fields. His interest in paleontology was known around town, and he had a good reputation. During the mid-1950s, it became apparent that he was going to have to find a place to store and curate more than 3,000 specimens collected during the salvage operations in the valley. From Armenta's monograph, we learn how central he was in bringing the academic community in Puebla up to speed.

> It became evident that this area's paleontological wealth required more extensive and formal studies, and for that reason, and at the initiative of the author, in 1956 the Department of Archaeology and Prehistory (subsequently the Department of Anthropology) of the Autonomous University of Puebla was founded; and in 1958, the Puebla Institute of Anthropology and History (subsequently Central Region Puebla-Tlaxcala), became a branch of the National Institute of Anthropology and History [INAH]....Thanks to those new organizations, the systematic exploration of the area was enlarged, and they were able to better study the fossiliferous deposits of Valsequillo, which contain abundant remains of mammoth, mastodon, camel, various types of horse, glyptodon, peccary, bear, dire wolf, various types of deer-like animals, weasel-like animals, felines, rodents, and other animals of the Pleistocene Period.[8]

Juan Armenta Camacho was not your average weekend or summertime hobbyist. Fossil hunting was his life's blood, a vocation he often paid for himself, including the publication of his 1978 monograph. Armenta's history of paleontology in Puebla showed that the region was known for its "giants." Not only were there tales of huge animals, but *people* 20 feet tall. The native Mexicans often gave these large bones as gifts to the Spanish conquerors, and invariably turned up as gifts to Spain royalty.

The articulated clusters of bones he found at the Valsequillo Reservoir were always suspicious to him. He had found stone artifacts, but they were always rejected because surface finds could never be dated. To establish a connection between the artifacts and the fossils, they would need to be found in place (*in situ*), buried together in the sediments. In all likelihood, the stone artifacts eroded out of the sides of arroyos, but it was near impossible to prove. Instead, he began to focus on bone fractures and their causes, and reading up on hunting practices by hunting tribes.

The fossils were gently buried in sands, silts, and small gravels. For Armenta, it was plain to see that floods were not the cause of deposition, nor fracture. Bones break differently when they are fresh compared to when they are mineralized. Armenta was seeing green bone fractures, which break concoidally, similar to flint. When the mineralized bones broke, they crumbled. It was so obvious, he set out to prove it.

When larger bones are fresh they are very tough, as any marrow licker will tell you. Breaking them takes a lot of force, similar to the amount that would be used to break a rock. You can always cut it or saw it, which people did to make all kinds of things, from needles to spearheads. Bone served many uses, and some required fracture.

Every book Armenta ever read said that silty and sandy sediments always indicated a slow stream or creek deposit, not a flood capable of carrying mastodon bones! *What forces of nature could selectively pick out huge bones from their original resting place and redeposit them in a matrix of only sands and silts, and break them up at the same time?* It did not make sense.

Yet, this was exactly the position taken by some INAH officials as the cause for the many broken bones. For years he only heard, *Sorry, Juan, they all look like they have been naturally fragmented through violent floods and riverine transport; they are not artifacts.* So, he devised a series of experiments to test the natural fracture theory. Fresh beef and pork bones of various sizes were placed in cloth bags and dropped into the violent runoffs that roared through local arroyos after rainstorms, later to be collected downstream. Results: little or no damage, and no fractures. Similar observations were noted where fresh bones from city trash had been caught up in the raging torrents. None of these were fractured either, and these ranged from cow bones to more fragile chicken bones. Then he tried using a cement mixer, adding water, gravels, and pebbles along with fresh bones. Except for irregular polishing and a few bone splinters, the bones never fractured.

His experiments fell on deaf ears. He could never penetrate the official dogmas even when he described clusters of bones still in their anatomical position (articulated), such as entire leg components (such as tibia-femur-pelvic girdle combinations), or vertebrae columns still attached to the skull. In one instance, he found a complete, extremely fragile mouse skeleton in tact in the Tetela Peninsula deposits, the same that contained the art piece. Such a delicate specimen would *never* have survived creek or river transport. The Mexican authorities were unmoved. It had long been the consensus that the Valsequillo fossil beds were way too old to contain artifacts.

Armenta then studied the butchering practices of hunters and gatherers in Africa, because the African animals were fairly similar to the Ice Age mammals he was finding. He learned about what animal parts were taken back to the village and what parts were commonly left behind at the butchery site. He also studied the medical literature on traumatic fractures in large mammals suffered during the hunt, ranging from accidents to butchery practices. All of these indications told him that the fragmented bones could not be fully explained by transport during floods. For Armenta the broken bones, some of which matched bone tool artifacts elsewhere in the world, were likely due to the actions of man. He lamented:

> That thesis was not accepted by the authorities, who said that medical experiences are not applicable to Quaternary animals, and that these animals owed their death to floods (seeing that the zone was lacustrine), and that the lack of certain pieces, and

Juan Armenta Camacho examining a tusk entombed in the Valsequillo Gravels, a hundred-foot sedimentary column spanning the Pleistocene. Inset: The fragile, articulated skeleton of a small rodent found at Valsequillo testifies it was found where it was originally buried. This is an example of a "primary burial." Photo by Juan Armenta Camacho.

fragments with all their diverse forms and repeated modifications, including the supposed engravings, are owed to the transport action of the arroyos, to earth compaction, and to other natural causes.[9]

Riding back on the bus that day, nothing had really changed. While one or two of the experts in Mexico City may have been sympathetic to Juan's cause, they had not yet seen anything that could serve as absolute proof for Pleistocene artifacts at Valsequillo. Unbeknownst to him, all the absolute proof he would ever need was quietly tucked away in the bag beside him.

Surprise Discovery

Description

The specimen is a fragment of a mastodon pelvis, triangular in outline, whose rounded base corresponds to an anatomical edge. The other two sides of the triangle are sections of old fractures. Its two parallel faces are anatomical surfaces of which only one, the internal face, which is smoother than the external one, was engraved.

Dimensions

Height: 15 centimeters
Base: 19 centimeters
Thickness: 6 centimeters

Because this was the first time that an engraved piece of Quaternary age had been discovered in the New World, and owing to the large amount of publicity and international importance that has been given to it, the author considers himself obligated to supply the following research information.

Location of the Find

The piece was discovered by the author during a routine salvage trip, in a place 50 meters to the north of what was later to be the principle center of the Hueyatlaco archaeological excavations ("Valsequillo Project"). The find was situated at the foot of a small rise, where the Valsequillo Gravels crop out (elevation: 2,056 meters).

Stratigraphically, the piece was situated in the lower-middle Tetela Formation, where it was firmly embedded, showing only the anatomical edge. At the time it was found, the engravings were not observed. Not having any antecedent that would suggest their existence, the piece was not carefully examined. The work was recognized when the bone was being cleaned in the laboratory; thanks to the fact that the author accidentally used a tangential light, the engravings were thrown into relief.

Study of the Piece

Having no precedent in America for prehistoric engravings to serve for comparison—the only ones on record were some examples on view in museums in England, France, and Czechoslovakia, pertaining to other cultures and with other characteristics of workmanship—and given the lack of experience of the author in this specialty, he thought extreme caution necessary before making a public announcement.[10]

The engraved mastodon bone was in his possession for more than a year before the press got a hold of it. Puebla newspapers were the first to break the story, then LIFE Magazine announced it to the world in an edition that would stun the world (not the artifact, but the Marilyn Monroe cover), but still destined for greatness in the company it kept. That came a year later. Armenta realized he could have gone out right away if his true ambition was fame. A single phone call and—voila—LIFE and any other publication would have been on his doorstep for a photo shoot. All that eventually happened, but it wasn't important now.

For those unaccustomed to scientific etiquette, it is considered uncouth to go gabbing to the press the minute something of this magnitude is uncovered. It needs to be shared with your peers, colleagues, and others for both adulation and criticism. Call it a rite of passage. If you shout out on your own, it cheapens the find. In Armenta's way of thinking, it could be summed up in two words: bad form.

He had the foresight and the humility to request help from biologists, professional artists, geologists, paleontologists, and archaeologists from all over. Experts would be needed to authenticate and witness the find. In the first couple years after the discovery, he played host to a who's who list of Paleoindian experts of the day. From his Introduction:

Long before the "Valsequillo Project" [1962–66] was created, outstanding specialists repeatedly came to Puebla, who examined the field and laboratory work, verified the authenticity of the finds, and evaluated their cultural characteristics, including: Drs. D. Pablo Martinez del Rio, Hanna Marie Wormington,

Alex D. Krieger, [and] Manuel Maldonado-Koerdell,
who all supervised many aspects of the investiga-
tion; Luis Aveleyra Arroyo de Anda [and] Arturo Romano
Pacheco of INAH; Douglas S. Byers and Richard S.
MacNeish of the Peabody Archaeological Foundation;
Hans Jürgen Müller-Beck of the Berne Museum; Michael
D. Coe of Yale University; Helmut de Terra of Columbia
University; Jean Brunet of the University of Paris;
J. Cruxent of the Institute for Scientific Investi-
gations (Venezuela); Ruth DeEtte Simpson of the
University of California; Alberto Rex Gonzalez of
the University of Cordoba (Argentina); D. Pedro Bosh
Guimpera, Frederick Peterson, Kent V. Flannery, Carl
Schuster, Charles E. Rosaire, Ian Cornwall, and del-
egates of the Congress of Internationalists which
was held in Mexico during this time period.[11]

In between visits, he carried out his own research on the piece. To begin with, there was the question of when the engravings were made, relative to the death of the beast. Anyone could have come along after the bone was mineralized and engraved the characters. Or was the bone fresh when the engravings were made? This was the first thing to find out.

Genuine or Hoax?

The drawings on the piece included animals now extinct. Did this automatically mean that they were drawn by someone who saw them alive? Or could they have been drawn much later, after the bone had mineralized? Known archaeological sites in the Valsequillo region range from the Aztec period (1300 A.D.) back to about 6,000 years ago; you can still find recent artifacts and potsherds scattered about the surface. Maybe an Aztec farmer stumbled across the fossil and decided to engrave some pictures. Or perhaps it was a hoax.

This is where science kicks in. For Armenta, the first thing to establish was when the engraving took place. Was it scrawled when the bone was still fresh (green), or after it had mineralized? To figure this out, he experimented with fresh bone and mineralized bone. Was there some quality of the engraving action on the bones that would clarify the issue?

Armenta asked for assistance from colleagues at the Histology Laboratory of the School of Medicine and the Biology Institute (Autonomous University of Puebla). Experiments were carried out on fresh bone from the local butcher and mineralized bone from the Valsequillo Gravels. Microscopes then examined the differences.

In fresh bone, the burin (both flint and steel)
gave a groove bordered by minute facets and microscopic resilient filaments of organic material that

the burin was not able to extract. Meanwhile, in a fossil bone from Valsequillo, the [experimental] scoring by the burin was clean, and only altered by microscopic conchoidal chips, fitting for its mineral composition (which, according to chemical analysis, is apatite and calcite).

The best testimony that the bone...was engraved "fresh" is the microscopic filaments encroaching upon the engraved grooves that were fossilized at the same time as the rest of the piece, and that they have the same degree of mineralization as the rest of the bone.[12]

The next time you cook ribs, cut some of the bones with a knife before putting them on the grill. Get a magnifying glass, and what may have looked to be a clean cut will show stringy filaments still adhering to the sides of the groove. On the art piece, some of the grooves contained these filaments. The bone and the filaments inside the grooves were both mineralized to the same extent.

When the mineralized sample specimen was scratched, the grooves were fairly clean and filament-free because it was no longer fresh bone. The microscopic conchoidal fractures are a miniature version of what you get when you break a glass, shoot a BB through a window (the cone), or flake stone tools. The two kinds of wear, green versus mineralized, are totally different, observable, and measurable. Without a doubt, the bone was still fresh when it was engraved.

Next, Armenta took the piece to a professor of engraving at the Belles Artes Academy. D. Senen Sanchez Tostado reports:

It is appraised that it was worked with heavy lines and fine lines, both continuous, having twice scored points and small hollows. Parallel with some lines, a fine dotted line was observed that possibly was part of the sketch, just as some engravers still make. The figures are a fine piece of miniaturization, bearing an evident degree of stylization, as can be deduced by the cleanness of the lines and the sure execution of the curves. Whoever engraved it was a craftsman, knowing his material, and well mastering the burin.[13]

H. Marie Wormington: The Real Deal

When the art piece was first announced, Paleoindian archaeologist Dr. Hanna Marie Wormington was on the scene. A giant in a man's world, originator of the Blitzkrieg scenario of Siberian [Clovis] hunters screaming down onto the American

Plains, possibly wiping out Pleistocene beasts as they had babies by the busload and radiated throughout the Americas, reaching the southern tip of South America within a mere thousand years. Her classic book, *Ancient Man In North America*, with new editions every several years, was the standard reference on the subject.

Not bad for a girl who learned about archaeology listening to lectures outside the classrooms and seminar halls. (At Harvard, women weren't allowed to participate in these kinds of studies.) Persistence won her a Ph.D. and an appointment to Smithsonian West, aka the Denver Museum of Natural History. She opened the door for many wonderful scholars in the field, she broke the ceiling and provided ladders to those who had what it took to make the climb.

Fate helped because she happened to be in the right decade looking at the right stuff in the right place when Carbon 14 was invented. Finally, there was something to date the thousands of sites that were turning up all over the world. The only requirement was that it had to be organic, any remains from something that died: bone, charcoal, wood, even shell. Out west there were dozens of kill sites turning up with plenty of extinct animal bone to date.

The oldest dates routinely topped out between 11,000y and 10,500y. The First Americans were called the Clovis because they were defined by a distinctive spearhead first found in Clovis, New Mexico. They had entered around 12,000y, the transition from the end of the Ice Age (terminal Pleistocene), and were here for the birth of the modern period, the Holocene. Geologists regarded this warmer period as an interstadial, a short warm period between longer, colder periods. Right about the time they arrived, many megafauna became extinct around the same time: elephants, horses, camels, dire wolves—all large animals. All of a sudden...gone. Were they hunted to extinction? Was there some climatic catastrophe that robbed them of their foliage on a continental scale? Some of both? How to tell for sure?

Wormington was right in the middle of the debate, riding the cutting edge of one of the greatest unanswered questions in world archaeology: When was the other half of the world first settled? When did our species first arrive? When did they become capable of reaching the virgin land?

She remained cautious. The Blitzkrieg scenario had not been proven; it was little more than a hypothesis, a model. There were enough rumors, undatable artifacts, and other vestiges that hinted a greater antiquity. Without good dates, nothing could be said for sure. Now there were reports that an elephant bone from Puebla was engraved with extinct animals.

She had flown down to Puebla as soon as she heard about it, getting to know Armenta and looking at his collections. She returned, convinced that the Valsequillo Reservoir needed to be examined closely and carefully.

On the same day that *LIFE* published the photos of the artifact, U.S. Paleoindian experts, including her protege Miss Cynthia Irwin, received a letter from Wormington about her impressions from Puebla.

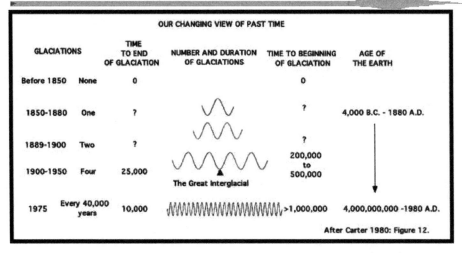

GLACIATIONS		TIME TO END OF GLACIATION	NUMBER AND DURATION OF GLACIATIONS	TIME TO BEGINNING OF GLACIATION	AGE OF THE EARTH
Before 1850	None	0		0	
1850-1880	One	?		?	4,000 B.C. - 1880 A.D.
1889-1900	Two	?		?	
1900-1950	Four	25,000	The Great Interglacial	200,000 to 500,000	
1975	Every 40,000 years	10,000		>1,000,000	4,000,000,000 -1980 A.D.

After Carter 1980: Figure 12.

What a difference a century makes. George Carter shows how our worldview of time has dramatically increased during the past hundred years. Although archaeologists did have recourse to tree-ring dating, the oldest dates trees could provide were rarely more than several thousand years. When Carbon 14 hit the stage we finally had calendrical dating tools that established when the Ice Age ended, when modern humans arose, and when the Clovis hunters arrived in the New World.

August 15, 1960 (excerpted).
Memo from H. M. Wormington, Curator of Archaeology, re: discoveries made near Puebla, Mexico, by Professor Juan Armenta Camacho.
I have seen much of the material that has been found and I have visited the site, and I do believe that Professor Armenta's finds are of great importance. Of major interest is the finding of a fragment of a pelvis of a proboscidian (no one knows whether it is mammoth or mastodon) with engravings that depict various forms of extinct animals. It was found in a formation (the Valsequillo gravels) that has also produced many crude bone implements, shaped by smoothing, and stone tools reminiscent of the chopper-chopping tools of southeastern Asia, which are also commonly represented in early Siberian sites. These gravels have also yielded the remains of 28 species of extinct animals. Dr. Manuel Maldonado-Koerdell, for whose opinion I have the greatest respect, has done the geological and paleontological

studies. He believes that this formation may be of
pre-Wisconsin age since it appears to underlie the
Becerra and the faunal evidence is consistent with a
Third Interglacial Age.

The Abelson test indicated an age of about 30,000
years for these bones. I know nothing about this test
beyond the fact that it is based on the rate of
change of six or seven amino acids. In the case of a
sample from another locality it did give a date of
15,800 while the C14 date was 16,000±. I have no
idea, however, how many tests have been run or how
much value this method may have.

Bone samples were submitted to the University of
Michigan Radiocarbon Laboratory some time ago, but it
will be months before a date is available. Humble Oil,
however, has agreed to accept samples for immediate
assaying, so a date should be available from there
before too long. Excavations during the last week have
produced charcoal which will also be submitted.

In summary: the carved bone must be of Pleistocene
age and is important as an early example of art in the
Americas. Geological and paleontological evidence suggests a probable Third Interglacial age, and the Abelson
test (of unknown validity) indicates considerable age.
Typological considerations would not be at variance
with such a date, and the study of stone and bone
tools will be of major importance. These statements
are not for quotation or publication. Any such statements should be obtained directly from Professor Juan
Armenta Comacho, Departmento de Antropologia,
Universidad de Puebla, Puebla, Mexico.[14]

Dr. Wormington's note to her peers was a warning to put on their mental seatbelts.
A third interglacial date (c. 30,000y–100,000y) meant that folks were in the Americas
well before the Clovis arrival of 12,000y. All this plus art! A dark cloud was forming on
the horizon, however. The bone sent out for dating did not have enough organic matter
left to date. Carbon 14 would be of little or no use, at least for dating the bone. For Yale
archaeologist Michael D. Coe, writing in his 1962 book, *Mexico*:

[The engraved bone] is the only specimen of art
representative of the Pleistocene Period that we have
for all the New World. It reminds one of the magnificent
incised art of the Upper Paleolithic of Europe, although infinitely more crude than any of them, and
reflects the obsession of both hemispheres for the hunting
of animals: 'art for meat' as it has been irreverently
called.[15]

Chapter 14

The INAH Field Trip

American archaeology was poised to take a step deeper into the past beyond the Clovis hunters. Once the art piece was authenticated by Smithsonian scientists, it was placed on immediate exhibit. Puebla newspapers continued celebrating their new status as "The Eden of the Americas." Meanwhile, Dr. Wormington and fellow Paleoindian expert Alex Krieger were busy looking for ways to fund a controlled excavation at the reservoir. Paleo-archaeologist George Agogino, from Eastern New Mexico University and director of the Blackwater Draw site (the original Clovis site near Clovis, New Mexico), offered the services of a good artist.

Dr. C. Vance Haynes was also involved by late 1960. He was one of the first American geo-archaeologists and worked out of the University of Arizona's Radiocarbon (Carbon 14) lab. He would become one of the staunchest defenders of the 12,000y "Clovis First" paradigm. In a January 1961 letter to Dr. Wormington, Armenta requested: "If it is not inconvenient, I would like for Dr. Vance Haynes to study the collection of artifacts, because he has kindly offered to reproduce some of them." A couple months later, Dr. Haynes and Armenta agreed that it would be a good idea to establish a national museum in the area devoted to the early prehistory of the Americas. In a June 1961 letter to Wormington, Armenta related:

> For lack of money, the project of the big Feria de
> 1962 has been dropped, and for the same reason, now
> there will be no possibility of founding here the
> Museo Panamericano de Prehistoria. The idea doesn't
> seem bad to me; Vance is of the same opinion. Perhaps
> you may accomplish it with the help of your friends;
> it would be a great work worthy of your prestige,
> which would perpetuate the enormous work of synthe-
> sis that you have accomplished. To create an institu-
> tion of this type has a special importance at the
> present, since the Prehistoric is the most continen-
> tal of all the cultures, and without distinction of
> nationality, all the countries of America feel proud
> of their heritage of the millenniums. Well, you will
> understand better than I the transcendence that it
> would have in the cultural life of the New World, and
> I do not believe you have need of my ideas. At any
> rate, they are at your disposition.[16]

Armenta's mind was a marvel. Transcendence of nationalism when doing archaeology, a common American heritage for all things prehistoric: what a concept. He was
way, way ahead of his time, and, similar to most folks disposed to enlightened thinking,
Armenta would pay a heavy price.

In late 1960, several INAH heavyweights asked Armenta to guide them on a field
trip to the spot where he found the engraved artifact. The field trip would include Dr.
Jose Luis Lorenzo, chief archaeologist at INAH, the same official who had ignored
Armenta's artifacts for years. For Lorenzo, Armenta was now a pest-turned-superstar.

Jealousy and envy, and the anger that accompanies the sudden need to save face,
were undoubtedly floating around in Lorenzo's brain. But there was something more
that ticked Lorenzo off: Lorenzo had assured Armenta and others that the reservoir's
fossil beds were just too old to contain artifacts. They were at least several hundred
thousand years old, if not a million. To his credit though, Lorenzo had not jumped on
the Clovis First bandwagon. He figured the earliest Americans could easily be 20,000y,
possibly even 30,000y. But 100,000y? 500,000y? *Patent nonsense.*[17]

Little more than desert scrubland in 1960, the Valsequillo basin became a reservoir during
the 1950s by damming up the Rio Atoyoc. Today, the area is rich in agriculture attracting a
growing population. The Rio Atoyoc drainage system had operated in Central Mexico for
eons. The basin was just one part of a much larger fossil rich region. In his monograph, Armenta
specified the significant fossil beds distributed in the Puebla-Tlaxcala Valley region.

> The Valsequillo fossiliferous deposits...form part
> of a biostratigraphic unit of wide distribution in
> the Puebla-Tlaxcala valley, according to the discov-
> eries that the author has made in the city of Puebla,

> in the quarries of San Felipe Hueyotlipan, and in the channel of the Zahapan River (where it intersects with the road to Tres Reyes) in the north, and in the east in the Barranca del Aguila (at an elevation of San Hipólito Xochiltenango), in the barrancas of Gorozpe, La Cantera de la Curva (near Tepeaca), in Pardiñez and in Tecali, to mention only the most abundant discoveries.[18]

The hardened sediments of the Valsequillo region contained a vast wealth of extinct bones that represented large sections of the Pleistocene. In 1960, the beginnings of the Pleistocene remained uncertain, ranging from 600,000y to 2.6ma—depending on one's opinion of the Villafranchian period. The Villafranchian was named from a geologic section in Italy signifying the rise of modern mammals, and was positioned between the Pleistocene and the Pliocene. For others, the Pleistocene was defined by the first appearance of the genus *Homo*.

The INAH Field Trip

The INAH-sponsored field trip was organized by Professor Arturo Romano (INAH, physical anthropologist), and included biologist Monika Bopp, engineer Federico Mooser, and archaeologist Jose Lorenzo, all from INAH. Ian W. Cornwall, a visiting British geologist specializing in ancient soils, also attended at the invitation of Ignacio Bernal, a noted and powerful INAH archaeologist (who did not make the trip). Armenta and his assistant, Luis Vasquez, served as guides to the artifact sites.

Among the earliest documents are short reports provided by Cornwall and Mooser, who wrote their impressions on December 7, 1960. The Valsequillo gravels were described by Cornwall as:

> A lime cemented breccia, below 7-8 meters of volcanic pumice, yields bones of Mastodon, Elephas Cameluss, a large Bovid, Equus, etc. together with the supposed implements, made from a pale tabular chert of Cretaceous origin. The breccia also contains a large percentage of black banded chert and a few very fine-grained buff-colored andesite pebbles.[19]

Ing. Mooser also described the implications of artifacts in the sediments. At one of Armenta's sites in the deep arroyo (barranca) of Alseseca, the sediments were equated with those allegedly containing the elephant bone art piece. For Mooser:

> The association of fossils found in these deposits
> indicates their age as Plio-Pleistocene; Osborne
> [Osborn] and Aguilera [previous investigators, ca.
> 1900] had already defined it as lower Pleistocene and
> possibly somewhat older. Thus the human implements
> would have an age of at least 600,000 years. In addi-
> tion, the petrology of the fragments of the deposit,
> mostly of silex [chert] of sedimentary origin
> (cretaceous)...indicates that when these deposits were
> formed the major volcanoes of the Clarion Fracture
> Zone had not yet been formed. Their typically porphy-
> ritic andesites are not present in the river beds.
> These facts imply that any human beings who might have
> lived at the time that the river deposits were formed
> never saw the volcanoes of Popocatepetl or Malinche.[20]

Mooser questioned the stone artifacts Armenta found in this arroyo, thinking they were probably nature-facts in light of the extreme antiquity of the sediments. "It seems likely that at the time the conglomerate was deposited, the silex fragments were shattered in such a way by fluvial [stream] activity as to give the impression of human artefacts."

Cornwall adds that the Plio-Pleistocene boundary is not clear, mentioning the two competing theories about the length of the Pleistocene. A European consensus figured the boundary to correspond to the beginning of the Alpine Gunz glaciation, or about 600,000y. The "1948 (London) Intl. Geological Conference had decided by a majority to include the whole of the Villafranchian stage (perhaps another 2 million years) in the Pleistocene." This would make the length of the Pleistocene about 3 million years.

As such, Cornwall was met with two choices:

❖ If the Plio-Pleistocene boundary was more than 2ma, there was no way these were artifacts because—in 1960—no hominids had been found to be that old

❖ If the boundary was 600,000y, then "it was possible that industries con-temporary with the European Abbevillian or the African Kamasian or the Indian Soan should be found. One would expect pebble-choppers and chopping tools as a first industrial manifestation at this early stage."[21]

If the 600,000y dates for the Valsequillo Formation were true, the artifacts would have to belong to *Homo erectus*, including the art pieces. Although a *Homo erectus* population might explain Armenta's crude stone artifacts, there was no precedent for *Homo erectus* art, and the engravings had convinced all that the hand that made them must have been a modern person similar to you and me: *Homo sapiens*.

This may have been a tenable proposition for Cornwall, but he would have been hard-pressed to find a New World archaeologist who agreed with him. The idea that prehumans could have made the trip to the New World 600,000 years ago was as ludicrous to the mainstream in 1960 as it remains now.

600,000-Year-Old Art?

Both Cornwall and Mooser commented on the sediments where Armenta found the art piece. Located on the Tetela Peninsula, the artifact came from the base of a bluff. Labeled Tetela 1, the piece was located just north of the site that came to be called Hueyatlaco. Another bone art specimen found nearby was labeled Tetela 2 and found at the nearby site called Tecacaxco.

After admitting a fairly low opinion of the stone artifacts collected by Armenta, Cornwall continues:

> The two exceptions were engraved fragments, which could not be explained away as products of natural agencies. Mooser pointed out that the more important of these at any rate, *did not* come from the undoubted stratigraphical position in the breccia, but from an *uncemented filling of a cavity* in the breccia, which could be of a much later date than the breccia itself. The latest possible date for this was the base of the Middle Pleistocene or Lower Pleistocene, marked by the...paleontological criterion for the base of the Pleistocene—the first appearance of the genera *Elephas, Bos* and *Equus* (as opposed to the Pliocene Mastodon, [and the] less advanced bovines and hipparion). The occurrence of a true *Elephas* alongside *Mastodon* in the faunal collection, suggests that the date of the breccia is close to this boundary—if it is as valid in the New as in the Old World, i.e. some 1 million–600,000 years before present.[22] (Emphasis in text.)

A date as early as 600,000y for art was hard to imagine. The only "plausible" explanation is that the art was carried out by someone much later. To resolve the disparity of the artifact and its original matrix, Cornwall suggested that, at a much later date, the deposits eroded, forming open pockets in the sediments—pockets that were later filled in. The art piece fell into one of these pockets prior to it being filled in during a later episode of deposition.

For this scenario, Cornwall suggests that flat-lying beds of river sediments begin to erode away in a peculiar way, turning the beds into a geological version of Swiss cheese. He does not describe how the pockets open up and the contents are mysteriously removed. Later, much later, this artifact, along with a batch of newer river deposits begin to fill up the much older pockets. It's a nice idea, one that would be revisited, but not born out by the layer cake appearance of the alluvial deposits.

Ing. Mooser (1960) wrote this account attempting to explain the problems of attaching the artifact to the Valsequillo geology.

> In lithology this locality [Hueyatlaco] coincides with that of the Barranca de Alseseca, and for this reason it is probable that both sites are contemporaneous. The great number of fossil bone fragments found here are the same brown color as those in the Barranca de Alseseca. However it is surprising to note that the particular bone containing carvings, instead of being brown, is *totally white*. This discrepancy suggests that the carved bone does not originate from this Plio-Pleistocene formation and that it was *not found in situ*. In a later survey it was established that the locality where the carved bone was discovered corresponds to a beach level of the present Valsequillo lake. The bone might very well have been washed out of soils far more recent in age and not out of the underlying conglomerate formations. For this reason it is impossible to correlate the bone with the conglomerate or to define its precise age.[23] (Emphasis added.)

Mooser's comments are instructive. He calls into question the integrity of the discovery because of its geological context. He believes the art piece may have been redeposited, falling out of some upper stratum and buried in a lower, more recent river bed. He also mentions the "totally white" complexion of the art piece in contrast to the brown-stained fossils captured in the beds.

Totally white? As soon as I saw this, my inner bell rang out. This is the only time the artifact was described as "totally white." This kind of white means bones bleached by the sun, the kind you see in the desert or Roadrunner cartoons. No fossil bones that I saw coming out of the site could be typified as "totally white"—light or pale yellow brown perhaps but not white. The dark brown color (stain) on many bones was caused by manganese leaching in the strata.

None of the surviving photos indicate a "totally white" appearance. The last known photographs of the engraved bone were taken in 1978 by David Hiser for *National Geographic Magazine*. He told me it was light brown in color. His photos were the last evidence for the art piece. After this, it drops from the planet.

The Valsequillo Gravels Formation was indeed old, but nobody could say with any precision its maximum and minimum age. If the formation is shown as a vertical column, the top would be the youngest age and the bottom would be the oldest. The ages discussed previously focused on how old the beds were. Soon, all focus would be on how *young* they could possibly be.

Geologically, there was thought to be an absence of an index feature (porphyritic andesites) in the sediments, which made the beds older than the nearby volcanoes. Paleontologically, all of the animals were tied either to the Early or Middle Pleistocene and the transition to the Late Pleistocene, dating to between 300,000y and 600,000y. Anyway you interpreted it, the Valsequillo Gravels were solidly positioned in the depths of the Pleistocene.

For anyone who has seen those huge specters on the horizon, Popocatepetl and La Malinche, you feel they must have been there since Creation. Yet, according to the field trip notes, there is the sense that anything coming out of the artifact beds must predate these volcanos. There was no sign of a certain rock that only turns up after they arrive on the scene. If there were artifacts coming out of these beds, they were made by folks who lived there before Popocatepetl and Malinche were pimples on the landscape.

Even for a fringe walker such as myself, this was a kick to the face. About a year into the research, Hal Malde, lead Valsequillo geologist from 1964–1973, calmed my angst. He told me that a few months after the 1960 field trip, sometime in the spring of 1961, Lorenzo and Armenta took another trip to the Gravels and located some of the igneous index rocks that were thought to be absent. As a result, the ages of the beds instantly became younger than the volcanic giants.

In the same January 1961 letter to Dr. Wormington, Armenta discussed the tensions that Sr. Lorenzo brought to the field trip, as well as the news that Lorenzo was now his boss. For Armenta, already walking a tightrope, the rope just got thinner.

Together with Ing. Mooser and Dr. Cornwall, we had the extremely great honor of the very eminent Sr. Jose Luis Lorenzo coming to Puebla to "study" the materials. His actions contrasted a great deal with those of his companions and, equally in the field and in the office, he made great show of a systematic disregard for everything that I have found. In front of all of the group and in a doctoral tone he pronounced that the horizon of the finds "is a Miocene conglomerate." He inspected the site where we found the principal bone with drawings and mockingly opined that the bone had been artificially buried there and that in no way could it be considered to be of the same epoch as the rest of the fossils of the deposit. In the office he studied the photos of the drawings and at once accepted, without any doubt, that they were made by man, but at once again demonstrated his disdain and came to the conclusion "The drawings are not of proboscids but of pre-hispanic motifs, such as those that are seen in some codices." In conclusion, he indicated to me that I should send the bone to him in Mexico City in order that he might study it (!). After that performance it would not surprise me if Lorenzo publishes some article before I may do so.

> But there is yet another small piece of news: last week Jose Luis Lorenzo was named Director of the Departamento de Prehistoria, of the Instituto Nacional de Antropologia, and, as such, now is my absolute chief.
>
> As a consequence of all this, it is very possible that within a few days I will not belong any more to the Instituto and will have to look for a new job and abandon everything I am doing. As I do not have any savings and it is urgent that I have a new job, possibly I will begin working as a laborer in a textile factory or perhaps I may dedicate myself to photography. In any case I believe that the change will have a stimulating result for me.
>
> Of course, in spite of ceasing to belong to INAH, I will finish the reconnaissance paid for by the American Philosophical Society and I will furnish the corresponding report.[24]

At this point, there was enough coming out of Valsequillo to demand a controlled archaeological excavation of the sites. They just had to find them.

Armenta had no background in controlled excavations, and it was necessary to find someone who did. It just so happens that Cynthia Irwin, a Harvard graduate student working on her Ph.D., did. She was a proven director of Paleoindian surveys and excavations in the United States. Further, she had taken up an interest in Central Mexico. She was already working in Puebla in 1959 studying Mexican ceramics and early projectile point types. She had met Armenta the following year and had a chance to look over his finds. Plus, she had a great mentor, Dr. Hanna Marie Wormington, the diva of American Paleoindian studies.

Stateside, a grant was being prepared for an exploratory expedition.

Chapter 1.5

Cynthia and Juan Versus the Communists

A 12-year-old girl walked into the Denver Museum with her twin brother, Henry. He had been working as a volunteer in the archaeology lab, and this was the day he took his nagging sister with him. They passed an exhibit everyone passed: J.D. Figgins's block section from the site that proved once and for all that humans were in the New World during the Ice Age.

Jesse Figgins, a paleontologist, had been the curator of the Denver Museum of Natural History during the 1920s when he found exceptionally well-made spear points near Folsom, New Mexico. They were embedded in extinct bison bones, bones from the Ice Age, from "before the Flood." The exhibit symbolized a new dawn for archaeology in the Americas. At the time, nobody knew exactly how old the artifacts were. One 1927 headline roared a date of "500,000 years!," and it probably wasn't alone. Until the Carbon 14 dating technique was invented, geological estimates for the Ice Age were far-ranging. The most conservative geologists estimated the end of the Ice Age to be around 25,000 years ago (25,000y). Carbon 14 knocked that date in half, and the 12,000y cellar for the earliest humans in the New World was set. And it all started at the Denver Museum. Cynthia Irwin was sold on the spot.

Left:
J.D. Figgins.
Right:
Dr. Ales Hrdlicka.

Left:A headline showing we had no idea how old things were during the 1920s. Bottom: The discovery of extremely well-made Folsom points with "antidileuvian" bison caused a revolution against Hrdlicka's 5,000y antiquity for New World prehistory.
Photos: DMNS.

When Figgins retired, his protégé, Dr. Hanna Marie Wormington, took over. Wormington seems to have taken a shine to this sharp-eyed youngster. Cynthia's mother, Cora, was also trained in archaeology, so Cynthia came to the museum already aware of basic ideas and principles. The relation to Wormington was the classic mentor-student, all the more so because Wormington knew that women deserved all the help they could get in the "man's world" of archaeology. Mutual affection, loyalty, and professional duty were strong bonds between the two that lasted for the rest of their lives.

Cynthia Irwin-Williams's fascination focused on two main topics: the earliest settlers of the Americas and the transition from the Archaic cultures, to complex agricultural societies in the Southwest. The advent of ceramics seemed to parallel the archaeology of sedentary farming communities. During her Radcliffe and Harvard years in the 1950s, she was involved in a number of high-profile Paleoindian sites in the States. Probably the one experience that had its deepest effect on her was an early stint in France examining Middle and Late Paleolithic sites. She cherished her 1958 work in the Dordogne of France for a number of reasons.

French archaeologists of the day, such as Francois Bordes, were years ahead of their peers in most other nations with respect to stone tool (lithic) technology. They actually knew how to make the flint tools, called flintknapping. Identifying and understanding how stone tools are made and used are absolutely critical to the study of archaeology. Stone materials last longer than any other artifact material, and are typically the only material that survived in Ice Age sites.

It was a terrific summer in France, and pivotal for her personal life. One of Irwin's trademarks became her beret. Later in her career, her compatriots and crews in the American Southwest, where she lived and worked, could not wait until Bastille Day, an official party day for anyone who worked with (or near) a Cynthia project. These memories are legendary for those who worked with, knew, and came to love her. She also became respected as one of the best, most insightful "dirt" archaeologists to ever pick up a trowel.

By 1961, with guidance and advice from Drs. Wormington, Krieger, and others, she had managed to impress the male archaeologists at Harvard's Peabody Museum, one of the premier archaeological and anthropological institutions of the time—and traditionally known to refuse female archaeology students. When Cynthia Irwin began her duties at Valsequillo in 1962, she was 26 years old, and a year shy of her Harvard Ph.D. and marriage.

She had also authored several professional papers for peer-reviewed journals on Paleoindian sites, and also a general article for *National Geographic* in the June 1962 issue called "Ice Age Man." Another article that came out the same year was a typology of projectile points from Mexico (*Acta of XXXV Congress of Americanists*). Both were written prior to her work at Valsequillo.

Cynthia Irwin was a rising star, with a bullet.

Bottom: Dr. Cynthia Irwin-
Williams. (CIW Collection)
Right: Her mentor and friend, Dr.
Hanna Marie Wormington, diva of
Paleoindian studies. (DMNS)

Communists Invade Puebla

The year 1961 was spent securing a grant from the American Philosophical Society (APS). As agreed by Drs. Wormington and Krieger, both Cynthia Irwin-Williams and Juan Armenta Camacho would work together writing up the proposal. However, by the fall there was a problem. Having not heard from Irwin-Williams, Armenta submitted his own proposal without any mention of Cynthia. Cynthia had also submitted a proposal without any mention of Armenta. *What was going on?* Did a rift develop between the two? Had Irwin-Williams decided to go it alone without Armenta? Was this a troublesome portent right at the beginning?

A September 25, 1961, letter from J.O. Brew, Peabody Museum director, to Frank H.H. Roberts of the Smithsonian Institution cleared up the confusion.

[This letter] has to do with the conflict between the two applications for grants to the APS for excavation in the State of Puebla, Mexico, one by Juan Armenta Camacho, the other by Cynthia Irwin. This is actually the same operation. The reason two applications were received is almost incredible. The story is as follows.

Armenta and Cynthia Irwin reached agreement some time ago to do this work together with Cynthia, as the experienced excavator, in charge of the field work. Then came the local Communist uprising which centered in Puebla. The University was seized by the Communists and for three months Armenta received no mail (incidentally, he has not yet received the missing mail). Cynthia had written to him sending copies

> of her applications and a full account of everything
> she had done.
>   Since Armenta had heard nothing from her, he went
> ahead on his own and sent in applications.[26]

Cynthia's brother, Henry, also a professional archaeologist, had married in early September 1961 and went to honeymoon in Mexico, carrying a message for Armenta about the project and the problems they were having establishing contact. When hearing about the Communist takeover, Henry informed his sister of the situation. With this resolved, the preparations were set.

Alex Krieger, similar to Marie Wormington, was a giant in American Paleoindian circles. In letters to both Wormington and Irwin-Williams, he demonstrates both an excitement about Armenta's discoveries and a cautious wisdom. In the midst of this tension and excitement, he was comfortable with the uncertainty regarding the true antiquity of the Americas. "That's what we are trying to find out, I think!"

Armenta had sent Irwin-Williams a box of bone and stone specimens, who then sent them along to Krieger. From descriptions, the lithics were broken cobbles and pebbles. In Krieger's return letters to Irwin-Williams and Wormington, he first described the stones, then the bones. Some look okay as artifacts, others not. Nothing is certain. Overall, he seemed more impressed with the suspected bone artifacts than he was with the suspected lithics.

> 10-9-1961
> Dr. Krieger to Dr. Marie Wormington
> Last week I received a box of Valsequillo articles
> from Cynthia. There are a few specimens of stone which
> can pass for artifacts, and a few others that were
> chipped once (by man or nature) and then strongly smoothed
> over by stream wear. Some of the bones are such advanced
> fossils it is hard to see how they could be anywhere
> near Wisconsin age; they have some crudely pointed ends
> and 'bevels,' all of which are waterworn....I feel sure
> that Juan's sometimes excessive enthusiasms will be
> well watched and that his excavation (assuming he gets
> the grant) will tell all of us just what is good and
> what is not good about Valsequillo."[27]

In his October 10, 1961, letter to Wormington, Krieger reveals a great eagerness about the discoveries, hoping that Valsequillo gets some archaeological attention right away.

> Also enclosed is a copy of my letter of today to
> Cynthia about the box of stone and bone specimens.
> This is for you to keep. It says all I care to say at
> this time. We just have to understand the provenience
> of these things a lot better, and the only way is by

> excavation, which is why I have been trying so hard
> to get Juan Armenta Camacho—or anybody—a grant."[28]

In a letter to Irwin-Williams written on the same day, he spends the first two pages listing the pros and cons of the specimens. Cautiously and noncommitted, he summarized:

> I think this is about all I can say just now about both the stone and bone specimens. There will be archaeologists who will pass the whole thing off as "natural," but then Marie has told me that this box does not contain some of the objects she has seen, which are more convincing. The big thing is to determine the age of the gravel. Even if it underlies the Becerra it may still be Wisconsin in age. (*And even if it were pre-Wisconsin, it would not scare me too much, for none of us can claim to know when the first men arrived in America: that is what we are trying to find out, I think!*)....So maybe they are all nothing but "waterworn scraps," but I don't think these things are to be so lightly brushed off, and anyway it was the paleontologists and the zoologists back in 1904-06 who told the anthropologists that these bones were *not* naturally shaped. It was not my idea; I only tried to revive the arguments, particularly after the paleontologists did some more research after 40 years and decided that the fauna there was partly Middle and partly Late Pleistocene, rather than the "Early Pleistocene" as thought at the time of discovery."[29] (Emphasis added.)

The underlying tone of the letter seems to be conveying to Irwin-Williams that he had complete confidence in her regardless of what, if anything, turned up. Also in this letter, there is the idea that the sediments may have been laid down during the Middle and Late Pleistocene, based on index fossils that had been reported on for the last 40 years by INAH's Manuel Maldonado-Koerdell. This countered the Plio-Pleistocene vintage placed on it by Ing. Mooser and by INAH's Jose Lorenzo. It was Maldonado-Koerdell's interpretation that Valsequillo was hundreds of thousands of years *younger* than previously thought—still old, just not that old.

Dr. Wormington had seen more convincing pieces in Armenta's collection on her visit to Puebla, and was equally certain of the mineralized bone with the engravings. She was undoubtedly impressed by the geological estimates of the sedimentary beds surrounding Valsequillo. Only controlled excavations would tell.

The debate regarding the antiquity of the sediments would serve as an academic wedge once the excavations got under way. Sr. Lorenzo's preconception of antiquity in the New World was essentially in line with Wormington, Krieger, and so on—it could extend as far back as 30,000y. His conviction that the Valsequillo beds were much older than 40,000y biased Lorenzo against the archaeology long before the gringa lady from Harvard got involved.

Since the 1960s, very few inner circle Paleoindian specialists in the United States braved the kind of open-mindedness expressed by Krieger and Wormington in 1961. A decade later when I got involved, you did not want to be caught advocating pre-Clovis, pre-12,000-year-old archaeology—not if you wanted a career. It was a treat to see how these two giants reacted so openly and willingly to the possibility of Pleistocene man in the Americas during or before the last Ice Age. The "sure, why not a 30–40,000y antiquity for the New World?" point of view was not something new after all! It was an attitude alive and well 40 years ago in the minds of some of the best.

When I began my archaeology schooling during the early 1970s, the price for claims of 14–40,000y sites was academic hellfire. Indeed, one of my first instructors threatened us with expulsion from the anthropology program if we expressed interest in such crazy things. To find out that such opinions were quite openly expressed just a decade before mystified me. *What happened between the early '60s and early '70s to forbid the very act of engaging in questions about pre-Clovis occupation of the Americas? Why were students never told of the Valsequillo findings?*

Chapter 1.6

Valsequillo's First Spearhead

In February 1962, a couple months before the first Peabody-INAH expedition began, Armenta sent a letter to Dr. Wormington. He had found the first spearhead known from Valsequillo. Similar to most breakthroughs, it was a chance discovery. While making his rounds, on the right bank of the Rio Alseseca near Rancho Arenillas, he found the point lying loose on the floor of the wash. It had a wide, flaring base and was made out of chert, a flint-like material. It was the first, absolutely unmistakable artifact he had found in the region since he first began his fossil hunting almost 30 years before.

Wondering where it came from, Armenta began looking at the surrounding sedimentary walls of the arroyo. He spotted a mammoth jawbone, a mandible, solidly embedded in a nearby stratum. On closer inspection, he saw a crack in the exposed surface of the jawbone. It was a wound that had been partially healed. Putting one and one together, he wondered whether the spearhead and the crack were related. The point fit into the crack perfectly!

For Armenta, the projectile point seemed to have penetrated the jaw and remained long enough for the bone to have partially healed around it. This would require that the mammoth was alive when the penetration occurred. The edges of the crack resembled wounds in modern-day animals that had escaped capture from the hunters. There was little doubt the point had been put there by a hunter's spear, but the mammoth did not succumb to the attack, and lived long enough for the bone to heal. It was not only the first known projectile point recovered from the reservoir, it was also additional proof for Pleistocene hunters in the Valsequillo area, as depicted on the Tetela engravings.

From Armenta's 1978 monograph (p. 25), he describes the nature and implications of the find.

The first Biface was found lying on the bottom of a Valsequillo arroyo in early 1962. A few meters away, Armenta located a mammoth jaw exposed in the wall of the creek. It had a semi-healed wound. A perfect fit? The photo on the right shows a "squared edge" on the right side of the point where it was damaged and splintered off, probably during impact.
Photos: Juan Armenta Camacho, 1978.

The artifact was driven into the animal in life, and was preserved in place for a long time, during which the bone developed scarring osteosis (or callosity) massive enough to cover part of the injury. Some osteologists point out the possibility that the scarring process had infectious complications, which left as its mark the corrugations which can be observed on the parasinfisial edge.

In order to reconstruct the circumstances in which those injuries were produced, by way of a working hypothesis and as only one possible explanation, the author postulates that the men were hunting a mammoth, possibly trapped in a mudhole, and stuck it with force in the snout, to the point of breaking the alveolus, in order to force open the throat, and give opportunity for their projectiles to penetrate down to the back of the neck in order to produce a fatal hemorrhage. But, to the misfortune of the hunters—and to the great fortune of the prehistorians—their aim missed, and the projectile was driven into the edge of the mandible, detaching the artifact from its support [spear shaft]; and the animal carried it in its escape, keeping it for the rest of its life.

By confirming this hypothesis, the mystery of how they were able to bring down these Quaternary colossi would become a little clearer, some of which reached a height of 4.5 meters and whose enormous mass appeared invulnerable to the weak thrusts with rock points of the gallant little men who hunted them many, many times. At Valsequillo, remains of 93 mammoths and 26 mastodons have been found, hunted by man.[30]

The spearhead did not match any other known type in Central Mexico. Irwin-Williams had just written a paper on point types in Mexico. It belonged to no clear category. Unlike the previous cobble artifacts collected by Armenta, its human workmanship could not be questioned.

If anything was questioned, it was the relation of the point to the crack in the mineralized bone. The fact that it was found loose on the floor of an arroyo was enough for Sr. Jose Lorenzo to doubt it as he did everything else Armenta found. No one could doubt it was an artifact, but Lorenzo and others at INAH had no problem disposing of its hypothetical connection to the crack in the mineralized bone. Because it was found loose at the bottom of the arroyo, the point had obviously dropped out of one of the younger higher strata above.

For U.S. archaeologists, the point was another golden carrot dangling from a stick.

Part II

Revolution

Chapter 2.1

The First Peabody Excavations, 1962

The First Controlled Excavations: April 23–July 15, 1962

The $4,000 grant from the American Philosophical Society was in the bank, and the first Valsequillo expedition was underway by the end of April, and lasted until mid-July, during the dry season when the water is lowest. Irwin-Williams would be in charge of all excavations; she had the background and expertise. Armenta arranged for the crew and the hardware required for the excavation: shovels, picks, and screens that sift loose dirt for artifacts and bones. He also arranged for the storage of all collections at the Museum of the Revolution in Puebla.

From her report to INAH summarizing her first season, Irwin-Williams describes how the project came to be and what kind of archaeology would make it a success.

> The region of the Valsequillo Reservoir, near Puebla, has long been known as an area which offers excellent opportunities for Pleistocene (and earlier?) research. The deeply bisected topography exposes a thick complex geologic section. The numerous deposits, some fossiliferous, represent a wide range of phenomena and vary in character from alluvial and

colluvial through lacustrine and a variety of volcanids. Prof. Juan Armenta Camacho had carried out surficial reconnaissance in the region for many years and had amassed a large collection of archaeological and paleontological materials. His studies led him to conclude that certain bone and stone objects possibly of human manufacture, had originated in a formation known as the Valsequillo Gravels. Due to the complexity of the geologic column (of sediments), scientific opinion concerning the age of the Gravels varied considerably but all concurred that they were of the Pleistocene or an earlier epoch. The character of the faunal remains from the Gravels likewise indicated considerable antiquity. The assemblage appeared to include camel, horse, mastodon, mammoth, glyptodon, dire wolf (?), extinct taper, and peccary, and other extinct carnivores and ungulates.

The possible presence of archaeological remains in the Valsequillo Formation was of significance, and if the Gravels proved to be of considerable antiquity, they might furnish precious clues concerning the early inhabitants of the Western Hemisphere. In addition, in 1959 Armenta reported finding on the surface a fragment of a proboscidean pelvis bearing engravings of extinct animals.

In short the situation concerning the potential archaeological material was this: We had questionable artifacts or "eoliths" almost certainly from the Gravels; we had an indubitable bifacial artifact out of place [the first Valsequillo spearhead], and the engraved bone also out of place. Our goal then was to discover the existence or lack of it, of fresh unrolled artifacts of unquestionable human manufacture, preferably fashioned of a distinctive non-local material, and most important, *in situ* in the Valsequillo Formation.

Only *direct association* of artifacts and flakes of indubitably human workmanship with extinct fauna *in situ* in the Valsequillo Gravel Formation, was considered as admissible evidence, and as an indication of a site to be excavated.[1] (Irwin-Williams's emphasis.)

What she is describing is the best scenario any paleo-archaeologist can hope for. In bumper sticker language she is saying: Perfect or Bust. The artifacts and bones must be found together in direct association and interred where they were originally discarded by ancient hunters. Artifacts or associated bone that look "rolled" will not qualify as *in situ* artifacts. "Rolled" indicates redeposition. If stone artifacts were washed into the Valsequillo Formation during a flood, they would exhibit rounding, similar to placing a sharp rock fragment in a rock polisher for a couple days. Mineralized bones would also display a rounded appearance, if they survived the trip.

The possibility of contamination has always been a bane for archaeologists. Gophers, prairie dogs, and other burrowers mix up layers of dirt containing thousands of years of artifacts; this is called bioturbation. These burrowing holes, or "krotovina," can transport newer, surface artifacts down to layers with older artifacts, and older buried artifacts can be worked up toward the surface. Worse, the same can happen to datable organic materials, such as small bones and charcoal. When out of place carbon is dated, they can lead to gross misinterpretations of a site.

Redeposition can also occur with landslides, but more commonly with floods. A flood can impact a bone bed and transport those bones, artifacts, and anything else it can carry downriver to be deposited in a secondary context. Geologists learn how to differentiate the contaminating events, and paleo-archaeologists have to be aware of these possibilities before lifting a shovel.

When buried flint flakes are found with rounded, water-worn edges, bells and whistles go off in the archaeologist's head. This is what Irwin-Williams was looking for. If artifacts such as flint flakes or tools were found in a primary context—buried where they were originally lost or discarded by humans—their sharpness should still be in tact.

The Fieldwork

Together, Armenta, Irwin-Williams, and crew spent half of the time surveying the shore perimeters and canyon recesses. They recorded about 80 to 90 suspicious paleontology sites that may be kill and/or butchery stations. The bones had fractured when they were green, and only certain parts of the skeletons seemed to be present. The nature of their sedimentary tomb was sands and silts with some pea-sized gravels deposited gently by slow streams. For a river to severely break large green bones, it would have to be a raging torrent, and there was no evidence of that. The small grain size

Opposite page: Valsequillo Reservoir. An archaeological heaven on earth showing Tetela Peninsula, primary tributaries and sites. El Horno is an island site off the western shores of the peninsula. Hueyatlaco and Tecacaxco are on the northeastern shore. The 1964 aerial was taken by Hal Malde at a time when the reservoir was quite low. All sites are presently underwater with a brief appearance by Hueyatlaco during the late spring. The "Footprints" site is a new discovery by Dr. Sylvia Gonzalez and the center of a primetime controversy.

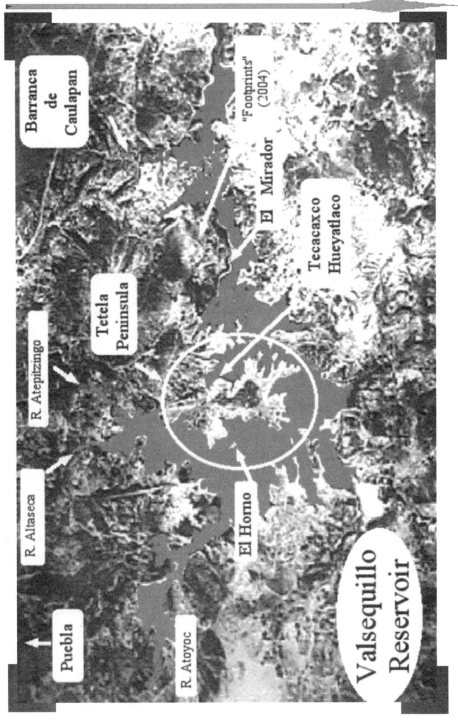

Barranca de Caulapan

"Footprints" (2004)

El Mirador

Tecacaxco Hueyatlaco

Tetela Peninsula

R. Atepitzingo

R. Altaseca

El Horno

Puebla

R. Atoyoc

Valsequillo Reservoir

is what made Valsequillo paleontology so popular—it meant the fossils were buried in their original place. The drawback was that so few whole skeletons had ever been found. Underneath the Formation was the Xalnene Tuff, a hard volcanic flow from the nearby Cerro Toluquillo, possibly more than a million years old.

Kill sites and butchery sites may or may not occur at exactly the same place. Given the size of the elephants, or even the smaller horses and camels, once killed, the hunters are not likely to carry the complete animal home in triumph, but only selected parts. More likely, a mega-animal is cut up on the spot and then the blood-soaked flesh and skins are washed off in a nearby creek. The Valsequillo region would have been ideal for onsite processing.

Irwin-Williams and Armenta decided on four sites for excavation. All have evidence for bone securely interred in the hardened sandy silts of the Formation. Two of the sites had stone artifacts stuck in the same exposures, and a third yielded a bone artifact. The fourth site, Hueyatlaco, embraced a broad section of the Formation with eroding elephant and horse bones; there were no exposed artifacts, but Armenta's engraved bone had been found 100 meters north at the same altitude, 2,055 meters above sea level (masl).

El Mirador: Elevation 2,049 masl

As surface sites went, El Mirador on the reservoir's northeast shore was most interesting. A projectile point was found. Fashioned out of a well-struck blade, the edge was retouched into the shape of a point. It was stuck in gravel that also included Pleistocene bone. Found by one of the trainees, the *in situ* point was documented and recovered by Irwin-Williams. The point was unlike any Pleistocene point she had ever seen in the States or Mexico.

Dr. Irwin-Williams wrote about El Mirador in her 1962 INAH report. No field notes or photographs have survived. The specimen shown in the photo is a plastic cast of the original.

> The site of El Mirador comprises a poorly known assemblage of extinct fauna including mammoth and horse, and the one associated human artifact. The association occurs in a coarse, poorly sorted gravel containing a large fraction of rounded rhyolitic cobbles and pebbles. This gravel has not yet received extensive geologic study, and it may or may not be equivalent to the Valsequillo Formation. The site is situated on a peninsula of the same name protruding into the Valsequillo Reservoir, ca. two kilometers east of the town of La Colonia Buena Vista de Tetela. It was discovered during a survey of the area in 1962 when Sr. Hector Montiel, an assistant at the museum

of the Revolution in Puebla, reported finding a flake of human manufacture *in situ* in the gravel, about ten centimeters from a horse vertebrae. After verifying the character of the exposed surface of the flake, its stratigraphic and horizontal positions were recorded, and the specimen was removed for further study. *A photographic record was kept of all the stages of removal.* Despite the very promising character of the locale, the shortness of time, and the relative remoteness of the spot and difficulty of transportation, made it impossible to conduct further tests at El Mirador in 1962.[2] (Emphasis added.)

The Specimen

The object recovered from El Mirador is of considerable interest: It is evidently a hafted knife or projectile point. The basic flake is rather long, thin and naturally blunt-pointed. The butt end of the flake has been considerably narrowed by coarse flaking confined for the most part to one face. The natural tendency toward pointedness of the distal end has likewise been emphasized by unifacial chipping. The butt end of the flake has a well developed faceted striking platform. The dorsal face displays multiple longitudinal ridges. The combination is suggestive of a crude prismatic core technique.[3]

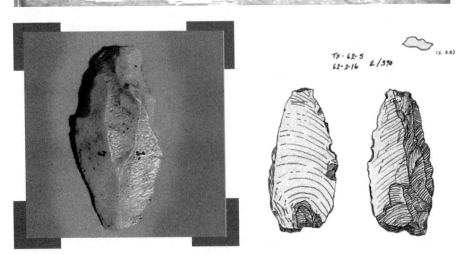

"Blades" are flakes twice the length of their width. On the left, a cast of the El Mirador point. On the right, sketch of the retouched points from Tecacaxco. Sketches: CIW Collection. Photo: author.

Most of the exposures of the Valsequillo Gravels were actually made up of sands and silts, and only occasionally of very small black chert gravel. The fact that the El Mirador matrix contains pebbles and cobbles suggests that a much stronger and faster river current had been active. Only further investigations would inform the scientists how this deposit related to the Valsequillo Formation deposits; but this study would have to wait. El Mirador was remote, and they put off excavation until a future expedition. Excavations at the Tetela Peninsula sites would be easier to manage in the few weeks that remained.

The Tetela Sites

The sites in the Tetela area were named El Horno (an island site) off the northwestern shore, Tecacaxco, and Hueyatlaco, located about 400 meters from one another on the eastern shore of the peninsula. All three were contained in the Valsequillo Formation but at different elevations.

- ✳ El Horno: 2,040 masl.
- ✳ Tecacaxco: 2,054 masl.
- ✳ Hueyatlaco: 2,055 masl.

The sediments on the site's surfaces were typified by similar indurated (hardened) sand, silt, and clay, and in places mingled with black chert in layers or lenses of fine gravel. Although nearly white when dry, the deposits when first uncovered during excavation range in color from beige to light brown or gray.

Valsequillo was still a relatively unstudied region and firm dates were hard to come by. Competing theories regarding the Valsequillo Gravels were based upon index fossils and other general criteria. The theories ranged from Early to Middle or Late Pleistocene, spanning 600,000y to 10,000y. Carbon 14 proved to be ineffective due to the mineralization of the local bone. Being a new and unstudied terrain, a lot of guessing was going on. It was true that some rather ancient Pleistocene animals were turned up by paleontologists, and in most circumstances they could be of help in pinpointing the antiquity of the deposits. However, could it be that the ancient creatures that became extinct hundreds of thousands of years earlier in the States had actually survived into the later Pleistocene? Mexican paleontologists were aware that the critical climate-changing events that presumably killed off some species up north in the United States may not have been in play in the more temperate climates available in Central Mexico.

One thing that was not in doubt was the stratigraphy itself. The Valsequillo Formation had a top and a bottom. The Law of Superposition stated "what lies above is younger than what lies below." The stratigraphy gets younger as you approach the top. This is as true for the Grand Canyon as it is for a city dump.

At many places around the reservoir, the Valsequillo Formation rests on a resistant volcanic unit called the Xalnene Tuff (pronounced "hal-nenny," also known as Toluquillo Tuff). The Xalnene is a cemented well-bedded aggregate of basaltic particles as much as a meter or two thick at Tetela. Many of the village houses have been built of the Tuff, taken as slabs from quarries at its source—a nearby volcano. Geologically, the Xalnene Tuff lies within a thick section of lake beds much older than the Valsequillo Gravels. As mapped by Hal Malde, most of the upper lake beds above the Xalnene (and in places still deeper) were eroded before the Valsequillo was deposited. That is, the base of the Valsequillo is a major stratigraphic break, what geologists call an unconformity, in the broad geologic history of the region.

El Horno: Elevation 2,040 masl

In prereservoir days, El Horno was located on a low peninsula along the west bank of the Rio Atoyoc. When Irwin-Williams was there it was an island. In 2001 it was underwater, but outlined by water lilies and walking birds. Geologically, El Horno was a vastly important site. El Horno was located at the base of the 100-foot Valsequillo Formation. It was the lowest site with an elevation of 2,040 masl.

El Horno, 1962. A rare photo of the island site excavations. It was a single component site largely centered around a butchered mastodon eroding out of the surface. This elephant toe bone, a phalange, had a carved ring around it, common to necklaces. It is the piece that convinced Irwin-Williams of the chance that artifacts would be found among the bones. She was right. Photos courtesy of the CIW Collection.

At El Horno, where the base of the Valsequillo Formation is in a channel cut 10 meters below the Xalnene Tuff, the bones and stone artifacts rest on the upper part of the underlying Amomoloc lake beds. Indeed, as described by Irwin-Williams (1962, p. 15), some bones, fine gravel, and "certain objects" had sunk into the soft red clay of the Amomoloc. Relative to the other three sites, it would mean that El Horno should be the oldest. One thing that was absolutely certain in 1962: It would be the first site to be covered with water when the reservoir began to fill.

The site primarily consisted of a single mastodon. It was discovered during a survey by a museum staffer from Puebla who found an elephant finger bone (a phalange), with a carved groove around it. On inspection, they determined that the v-shaped cut marks were caused by a sawing action, an obvious artifact. It was enough for Irwin-Williams to choose El Horno as an excavation site. From her 1962 INAH report, she writes:

> The adjacent phalange, evidently from the same animal, showed some evidence of butchering. When the locality was visited, it was evident that a considerable portion of a single proboscidian [elephant] was represented. Although much had been eroded away, much still remained in place in the Valsequillo Formation. The only evidence of the presence of man was the cut phalange, but on the basis of this slight but intriguing clue, it was decided to conduct test excavations at the locale.
>
> On June 13, 1962, the datum point was established and a grid of one meter squares was laid out. The first act was to photograph and map the existing surface out of which the fossils were eroding. Subsequently a small test trench indicated the presence of three observable depositional units [stratigraphic layers].
>
> 1. Recent lake shore deposits (0–18 centimeters thick), including glass, metal, ceramics, and redeposited fragmentary fossils evidently belonging to the proboscidian.
>
> 2. A well defined white silty deposit, labeled Zone A, (0–45 centimeters thick) containing undisturbed mastodon fossils.
>
> 3. A red clayey deposit with occasional small gravel lenses designated Zone B (40–60 cms in excavated thickness) including a few fragmentary fossils pertaining to the proboscidean, and several artifacts.
>
> In addition certain fossils lay partially in Zone A and Zone B. Apparently the underlying deposit B had been in a soft unconsolidated state at the time of the advent of the mastodon, and certain objects had sunk or partially sunk into it.

The initial procedure was to remove the entire recent lake deposits exposing the early layers and negating the possibility of contamination with modern materials. Subsequent excavation was carried out with small hand tools. Each fossil or artifact was photographed and recorded in terms of its exact geological context, its depth below datum and its triangulated horizontal position. The fossils were treated with a solution of Bedacryl and allowed to remain in place until the termination of the work on July 14, 1962....[It] was possible to complete the project before [the rising reservoir waters] reached the level of the actual excavation.

The Materials and Their Context

The fossils found in place pertained for the most part to a single mastodon comprising somewhat less than a third of the complete animal and including principally the pelvic girdle minus the sacrum; several ribs, one tusk and fragments of the other one; numerous tooth fragments and various fragments of long bones. In addition a large number of fragmentary fossils representing long bones, ribs, cranium, and metapoidals were redeposited in the modern lake sediments. Fossils not pertaining to the mastodon were rare but included horse and a small artiodactic [deer].

A total of thirteen specimens of chipped stone were recovered *in situ* with the El Horno mastodon. Six of these occurred in Zone A: two directly beneath the pelvis, three in an area containing several ribs, and one a short distance from the pelvis. Five of the remainder were recovered from Zone B, three in relatively isolate positions, one near the tusk, one in a cluster of tooth and bone fragments. The remaining two occurred at the contact with the modern sediments a short distance from the main concentration of fossils and their association can be considered somewhat less certain. In addition, while constructing a drainage, two specimens were recovered out of place near the tusk.

Of the total of thirteen specimens of chipped stone recovered *in situ* with the El Horno mastodon, six showed definite evidence of retouching and can be considered intentionally formed artifacts. Another two exhibited signs of utilization on one or more edges, and probably served as cutting edges, or scrapers. The specimens were numbered chronologically in the order of discovery.

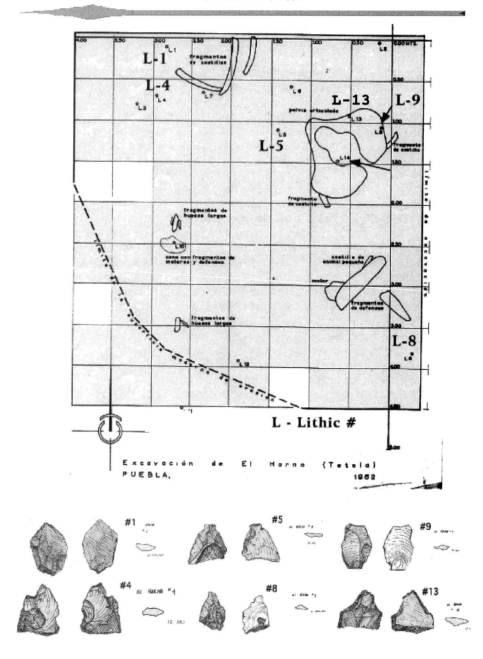

Juan Armenta Camacho's planview of the mastadon butchery feature at El Horno, 1962. The line drawings of the El Horno lithics are from the CIW collection.

Summary

Between June 8, and July 14, 1962, excavations were carried out at the Site of El Horno, in the Valsequillo Zone, Puebla, Mexico. A total of fifteen artifacts and flakes of indisputably human workmanship were recovered, eleven in direct association with the bones of extinct animals, primarily mastodon.[4]

El Horno was a bona fide subsurface archaeological site. The close associations of the bones and the lithics pointed to a primary, undisturbed archaeological deposit. The stone artifacts underneath the mastodon's pelvis and the other lithics had been buried at the same time as the bones. There was no evidence of intrusion or that the artifacts were somehow added later. Nor was there evidence that either bone or stone artifacts had been redeposited. The couple artifacts that were found loose did not disqualify the others. As Irwin-Williams said, "Their association can be considered somewhat less certain."

Irwin-Williams's previous experience with the complexities of Paleoindian sites had cultivated a strict care and attention to detail. Because of the potential importance of these sites, the evidence and its presentation needed to be immaculate. "How" you uncovered something was just as important as "what" you found. This is why copious notes and photographs are taken. All told, El Horno was a great start.

The sediments in Zone A and Zone B were silts, clays, and some fine gravel. Together, they strongly suggested that the archaeological feature was buried by a very slow-moving water, similar to a stream or small creek emptying into a pond or lake. For a hunter butchering and washing his prey, a most excellent environ. For the archaeologist, silt and clay matrices are very strong arguments against redeposition of the stone artifacts and large elephant bones during a violent flood event.

El Horno was a bullseye. There was no doubt in her mind that it represented an undisturbed remnant of a Paleoindian success story. Later, in 1968, part of the butchered mastodon was dated by the Uranium Series method as older than 280,000y.

Tecacaxco: Elevation 2,055 masl

Tecacaxco was a site consisting of a single stratigraphic level. One identifiable tool and numerous flakes were found associated with extinct bones. A single photo and a planview of the site's excavation survive. From the same 1962 INAH report, Irwin-Williams writes:

The Site

The site of Tecacaxco is located on a high terrace of the Valsequillo Reservoir below the northeastern edge of the town of La Colonia Buena Vista de Tetela. It is situated at an altitude of about 2,055 masl, where the local facies of the Valsequillo Formation outcrops at the head of a small steep arroyo draining into the reservoir. It was located during the extensive reconnaissance of the Valsequillo Zone carried out between May 15 and June 12, 1962. Sr. Prisciliano Garcia, one of the local workmen assisting in the survey [and hired again in 2001], reported finding a "fresh" flake in the Valsequillo gravels. The object was photographed, and mapped *in situ*, and then removed. Subsequently, another similar flake was encountered, and it was decided to conduct preliminary excavations at the site."

Observation and Procedure

The archaeological site consists of a homogenous deposit of a poorly sorted facies of the Valsequillo Formation. Characteristically it contains numerous fragments of the underlying volcanic deposit known as the "Xalnene." No internal divisions were immediately observable within the artifact bearing stratum. It is stratigraphically entirely exposed at its upper surface (except for a thin recent cover of dark soil). Geologic trenches are needed to establish its exact relation with the other later local deposits.

On June 12, 1962 a datum point was established and a grid of meter squares was laid in. Due to the nature of the outcrop, initial excavation was done on both sides of the gully and the two divisions of the site were tentatively designated Tecacaxco 1 and 2. However, the second (southern) portion proved after extensive tests to be wholly unproductive, and attention was focused ultimately on Tecacaxco 1. Here excavation proceeded to a maximum depth of 1.3 meters below the Sub-Datum established on the uppermost surface of the deposit. Fragmentary fossils occurred throughout, but artifacts were absent in the lowermost 40 centimeters. In addition a small test trench was begun on a low knoll west of the main locale, but could not be completed in 1962.

Initially all modern soil and debris were removed to avoid mixing. All subsequent excavation was done with a variety of hand tools, and all excavated material was sieved in a one-fourth inch mesh rocker screen for maximum security. Each fossil flake or artifact was photographed and recorded in terms of its geologic context, depth below datum and triangulated horizontal position.

The Material

A considerable quantity of fragmentary fossil faunal remains was recovered. These were scattered throughout the excavated section, though they decreased in number in the deeper levels. The chipped stone artifacts were likewise scattered, though they too decreased in number with depth and were absent in the lowermost 40 centimeters.

Though the faunal remains have not been analyzed, preliminary field identification indicates at least the presence of mammoth, mastodon, horse and camel.

The only definite artifact [sic tool] recovered from the Site of Tecacaxco in 1962 was a small thin roughly oval flake which displayed extensive chipping along one edge. The tool could have served for either cutting or scraping.

The relatively numerous flakes from the site may be described as follows. Many of the flakes show prepared, usually faceted, striking platforms. Some in addition seem to be the result of several parallel strokes, as in a crude prismatic core technique. These tend to be elongated and to have one or more visible median ridges. In other examples however, the blows resulting in the configuration of the dorsal surface had been struck from several directions.

Summary

At Tecacaxco chipped stone objects of definite human manufacture were recovered from a deposit belonging to the Valsequillo Formation, together with fossilized faunal remains representing several extinct species.[6]

The stone artifacts are described as possessing "median ridges" and "facetted striking platforms." These flintknapping practices first turned up during the Late Pleistocene period in the Old World, along with the advent of modern man (about 35–40,000y, known as the Upper Paleolithic period). Median ridges (arrises) and prepared (facetted) striking platforms were proof that our direct ancestors had improved on their practical understanding of fracture mechanics. These features were also present on the blade-point found at El Mirador, but not on the flakes and tools from El Horno.

Tecacaxco was a single component site bottoming out on the Xalnene Tuff. Photo: CIW Collection.

Hueyatlaco: Elevation 2,056 masl

Hueyatlaco was chosen because of a large fossiliferous outcrop of the Gravels. No artifacts were found on the surface, but it was a football field away from the location of the famous engraved mastodon pelvis and another engraved piece found soon afterward.

The site of Hueyatlaco is located on a high terrace of the Valsequillo reservoir below the eastern edge of the town of La Colonia Buena Vista de Tetela (98° 10' longitude, 18° 55' North latitude). It is about one-fourth kilometer south of the site of Tecacaxco, and like the latter lies at an altitude of about 2055 meters above sea level. It is situated about one hundred meters from a larger but more isolated outcrop of the Valsequillo Formation, near which Armenta reported finding the engraved fragment of proboscidean pelvis in 1959.

No flakes were visible on the exposed surface of the outcrop during the reconnaissance of 1962. However, on the basis of the occurrence of the engraved

bone and the evidently rich fossiliferous content of
outcrop where exposed, it was decided to carry on
test excavations in the area. The actual site for
these excavations was chosen in preference to the
large isolated outcrop near where the engraved bone
was found because it was felt that this locale would
be less difficult to tie into the overall stratigraphy sequence, and that its geologic position would
thus be more certain.

Observations and Procedure

The site itself comprises a prominent outcrop of
the Valsequillo Formation, divided into two sections
by a shallow arroyo, which also serves as a local
cattle trail. The two sections were termed Hueyatlaco
1 and Hueyatlaco 2, respectively. Preliminary excavations were conducted at both sections.

The geology of the locale is very complex, and as
noted above comments made at this time are extremely
tentative and are descriptive in character rather
than interpretative. The local facies of the Valsequillo
Formation is apparently fluviatile in character. It
varies from a fine silt and sand representing a weak
current (possibly near the edge of a larger body of
still water into which the stream flowed), to a fine
gravel, representing a swifter flow. All of the deposits encountered at Hueyatlaco 1 and most of those
at Hueyatlaco 2 were of the fine silt-and-sand variety: There is evidence at Hueyatlaco 1 of this deposit cutting an earlier red clay level. Although
minor sub-divisions in the Valsequillo Formation may
be based primarily on fluctuations in current their
exact significance cannot be ascertained without a
thorough study of the intimate details of the site's
stratigraphy by a qualified geologist. *Somewhat more
certain is the fact that the character of both the
faunal remains and the artifacts recovered indicate
that they have been moved little or no distance from
their point of origin. The fossils are unrolled and
often unbroken, and the artifacts are fresh with no
signs of water-wear.*[7] (Emphasis added.)

The "fresh" appearance of the lithics was a key observation. Had the stone tools
been carried in from some other place (redeposition), they would have suffered wear
and tear during the journey. Their surfaces and edges would have been rounded and
polished, similar to the smoothness of river cobbles, and perhaps they would have
suffered random edge damage. The absence of any evidence of water-wear, and the

close proximity to the Pleistocene bone was a strong indication that they were covered in place, and in association to, the bones in a primary burial matrix that had remained undisturbed until excavation. Perfect.

> A datum point was established on June 12, 1962 and a grid of meter squares was laid in at Hueyatlaco 1. Subsequently when the material recovered warranted it, a similar grid was established for Hueyatlaco 2. All modern soil and surficial debris were removed where present to avoid mixing. Subsequently, excavation proceeded with various hand tools and the excavated earth was passed through a one-fourth inch mesh rocker screen. Each fossil flake or artifact was photographed *in situ* and recorded in terms of its geologic context, depth below baseline, and triangulated horizontal position. In two cases, the association of an artifact with the remains of extinct fauna was particularly close and the objects were left in place and removed in a block for further examination and/or exhibition at the Museum of the Revolution."[8]

The feature blocks were cut free with a saw, and then taken to the museum. The blocks showed beyond a shadow of a doubt the intimate relation between artifact and mineralized bone—and they were portable. Unmentioned in her notes, a feature block was also extracted from Tecacaxco—perhaps by Armenta.

> **The Material**
> A large number of fossilized remains of extinct fauna were recovered. These were concentrated in the Valsequillo Formation: although sections of the underlying formation were explored at Hueyatlaco 1, they failed to yield such remains. Although no formal analysis is available at this time, preliminary field identification indicate the presence of at least mammoth, mastodon, horse, and camel.
> The artifacts recovered from Hueyatlaco occur in the same stratum with the faunal remains, often in close association with them. Since no formal analysis has been done on the material to date, the following brief discussion is based on observations made during the field season. The artifacts will be considered chronologically at Hueyatlaco 1, and then at Hueyatlaco 2.

Hueyatlaco 1 Artifacts

#1: This extremely interesting artifact has been extensively worked on both faces. The careful shallow flaking and secondary retouch produce a cutting edge along one side of the ovoid object. Part of this edge has been subsequently truncated by a blow struck along the edge of the artifact. The truncation presents numerous similarities to the burin form, but whether the tool actually functioned as a burin cannot be ascertained with assurance until a larger sample of the assemblage is available. The artifact was recovered from the silt sand facies of the Valsequillo Formation at Hueyatlaco 1.

#2: This second artifact was a thick oblong flake showing extensive modification of the one edge. The chipping varies from shallow to rather steep, producing a somewhat irregular scraping edge. (The irregularity may be purposeful as the resultant form is roughly analogous to the spur-perforator found in the pre-ceramic collections from Queretaro and Hidalgo.)

#3: This is an elongated thin naturally pointed flake showing modification at the distal end and along one side. The naturally pointed tip has been further sharpened by fine (pressure?) flaking and the adjacent edge shows considerable evidence of utilization. The character of the flake is of interest. It displays two parallel longitudinal dorsal ridges and is obviously the result of a series of parallel lows, possibly on a simple prismatic core; it retains the striking platform (unfaceted).

#4: This very interesting object apparently represents a multi-purpose artifact combining the functions of a concave scraper and perforator. It is made on an irregular random flake, and displays careful steep (pressure?) flaking on one end and the adjacent angle to form a concave scraping edge and a blunt perforator. *It was uncovered in situ about one centimeter from a large portion of a horse mandible, in the silty sand deposit at Hueyatlaco 1. In order to preserve this interesting and significant association, the group was removed in a block and deposited at the Museum of the Revolution in Puebla.*

#5: This least definitely worked chipped stone artifact was also recovered from the silty-sand of Hueyatlaco 1. It is an ovoid tabular flake displaying some preliminary flaking on its dorsal surface, and concentrated steep (pressure?) retouch on one diagonally oriented end. It could have served as a scraping or planing tool.

Hueyatlaco 2 Artifacts

#1: This is a bifacially worked elongated or lanceolate object, very possibly functioning as a projectile point. The chipping is rather coarse and steep and tends to be concentrated on one slightly convex face of the artifact. The reverse face has a steep longitudinal ridge running its length, and shows relatively less work. The artifact evidently made on a thick carinated flake, and retains the unfaceted striking platform at the proximal end. It was recovered from the silty-sand facies of Hueyatlaco 2.

#2: This is a small chert cobble showing bifacial percussion flaking around approximately one-third of its circumference. The edge produced is sharp and somewhat sinuous. *The object was uncovered in situ driven into a large fragment of a mastodon mandible* near the tooth row. A mastodon rib lay nearby. The group occurred in a fine gravel lens of the local Valsequillo deposit at Hueyatlaco 2. Since the artifact was in such direct contact with the mastodon remains, *it was decided to preserve this association intact. The group was removed in a block to the Museum of the Revolution in Puebla.*

Summary

Although only preliminary tests were carried on at Hueyatlaco, there is good evidence for the association of man-made artifacts and the extinct fauna of the Valsequillo Formation. Further investigations should be undertaken to gain a representative sample of the archaeological assemblage.

General Conclusions

After extensive survey of the region of the Valsequillo Reservoir (Puebla), four sites were located in which there is good evidence of the association of man-made artifacts with the extinct fauna: In three cases within the formation known as the Valsequillo Gravels, preliminary excavations were carried out at these three localities and produced a small but interesting series of artifacts. It is hoped that further archaeological investigation will produce a more complete sample and that a more detailed analysis of the material will be possible. It is also hoped that geological and paleontological research in the area will yield data on the exact antiquity of the deposits and the environment they represent.[9] (Emphasis added.)

The First Season

The first season was an unqualified success. In a few weeks, Cynthia Irwin-Williams and Juan Armenta Camacho had located several sites with bone and artifact features glued to the same column of ancient sediments. All three tested sites contained undisturbed primary archaeological deposits. Armenta's familiarity with the area, and Irwin-Williams' fundamental understanding of how sites were buried, proves to be a powerful duo. The Valsequillo Gravels were made up of relatively tranquil stream deposits. They rarely followed the same direction, and it would be necessary to recon-struct the size of the channels and directions of current.

The grain sizes in the matrices of the excavated sites were primarily sands, silts, and clay with occasional lenses of small gravels, just what you would expect from slow-moving currents. This was a critically important fact because, a few years later, folks would argue that the artifacts and/or bones *had to be* redeposited during a flood. The small-grained matrices of the formation would argue against this. How could a water current strong enough to carry only silts and sand also carry much larger and heavier articulated bones and sharp artifacts without also carrying many more gravels, along with pebbles, cobbles, and other items of similar weight and mass? Nature is not selective.

Irwin-Williams had excavated three sites all contained within this Pleistocene Formation. Hueyatlaco was 15 meters (~50 feet) higher than El Horno. She shuddered at the thought: *the archaeological potential of Valsequillo!* Had they only scratched the surface? It was not just a collection of solitary sites that was established. *The entire region was a mega-site.* Armenta's 80-plus kill sites, once suspected to be an enthusiastic-but-unprofessional exaggeration on his part, was now beginning to look to be a probability. An archaeological parallel to the Valsequillo basin would be Africa's Olduvai Gorge, where Leakey was also finding a range of sites contained in a geological column. Valsequillo was not as old as Olduvai, but it may be every bit as fertile for Pleistocene archaeologists.

El Horno, the island site, was located near the base of the formation (2,040 masl). It contained a mastodon butchering feature with more than a dozen lithics in firm associa-tion with the bones contained firmly in Pleistocene sediments.

El Mirador, at 2,049 masl, would be excavated in the future. A unique "edge retouched" point fashioned from a well-made blade was collected from a pebble and gravel matrix deposited by a much swifter stream.

Tecacaxco, a meter below Hueyatlaco, contained stone artifacts and mineralized bone in a meter-deep silt matrix deposited by a slow-moving stream.

Hueyatlaco, at 2,055 masl, was marked by a large remnant of the Valsequillo Grav-els. As she predicted, it containing a number of sedimentary layers deposited by slow-moving streams. The geology indicated excellent environments for hunting large animals and butchering the kills. The artifacts found were fewer than Tecacaxco, but highly significant. It was the only site so far that contained bifacial spearheads—projectile points that are flaked on both faces, similar to other Paleoindian spearheads, but much less sophisticated.

Hueyatlaco, looking south, the way we found it in 2001. Trench 1, in the foreground, was abandoned early on. In the background on the left, Trench 2 is being laid out across a remnant of the Valsequillo Gravels formation, a section I called Mario's Corner, after one of the directors. Below, a close-up of the Gravels, largly composed of sand and silt. The small black dots are the chert gravels, which were rare for the site. Photos by author.

Irwin-Williams's 1963 report to the American Philosophical Society bristles with enthusiasm—not only was the expedition a success, but there was probably a lifetime's worth of work out at the reservoir. The region was perfect, and she thoroughly understood that any effective future field work would require an integrated approach that merged archaeology with geology and paleontology. Bones had been sent off for C14 dating, but their mineralized condition frustrated any attempt at success.

Not a bad start to a career in archaeology. The Leakeys spent 30 years searching for the origins of man before turning up Zinj. It took Armenta 25 years of looking before he accidentally crossed paths with the engraved elephant bone. For Irwin-Williams, it took about 60 days to establish undisturbed subsurface Pleistocene archaeology. She had reason to be excited. The Valsequillo stone tools were much more primitive than the sleek, fluted Clovis bifaces.

Did they come before the Clovis? Were the Valsequillo hunters the ancestors of the Clovis? Did Clovis technology have its technological beginnings in Central Mexico instead of Siberia? Or were the hunters of Valsequillo totally separate and unconnected? Thousands of questions remained.

In archaeology, there are, and always will be, thousands of unanswered questions for every great discovery. It is the nature of the beast. What is rare is finding a single region such as a Valsequillo basin or an Olduvai Gorge where many of those questions might be answered in a single place. The few Clovis sites in the United States were often separated by hundreds of miles. On the Tetela Peninsula there might be a dozen paleo sites within walking distance. Unlike most, if not all, Clovis sites, the Tetela sites were less than five minutes away from the closest beer. Heaven.

For Armenta, after a generation of rejection by Mexican authorities, the success of the first expedition must have been sweet. Imagine the relief! Pleistocene archaeology at Valsequillo was now a scientific fact. Hundreds of photos, pages of notes, and stratigraphic profiles chronicled human artifacts in place next to mineralized bones—mineralized just as the engraved elephant bone was. Two features had been removed as blocks from Hueyatlaco and stored in Armenta's museum as permanent and unmistakable keepsakes. Even his most vocal critic, Sr. Lorenzo, located an artifact during one of his visits, an artifact belonging to a feature that was deemed so important that it was chosen as one of the blocks.

The Feature Block

Irwin-Williams had collected two feature blocks from Hueyatlaco, and apparently another from Tecacaxco (the notes are missing). In this form, the features were actually portable and could be exhibited at museums. More importantly, they were self-contained laboratories because the bones and lithic(s), as well as pollen and other microfossils, were still together in their original matrix. In effect, each block was a microcosm of the site. These blocks were the perfect, most responsible way to provide the evidence to doubters and to posterity, especially when tied together with a complete photographic record that chronicled their excavation, removal, and storage.

There is a saying: You can't have your cake and eat it too. Archaeologists know this all too well because they destroy what they dig. Once dug, you cannot put the site back together as you found it—except from notes, photos, and memory. Irwin-Williams's decision to preserve these critical features by cutting them out and removing them to the safety of a laboratory was brilliant, and undoubtedly necessary. The matrix would function as the geological fingerprint that would forever link the blocks and their artifacts to Hueyatlaco.

The idea of collecting a "feature block" must have been symbolic for Irwin-Williams as well. Since her first pre-teen strolls through the Denver Museum, she had passed by the Figgins exhibit countless times. Dr. Jesse Figgins was a paleontologist and curator of the prestigious Denver Museum, and in 1927 he set out to examine a bison site near Folsom, New Mexico. To his surprise, and everyone else's, he found some extremely fine projectile points in the midst of the Pleistocene bones. Folks had suspected that people were around before the Flood, but it had never been proven well enough to convince the skeptics. The skeptics, such as the Smithsonian's Ales Hrdlicka, were also the authorities, and the authorities held that people did not arrive in the New World until about 5,000y, or 3000 B.C. All talk of "antidileuvian" man in the New World was poppycock, and Hrdlicka and his fellows would not hear of it.

Figgins had now found absolute proof of the coexistence of man and extinct Ice Age beasts. Full of pride and excitement, he traveled east to report his find to *the man*.

Entering Hrdlicka's office, Figgins showed him the points and described their association to the Ice Age fossils. Figgins's enthusiasm was popped when Hrdlicka told him the bad news: Because Figgins had removed the points from their original context, he had ruined his proof of association. Instead, Hrdlicka told Figgins he should have left them in place alongside the extinct bones, and then arranged for a field trip with scholars to act as witnesses. Dumbstruck, but not defeated, Figgins left for home.

The following year, Figgins returned to the site, found some more points in direct association with the bison bones, halted excavation, and arranged for a field trip with scholars who would witness the association first hand; then he went one step further.

When possible, parts of a site are often left untouched so that others can follow to explore or verify the findings. At Wild Horse Arroyo, however, there was always the risk that another flash flood could come along between excavations and destroy the rest of the site—and Figgins's proof. So, using a saw, he decided to cut out and remove the points and bones in a block and take it back to the museum to preserve and display. It proved to the world that Man walked the Americas during the Ice Age. The exhibit, still on display, remains a symbol of the turning point in American archaeology.

The finds showed that antidileuvial man *did* exist over here! There *was* an unknown, deeper, older dimension to New World archaeology, and nobody was absolutely certain about how old that was...exactly. The headline showed we had no clue whatsoever when the hunters shot those bison. The half-million-year estimate of the tabloids was probably just as close as the 25,000y estimate of conservative geologists. It was not until the advent of Carbon 14 during the 1950s that the actual age for the end of the Pleistocene was established at 12,000y. Figgins's Folsom site turned out to be about 10,000y.

The first Clovis kill sites were carbon dated to 12,000y, right at the end of the Ice Age. No other site in the New World had dated any older. Other candidates would pop up now and then, but there would always be a problem, especially if there was nothing organic to date. Invariably, the sites and their artifacts would be dismissed by gringo officials in the same way Armenta's sites had been dismissed for years: The "artifacts" were either geo-facts, or not convincing enough. There was no ironclad evidence that anyone was over here before the Clovis.

Until now. Irwin-Williams, Wormington, Krieger, MacNeish, and a growing number of other paleo specialists figured they had a strong contender for the Clovis throne. Better yet, it was an entire region.

Additional Engraved Bones

Meanwhile, during this season, several more engraved bones turned up, which Armenta sited in his 1978 monograph. Two are associated with Tecacaxco, but are unreported by Irwin-Williams, and three were from an arroyo north of the Tetela Peninsula called Atepitzingo. The only information comes in the form of captions for photos in his monograph. Their exact proveniences are unknown—which is not to say they were not taken. Because all of Armenta's notes, artifacts, everything(!) were commandeered by INAH a few years later and subsequently lost, destroyed, or thrown away, this is the only information that has survived. What one chooses to believe will be a matter of the "eye of the beholder," because the actual pieces are no longer available for study. One of the Tetela specimens was directly tied to the Tecacaxco excavations, and this means its exact provenience *may* be available if the field notes turn up.

Page 84: The Xalnene Tuff is a volcanic feature that lies at the base of the Valsequillo Formation. The Xalnene flow can be seen on the terrace above the three workers at Hueyatlaco; its source, Cerro Toluquilla is upper right. Bottom left: ha house built with the tuff in Colonia Buena Vista Tetela. Bottom right: the tuff feature at the bottom of Unit/Trench 1; linear cuts made while collecting a sample in 2001. Photos: top: DMNS; bottom left: author; bottom right: Hal Malde.

Looking east at Hueyatlaco in 1962. Both stations are being worked. The site is composed of a large remnant of the Valsequillo Formation. The reservoir was reduced to the Rio Atoyoc, exposing some of the finest early man territory in the hemisphere. Currently, Hueyatlaco is submerged by several meters for most of the year.
Photo: CIW Collection.

85

Hueyatlaco, 1962. Giant steps down to the Rio Atoyoc. These remnants of the Valsequillo Formation held the archaeological world in awe. Hueyatlaco I in foreground. Hueyatlaco 3 trench (above) was abandoned in 1963. Photo: CIW Collection.

Chapter 2.2

Hueyatlaco,
1964 and 1966

By the time the 1964 project began, Irwin-Williams was a Ph.D., and married to David Williams, a nuclear chemist at Sandia Corp.

Record rainfall filled up the reservoir leaving only the highest site, Hueyatlaco, exposed. More than a dozen *in situ* stone artifacts were found in association with more mineralized bones from extinct animals.

Irwin-Williams had an initial hunch that Hueyatlaco would be productive from a geological perspective. She never dreamed it would be so archaeologically rich. She found artifacts in two parts of the site. Now, she was wondering whether there were any artifacts lower down (older) in the Hueyatlaco sediments. The artifacts and features from El Horno were 15 vertical meters below Hueyatlaco, so it was routine to think that deeper digging could produce older artifacts.

Her requests for a geologist and a paleontologist were answered in the persons of Dr. Harold E. Malde (U.S. Geological Survey) and Dr. Clayton E. Ray (Smithsonian). Hal Malde, a highly regarded field geologist, had just completed a nine-year study surveying and mapping 7,000 square miles of the Snake River region in Idaho. His early career was marked with an interest in archaeology, and when approached to conduct a study of the Valsequillo region, it was an easy decision. It would be a nice change and his family would enjoy the Puebla area. The archaeology also sounded fascinating. He had worked at other Paleo sites in the States, and the geology in the Valsequillo region could well prove older than the 12,000y terminal Pleistocene limits of those other sites.

Irwin-Williams realized that the true brain work for this project would be the geology. Geology and archaeology had been tied together before, but was often reserved for the really old sites of the Old World. The older you go, the more important geology becomes. With so few artifacts and bones, the older you go back, geology can at least tell you what kind of environment the archaeology was in; geology also told the archaeologist how the site was buried, what forces were at work, and so on.

In the New World, the 12,000y cellar date for the Pleistocene-Holocene boundary was a relatively surficial geology, more akin to geography. The Valsequillo geology could date tens of thousands of years old—probably before the last Ice Age. And unlike other claims for early sites and their typically viewed questionable artifacts, the Valsequillo artifacts were extremely obvious. Valsequillo provided a reverse problem: The presence of *in situ* artifacts was self-evident, a no-brainer, a textbook case. It was the ground they were buried in that would become the hub of the mystery.

Smithsonian paleontologist Clayton Ray would draw on years of experience working in the field. The kinds of animals that lived around the basin could be crucial for figuring out a general time frame for the sites. If there were any index fossils of creatures that died out prior to the Wisconsin Ice Age, then the argument for a pre-Wisconsin culture in Central Mexico would be substantial. There was one major obstacle in all this: Most of what was known about Pleistocene extinctions took place north of the border. Species that died out in the United States lived a lot closer to the glacial margins, and therefore more vulnerable to the finicky weather disasters of that region. Central Mexico may have been more immune to this sudden shift, maintaining a more stable, moderate climate. So, just because critters might die out in El Norte did not mean that the same critters in Puebla died out, too. They may have survived for another 10,000 years or 100,000 years or even longer. This had to be taken into consideration. Sadly, we are no better off now than we were in 1966 with figuring out the what's, the where's, and the when's of the Puebla Valley bestiary.

Without recourse to C14 dating, the task of dating the sites was now in the hands of Hal Malde and Clayton Ray. The fact that you cannot obtain a calendrical ("absolute") date from a site does not prevent you from going ahead and doing the fieldwork. Stratigraphy would prove to be a key.

To reconstruct what happened before the sites were abandoned, Irwin-Williams needed to know the geology and the fauna that attracted the hunters. It is also the reason she demanded that she alone would micro-manage all excavations of any artifact and feature after it was initially exposed by the field crews. In this way, there would be no mistaking its geological context. Photographs recorded every stage from excavation to collection.

Irwin-Williams's three summary reports are snapshots in time. They were all written before the sites were dated. The following artifact descriptions repeatedly cite their *in situ*, unrolled condition.[10]

"Dig Styles": Hueyatlaco, 1966. Dr. Irwin-Williams's excavation techniques would provide a three-dimensional reconstruction of complicated stratigraphic histories across the site. Methods such as these exploited the site's hardened sediments. The "Tower" (1966) was part witness column for the preservation of stratigraphic information, and part anti-Lorenzo measure after he ruined some of her feature blocks. Photos: CIW Collection.

Material Culture Recovered*

(*Number designations accompanying each piece indicates provenience by grid number and level below
baseline.)

Unit 1C

As noted above the majority of artifacts from 1C
were recovered in 1962 and have already been described. The only additions made in the last season
to this assemblage were an unretouched percussion
produced flake (G5/9) and a bifacially worked projectile point (F5/9) which may be described as follows: It is a rather short thick point, with abrupt
but not barbed shoulders and an asymmetrical stem,
which is shorter and more expanding on one side than
on the other. The base is slightly concave and the
blade forms an asymmetrical triangle with very slightly
convex edges. The character of the point is of interest: it is nearly twice as thick as the base, and has
been crudely blunted either purposely or accidentally. A flake has been struck off along one edge
which corresponds in structure to a burin stroke;
whether this was done purposely employing the blunted
end as a striking platform. Or is due to natural
causes is not known. The detail of the point face is
unusual: Near the point the cross-section is steeply
bi-convex; near the base, however, each face exhibits a shallow central concavity which is reminiscent
of cross-sections of fluted points. The correspond-
ing surficial areas exhibit a flat to slightly concave appearance. Concentric ripples and stress marks
indicate that the blows responsible for these surfaces were both struck from the basal end. The flakes
which define the form of the entire piece were probably done by well controlled percussion or occasionally by heavy pressure. All of this retouch cuts into
and therefore post-dates the flat concave surfaces.
There are two possible explanations for the situation: The piece could have been on an ordinary flake
with the thicker striking platform at the tip and the
thinner distal end at the base. However, the orienta-
tion of the ripple lines and stress marks indicates
that this is not the case. Alternately, employing a
thick flake, longitudinal thinning strokes could have
been applied on the original striking platform where
the base would be leaving the still relatively thick

distal end for the point. Finally an analogous thinning process could have been applied after the point was partly roughed out. The technique employed in the last two, more probable possibilities, is similar in principal though not in detail to that used on "fluted points." (No historic implications should be drawn at this time.)

On the whole, while the sample is small, some conclusions may be drawn from the assemblage recovered from Deposit C: There is evidence of a rather well controlled bifacial percussion technique, used to produce two known forms—a stemmed concave based point and a large bifacial cutting tool. Something reminiscent of fluting may have been employed for the point. The bifacial cutting edge displays in addition what very possibly amounts to a heavy burin blow off one side. Other artifact types produced by unifacial percussion and some pressure retouch include the concave end scraper-and-perforator, the side scraper and the gouge or scraper on the end of a flake. All of the above are produced on a rather poor quality chert, chalcedony with many imperfections. The single piece made of a less irregular white chert is a lightly retouched blade or blade flake; a larger sample or one of a better grade of raw material might indicate the existence of a coordinated blade industry. The character of the assemblage as a whole suggests a situation in which the important consideration was in killing game and in the processing of meat and hides. A brief hunting camp at or near a kill-site best fits these conditions.

Deposit 2C1

As Deposit 2C1 probably corresponds to 1C1, the single artifact recovered from it in 1962 belongs to the same complex just described. It is as noted a bipointed bifacial object, possibly a projectile point, and was produced by a percussion technique. It is on the whole rather cruder than the bifacial pieces in 1C1.

Deposit 1E

As noted above the single cultural item from E1 may have originated up in the immediately preceding level. The principal interest of the small flake (D3/17) is that it shows indisputable signs of calcination [burning], indicating the presence of fire by human or natural origin.

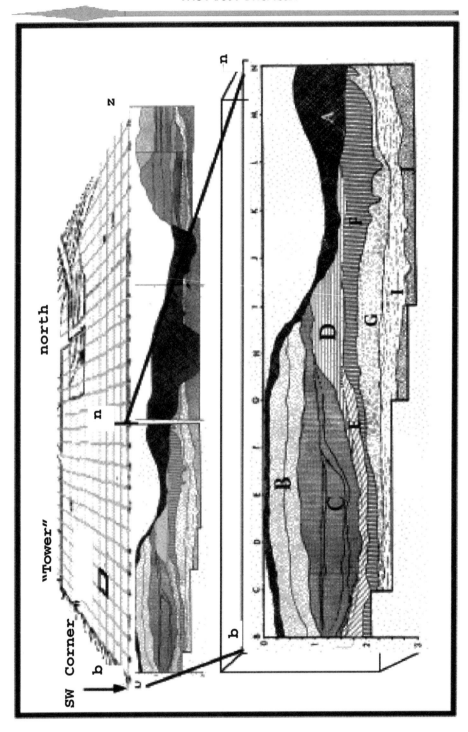

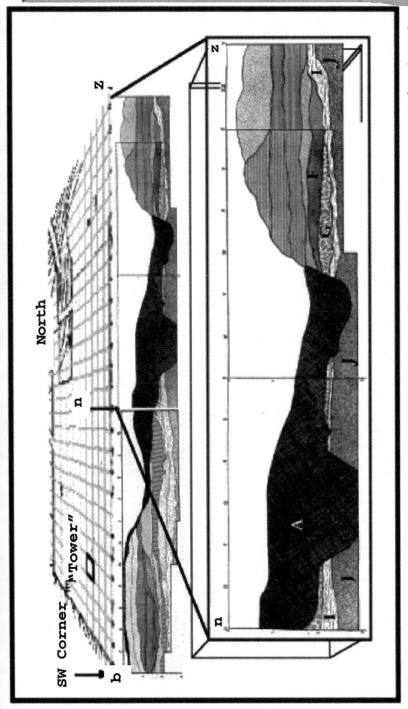

Hueyatlaco profile looking north (toward reservoir). Incomplete reconstruction based on surviving data, and combining CIW's planview with her profile sketches. Beds C and E were referred to as the "bifacial" beds. Bed I underlies the entire sit and was teh "unifacial" bed, referring to blade points that were retouched along a single face.

Deposit 1E2

Deposit 1E2 produced one of the most interesting associations of extinct animals and man-made tools at Hueyatlaco. Two artifacts were directly associated with the partial semi-articulated horse skeleton. The first recovered adjacent to the primary concentration of ribs and vertebrae, is an excellently worked bifacial bi-pointed projectile point (D6/19). It was produced by well controlled pressure flaking. It is somewhat thicker and rather blunter at the basal end than at the point. While bi-convex in cross-section, it displays a distinct longitudinal ridge on one face. The second artifact (E7/23) found under one of the associated vertebrae is the tip of a projectile point or knife which displays even finer craftsmanship than the first, and might have been produced by either pressure or percussion. On one side next to the break it has been retouched or resharpened. Two other man-made objects were recovered nearby the main complex and probably associated with it. One is a fragment of a large bifacial tool (C4/20) somewhat cruder than the above specimens, and rather reminiscent of the large broad flat flaking found on the biface from 1C1. It was almost certainly produced by percussion. The last is a large irregular nucleus (H4/20) from which numerous flakes had been removed by percussion.

There seems to be no question but that the assemblage represents a single "kill," and possibly a brief camp.

Deposit 2E3

Deposit 2E3, as noted above produced very numerous remains of mastodon, possibly most from a single animal, and a concentration of split jaws and teeth with two associated artifacts. The one recovered in 1962 in situ imbedded in a mandibular fragment, was a small bifacially worked pebble tool. The specimen found in 1964 between the cusps of a molar, was a thin flake with a single burin-like blow removed along one edge (Y5/20). Both of the objects, in contact with the jaw fragments and teeth, had evidently been employed in disassembling them. Again this meager sample attests to early hunting and butchering activities practiced.

Unit G

Unit G produced two of the most significant artifacts recovered in 1964: two small pointed objects probably projectile points. The first (Y1/22) was recovered adjacent to, and with its point almost in contact with, the fragmentary acetabulum of a proboscidean. It was made on a blade or blade flake and is an asymmetrically elongated diamond-shape in overall form. The contracting stem has been formed by abrupt rather coarse percussion flaking along the edges, while the point has been lightly trimmed along the edges by pressure, principally shearing. Work is unifacial and is essentially confined to the edges so that the faces are formed by the surfaces of the component flake. Of great interest is the fact that the lower one-third of the stem has been heavily ground and polished, both at the lateral edges and across the ventral face of the artifact. Microscopic examination shows that the dominant direction for the polishing stroke was at approximately right angles to the longitudinal axis of the piece. The second (X1/22) was recovered in situ under a camel rib less than a meter from the first. It is very similar in many respects to the latter, but appears to be broken at the base. It is roughly triangular in outline and plano-convex in cross-section. It was made on a blade or flake blade and the point has been trimmed by pressure, mainly unifacial and involving a shearing process. The existing base is formed by an abrupt hinge fracture. It is possible that the piece was used in this form. Alternately there may have been an elongated stem like that of the first points though the character of the flake indicates that such a stem would have been considerably thinner than the first. In addition to the two points, a single flake (U3/24) was found nearby; another (R3/23) in the trench between the two stations and a third (F4/21) at Hueyatlaco I. The character of this assemblage strongly suggests a kill-site and perhaps brief butchering activities. The artifacts themselves indicate the possible existence of a technology and typology radically different from those observed in succeeding levels. There is evidence of a rather well-controlled blade producing technique. At the same time the advanced percussion and pressure flaking

extending completely across the surfaces of the artifact, characteristic of materials of Unit C and E, is
totally absent. In view of the small sample no comment
can be made concerning the relative associated tools.

Unit H

As noted above Deposit H is a local phenomenon
confined to Hueyatlaco II and postdating Deposit G.
It produced a concentration of horse and camel bones,
associated with a single utilized or lightly retouched flake (X2/23).

Unit I

Despite a general paucity of faunal remains, Deposit 1I produced a single artifact of considerable
interest: a small pointed object. probably a projectile point (I2/24). Although it is made on a thin
flake rather than a blade. it bears numerous resem-
blances to the points from Unit G. The blade is roughly
triangular, and a short asymmetrical basal projection
on one side might be considered a stem. It has been
trimmed all around by shallow or abrupt pressure and
some percussion retouch limited entirely to the pe-
ripheral edges. It has a flattened hexagonal cross-
section. On the whole it is very similar to the Unit G
specimens and tentatively may be considered as belonging to the same typological group. It should be
noted that the single point found at El Mirador in
1962 is also quite similar and may pertain to the same
type. Again the specimen from Deposit I suggests hunting activities.

Summary

Summarizing the overall character of the cultural
remains recovered at Hueyatlaco, the following brief
commentary may be made: (1) The fluviatile deposits
laid down at Hueyatlaco indicate that a stream or
streams existed in the locality over a period of some
time. (2) These favorable conditions repeatedly attracted a large variety of extinct fauna to the site.
(3) Early men were also attracted to the spots where
several times during the prehistoric period represented, they hunted, killed, and butchered the available
game. (4) Each of these hunts was an isolated incident in time, providing a brief glimpse of the rel-
evant technology and typology. (5) Taken together
they yield a most skeletal framework for an early
prehistoric sequence. (6) The exact chronology of
this sequence must await further geologic and radiocarbon studies.[11]

Top: close-up of a Hueyatlaco biface from Bed E still in place. Bottom: the feature is shown with bone in the foreground; the arrow on the right points toward the biface. This is one of the very few photos with a menu board, a photo that was destined for the multi-volume work on the discoveries before the fiasco. At least a thousand of these "official" photos are missing. Photos: CIW Collection.

Hueyatlaco, 1966

During the 1966 season, the geologists continued exploring the reservoir, the Puebla Valley, La Malinche, and other volcanoes. Again, Hueyatlaco was the only site above water, and it received the full attention of Irwin-Williams. The bad news was that Lorenzo sunk a couple humongous trenches in her absence just upslope from her excavations without telling her—an outrageously unethical thing to do by any archaeologist anywhere when another archaeologist is working a site. The good news came later when the added profiles of Lorenzo's trenches provided a better handle on the site's geological composition.

A topographic map was produced that detailed the planview of the excavations, including the excavation of Hueyatlaco 3 begun in 1964. This was the Valsequillo outcrop that produced the engraved mastodon bone. It was located about 100 meters north of Station 1, across a swale feeding into the reservoir.

Archaeologically, it was a season of "meager" collections—that is to say, two lithics. One was a flake, but the other was a bifacially flaked projectile point. The latter was the first and only artifact that was "rolled," or rounded. It seems it was lodged in a small stream channel or rivulet.

Deposit 2E4 also produced the only diagnostic man-made artifact recovered in 1966: A large fragment of a bifacial knife or point. The object occurred in close proximity to the remains of horse, an immature mastodon, peccary and camel. However in view of its condition, the association may well be secondary. The piece represents a trianguloid section near the tip of a large knife or, less probably, a point. It was produced by the same kind of well controlled broad percussion flaking found on the bi-pointed projectile point from 1E2. It Is bifacially worked and bi-convex in cross-section. It had been broken laterally across the existing base, and also probably at the tip. Its width and angle of lateral expansion suggest a knife rather than a projectile point. The edges of the piece have been moderately battered suggesting some displacement from its point of origin. It is notable in this respect, since all of the other artifacts recovered from Hueyatlaco are fresh with no signs of rolling, and indicate little displacement from point of origin.[12]

98 ☞

When the report was submitted, there was still no hint of how old the sites were. All anybody knew for sure was that all four sites were encased in the Valsequillo Formation: a single, well-defined, mappable sedimentary column that measured about 30 vertical meters (2,040–2,070 masl). The Hueyatlaco artifacts were coming out at least 15 meters below the top. El Horno was located another 15 meters below Hueyatlaco. That's essentially what they knew. They also knew that the stone technology they were finding was more primitive than Clovis.

By the end of the 1966 season, the geological position of the Valsequillo Gravels in the southern Puebla Valley had been mapped by Hal Malde, but further search for datable deposits still lay ahead. That task would require a search among volcanic ash deposits found on nearby volcanoes, and among deposits in local arroyos that empty into the reservoir. That was the plan.

Irwin-Williams had every reason to believe she would be working there for years to come, in spite of Lorenzo's increasing mania. Armenta's surveys had located more than 80 potential paleoarchaeology sites representing several lifetimes' worth of work. Hal Malde and new recruit Virginia Steen, a soils and volcanic ash specialist, were hunting for geological features that tied into the Valsequillo Gravels. Clayton Ray was trying to obtain index fossils; everybody was on the lookout for something to date.

Valsequillo had hardly been scratched, but the art pieces, subsurface artifacts, and feature blocks had electrified the archaeological communities of both Mexico and the United States. Word was getting out. No definitive, official announcements had been released to the U.S. press because there were no dates yet. The newspapers of Puebla, on the other hand, were having a ball. Since 1960, the Puebla press heralded Valsequillo as the "American Eden," and Armenta was their hero.

Into this state of archaeological bliss, things quickly spiraled downward. It first arrived in the form of INAH's Sr. Jose Luis Lorenzo. How did Puebla receive the news that Lorenzo fired Armenta at the beginning of the 1966 season, confiscated all of his work, and effectively banned him from fieldwork? This remains unexamined.

Chapter 2.3

"He Did What?!": Lorenzo's Vandalism

It was a cool spring morning in the National Mall in 1962 when Sr. Jose Luis Lorenzo walked, unannounced and unexpected, into the Smithsonian Institution. He was on a mission. He demanded the engraved elephant bone be returned immediately, so he could take it. According to one official, it seemed a well-practiced tirade. Lorenzo behaved as if the Smithsonian had illegally stolen the pieces from Mexico and he had caught them red-handed. The truth is that Armenta had sent them up through his Puebla University museum in full knowledge of Mexican authorities. It was hardly a secret.

This was Lorenzo's own call, a flexing of his muscles. The staffers of the Smithsonian complied, and packed the materials up, and Lorenzo was on his way. The earliest art of the Americas never left Mexico again.

Born in 1921 in Madrid, Jose Lorenzo first arrived in Mexico during the late 1930s, as a Communist refugee from the Spanish Civil War. He became a leading force in Mexican archaeology. Extremely well-read and widely educated, he was highly respected, if not feared, by his students. During his long career, he was charged with some of the most prestigious institutions, agencies, and offices. His strong, often-dogmatic demeanor earned him the nickname "the Sun King" by his colleagues.

A short listing from Jose Luis Lorenzo's obituary includes:[13]

✳ Chief, Department of Prehistory, Department for pre-Columbian Monuments, Department of the School of Restoration and Museology at INAH.

✳ Chief, Latin American Regional Centre for the Preservation and Restoration of Cultural Property (UNESCO).

✳ Chairman, Archaeological Council, Instituto Nacional de Antropología e Historia (INAH).

J.L. Lorenzo may go down in history as one of the greats in Mexican archaeology; he was also one of the most powerful. At most every excavation permit requested by foreigners required his signature. For an archaeologist, it was indeed a god-like power. Many gringo careers depended on that signature. Playing politics was not an option. You did not want to be on Lorenzo's bad side if you had things to do in Mexico.

✳ If you were an archaeologist from Harvard, that was strike one.

✳ If you were a gringa archaeologist, that was strike two.

✳ If you were a gringa archaeologist from Harvard...you get the idea.

The truth is that Lorenzo was upset about Valsequillo and Armenta years before Harvard got involved. Lorenzo's loathing of Armenta had been alive and well since the mid-1950s. The Irwin-Williams/Harvard tag team only exacerbated an already-stressful, purely Mexican soap opera. On the other hand, Lorenzo had a fond respect for C. Vance Haynes, so it was not an anti-gringo bias across the board. Why Harvard seemed to get his goat is unknown to me.

Folks who knew him say that Lorenzo was all about Lorenzo. Some regarded his problem as an outgrowth of his Communist upbringing and/or his attention to class. In the end it doesn't seem to matter. He could use the "Mexican vs. U.S." card whenever it suited his purpose, but this was not the only way he pulled rank. His treatment of Armenta was a lion toying with a lamb, until the struggling lamb happens to kick the lion squarely in the nuts. This happened when Armenta discovered the engraved art.

The international publicity that greeted the art piece changed everything. Armenta was receiving a lot of attention from high-level scholars from around the world. Armenta's long-held suspicions were becoming true. He was right all along. How did this make Lorenzo feel? Did Armenta's authentic fame bruise the Sun King's ego? Until someone steps forward with something else, it will be difficult to conclude anything else other than "professional" jealousy and envy irrationally fostered Lorenzo's unforgivable behavior in the years ahead.

Unspeakable

In late 1963 Irwin-Williams received an urgent letter from Armenta. It was a nightmare. Lorenzo had deliberately destroyed two of the feature blocks from the 1962 season. Armenta and a couple assistants were present when the foul deed was done. They were transfixed, caught in a paralysis of disbelief and totally helpless to prevent the atrocity.

Autonomous University of Puebla,
Department of Anthropology
Memorandum
Salutation: To: Dr. Cynthia Irwin-Williams
From: Juan Armenta Camacho
Topic: The destruction of a specimen
    I regret to tell you that yesterday Prof. José Luís Lorenzo, for the second time, removed an artifact from the matrix in which it had been recovered. As you will remember, the first time was the retouched flake from Tecacaxco that we lifted as a block, and which he pulled out in our presence [in the lab], apparently deliberately. But yesterday he [removed] the scraper that HE HIMSELF discovered at Hueyátlaco during one of his visits, and that by its very close association with a horse snout was one of the best evidences we had for the presence of hunters.

    To me, it appeared that this was an exceptionally important scientific specimen (similar to the Folsom point, at the Denver Museum), and, furthermore, it was the first that was recovered associated with extinct fauna in all the prehistoric work done in Mexico. For that reason I ordered Juan Hernandez to clean in a special way the block that Hector Montiel lifted out so carefully, and with which he took so much time, since it was evidence that would end all discussion and that it might have been a very objective lesson for those who saw it in some museum. Juan Hernandez dedicated more than two weeks to that piece, and did an excellent job. We had planned to preserve it with much pride.

    But yesterday Prof. José Luís Lorenzo came, accompanied by a friend, and to my great surprise and bafflement, pulled the artifact from its matrix in order to examine it and show it to his friend. Crushed by having just seen this happen, I asked him why he had done such a thing (which not even the most ignorant of our peasants would have had the insolence to do) but he, joking (irritated?), discounted the importance of the affair.

    This incident has, frankly, bothered me a lot, and I ask myself even now if it was an act of absolute ignorance or of intentional bad faith.

    I'd be thankful that, if possible, I could take necessary measures to prevent a repetition of such an absurd and inexplicable thing.
Faithfully,
Prof. Juan Armenta Camacho[14]

No record of Irwin-Williams's response to either Armenta or team members exists. Armenta's letter does clear up *why* there was no report of a feature block from Tecacaxco: Lorenzo had ruined that one as well. In front of Irwin-Williams and the whole crew, right after they had carefully removed the block, Lorenzo whimsically picked out an artifact that had been thoroughly stuck in the feature. The omission of this incident in the reports destined for INAH was plain politics. You do not write a report that says the official who signs your permits intentionally destroyed something priceless.

Once again, the magic of an artifact's undisturbed context had been raped of its significance. Other accounts tell of Lorenzo flinging the artifact across the lab in disgust—it was as if he despised the artifact—an artifact he himself had identified in the field! Lightening had struck twice in the same way. This was sheer vandalism, sheer sabotage, sheer madness—not ignorance.

Of all the blocks collected, the one from Hueyatlaco was the most valued, because it was the obvious rival to Figgins's Folsom feature back at the Denver Museum. It was destined to share an exhibit in the national museum next to the engraved mastodon bone. Two weeks had been devoted to making the feature block a pristine, immaculate exhibit; ironically, the intense effort was in preparation for Lorenzo's visit. In a flash, it was ruined. Useless. Plenty of photos had been taken, both in the field and the lab, and piles of records written, but it would never be the same. Later, all these notes and photos would all be confiscated by Lorenzo and INAH. They have never been seen again.

Any other archaeologist would have been arrested and jailed for the vandalism, or at least stripped of his credentials before being shown the door.

By the end of the1966 season Lorenzo had already:

❋ Mutilated at least two of the feature blocks.

❋ Prevented Armenta and his assistant paleontologist, Mario Pichardo, from participating in the 1966 season of field work, seriously impacting the team's goals for that season.

❋ Demanded that Armenta forfeit his 30 years of notes and more than 6,000 bone specimens to INAH, including the engraved bone artifacts he had found.

❋ Sunk a couple gaping trenches just meters upslope from Irwin-Williams's excavations at Hueyatlaco.

On the surface, Irwin-Williams was forced to be a nice, polite diplomat. Underneath, she was fuming. Other members of the team felt the same way. Clayton Ray was depending heavily on Pichardo. When he heard that Lorenzo told Pichardo to get lost, Ray appealed to INAH's archaeological hierarchy to reinstate him. As Ray conveyed to me, INAH said their hands were tied, but finally assured Ray that "a replacement would be sent." It never happened.

When Irwin-Williams arrived in 1966, two gaping trenches met her eyes when she walked across the upper slope of Hueyatlaco. In her absence, Lorenzo had decided to dig two monster trenches up the slope and about 10 meters south of where she left off in 1964. Written and unwritten codes among archaeologists state that you do not screw around with another person's site, especially behind his or her back. At the beginning, Lorenzo had told her these were her sites and nobody else would be allowed to dig there. And now this? What could she do? The Sun King had already gotten away with murdering a couple feature blocks, and then fired Pichardo and Armenta.

Juan Armenta Camacho, the heart and the soul of the discovery, the human reason for the Valsequillo Project, was now barred by Lorenzo/INAH to participate in any future involvement with paleontology and archaeology. He was out of the picture before the third season started, and his field days on the frontlines of prehistory were over. And all because he was successful? His unforgivable crime? Take your pick: He did not have a degree (though he began the anthropology department in Puebla)? He was not a real member of the academic club? He was getting more attention than Lorenzo? Reasons were never given. Maybe Lorenzo took him out just because he could. Whatever the reason, it was a disgrace. INAH stifled a wonderful man with an incredible mind. They/Lorenzo eventually lost or destroyed his First American treasures. Lorenzo was not through, however. The best was yet to come.

At the time, Irwin-Williams was still looking ahead to many more years working this archaeological heaven. She never worked Valsequillo again.

Chapter 24

Barranca de Caulapan and the First Dates

Early in the project an attempt was made to date Hueyatlaco using the 14C method. It was not successful. No carbon was preserved at the site. What was thought to be charcoal turned out to be manganese dioxide concretions. Bones sent to the research laboratory at Humble Oil, Houston in 1962 and to the University of Arizona in 1968 were undatable: no collagen or organic matter was preserved. It was thought at the time that this lack of carbon was caused by some odd quirk in the groundwater chemistry.[15]

—Dr. Virginia Steen-Mcintyre, Tephrochronologist

Caulapan

The geology was being pursued by Dr. Hal Malde and Virginia Steen. Their surveys took them to a number of locales around Puebla, including the volcanic slopes of La Malinche. La Malinche seemed a likely source for the prominent Hueyatlaco Ash lens several meters above the archaeology beds. Each ashflow has a particular makeup and chemistry, a fingerprint that can be tied back to a specific eruption. If they could locate ash on La Malinche that matched the Hueyatlaco Ash, then all they had to do was date the ash to find when it fell. Simple enough in theory, but the methodology was intensive. Virginia Steen was a specialist in tephrachronology and had developed innovative methods that enhanced the discipline.

On the flanks of La Malinche they took samples of ash, locating contact points between ash eruptions and the ground. When hot volcanic ash falls to earth, it burns up ground cover (trees, bushes, and grass) producing a charcoal lens. Dating the charcoal with C14 tells you when the hot ash fell.

Elsewhere they surveyed along cliff sides, road cuts, and the walls of local arroyos where fossils were known. The steep arroyos (*barrancas*) feeding into the reservoir were evidence of severe downcutting. The most promising barrancas were the Rio Alseseca, Rio Atepetzingo, and Barranca de Caulapan. Malde first walked Caulapan in 1964. Located about 6 kilometers from Hueyatlaco, the sediments contained shell clusters, which you can date.

From a paper given in Chile in 1969, Irwin-Williams states:

> The Barranca de Caulapan is one of several tribu-taries flowing into the Valsequillo Reservoir east of the Tetela Peninsula. Although the group of deposits at Caulapan is separated from the Tetela group by about 5 kilometers, geologic mapping by H.E. Malde indicates that they may be of equivalent age, and represent all or part of the temporal range of the Valsequillo Formation. A series of molluscan fossils from the Caulapan section were submitted for radio-carbon dating.[16]

Caulapan may contain the remnants of a portion of the Valsequillo Gravels. Here, similar to Alseseca and Atepitzingo, you can walk along the sides of the arroyo and find consolidated remnants of alluvial deposits, ranging from gravel to sand and stretching upward of 24 meters to the top. Look more closely and you find mineralized fragments of bones and pockets of shell.

Prior to the 1966 season, Armenta and Irwin-Williams found an *in situ* chert flake tool in the beds of Caulapan described as: "a thick flake exhibiting limited pressure retouch and/or utilization." The stratum containing the artifact was located about 10 meters up from the base of the Caulapan column. Shell and bone were collected from the same stratum. The bone was too mineralized, but the shell could be dated.

At the time, Malde had believed that the Caulapan column was possibly related to the beds at Hueyatlaco and the other Valsequillo sites. A one-to-one correspondence was still unknown, but suspected. They were treading on new ground because the region had never been geologically mapped and estimates regarding age were far ranging. Only rigorous examinations would tell. For now, all he knew for sure was that they were both Pleistocene.

If the beds were related to those at Hueyatlaco, then dating the Caulapan beds would indirectly date the Valsequillo sites. At least it would be a start. Meyer Rubin of the USGS radiocarbon lab had the results in late 1966: 21,850 years BP±850: Carbon 14 Sample W-1895.

Barranca de Caulapan. CIW's profile sketch shows locations of 1967 C14 shell dates. The artifact, the shells for the 22,000y C14 date, and bone for the 21,000y Uranium Series dates were taken from the zone between the two bars in the photo with geologist Bob McKinney on a 2001 visit. Photo: author.

CAULAPAN PROFILE and 14C SHELL DATES

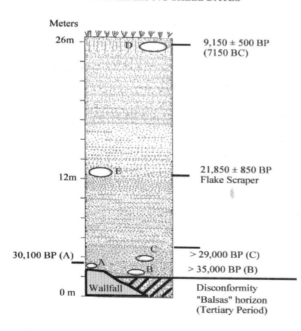

Meters

26m — 9,150 ± 500 BP (7150 BC) — D

12m — B — 21,850 ± 850 BP Flake Scraper

30,100 BP (A) — A — C — > 29,000 BP (C)

B — > 35,000 BP (B)

0 m — Wallfall — Disconformity "Balsas" horizon (Tertiary Period)

The dated shell from the Caulapan bed with the stone artifact was returned at 21,850 years BP±850 years (sample #W-1895). This was roughly 10,000 years older than any accepted evidence for humans in the New World. The dates placed the entire team on red alert. Valsequillo was now a pre-Clovis contender, if not a paradigm buster.

The surviving reports, letters, and memos offer a rare glimpse into the kinds of decisions, concerns, patience, and duty during an incredible discovery. The first priority: Get it right. They needed to be careful. The various strings of data and evidence needed to be tightly woven together.

On December 5, 1966, Dr. Malde wrote a letter to the Valsequillo team of investigators including Irwin-Williams, J.O. Brew (Peabody Museum director), Clayton Ray, Virginia Steen, Meyer Rubin, Dwight W. Taylor, and Paul S. Martin. It includes a key discussion on shell dating.

> Subject: Valsequillo Radiocarbon Dates By U.S. Geological Survey.
> From: Harold E. Malde
> December 5, 1966
> Meyer Rubin recently sent me the dates on the Valsequillo shells and the La Malinche soils, and I have been busy ever since preparing a comment about his astonishing determinations, with the enclosed result. This commentary is sent to you for criticism so that we can eventually assemble a mutually satisfactory statement about the significance of the dates. Please criticize my caution (or lack of it), my omissions and inaccuracies, and whatever else tickles you.
> When we agree on what to say in print about these dates and have submitted a manuscript for publication, I think we can then feel at liberty to discuss the dates with our colleagues-not before. I know that I can rely on all of you. If we don't keep our mouths shut, the repercussions could be frightful. Think of the consequences if a newspaper gets hold of this and each of us gives a different statement. We need a concerted, dispassionate response, bolstered by as much concrete data as we can muster. When we agree on what to say, we must immediately send a copy of our statement to Richard G. Ray so that the National Science Foundation will not be caught off-guard.
> Please observe that my enclosed notes have not been sent to Juan Armenta because of a fear that they might by some mischance become prematurely known to interested parties in Mexico, but of course Juan should eventually be the first in Mexico to have this news.

In my commentary about the dates I tried to include enough background information and geology to
make the dates comprehensible. Thus, even though the
dates would be first published without the support of
a detailed report, they would not appear naked and
accompanied only by categorical statements about the
inferred age of a particular archaeological site.
For this reason the dates should not be attached
isolated to a current manuscript-for instance,
Cynthia's contribution to the Extinction Symposium—
and indeed should not be released in any preliminary
form. As you ponder the impact of these dates on
American archaeology, I think that you will agree
that an accurate appraisal of the dates, not hasty
publication, is in order.[17]

One of the first responses came from Dr. Paul S. Martin of the University of Arizona's
Geochronology Lab in Tucson. He was also a Clovis First champion of the first order,
and was convinced that the 12,000y Clovis hunters caused the extinctions of the
megafauna at the end of the Pleistocene. In the letter, he lays out the standard Clovis
First response to pre-Clovis contenders, a response that typified U.S. archaeology for the
next 30 years.

From Paul Martin to Hal Malde
re: 20.000 yr. dates
12-7-1966
Dear Hal,
About the astonishing news of Early-Early Man at
Valsequillo, I'm afraid I'm not convinced, certainly
not at the 95 percent confidence level, that you've
got him. I should have been more attentive during our
days in the field. But let me offer the gratuitous
opinion, which I'm sure you've anticipated. Until
the field evidence is fairly direct, and fairly
simple...with charcoal, artifacts and extinct fauna
all together and in place, you won't disarm the
skeptics.
Let's assume your interpretation is indeed correct—that W-1895 in Barranca de Caulapan is tempo-
rarily equivalent to the artifacts and fauna at
Hueyatlaco and/or that the pumice at Hueyatlaco is
indeed the one equivalent to the ash flow that buried
W-1911 and W-1908 on Malinche. Why after several
years of field prospecting by Cynthia et al plus Juan
Armenta's enthusiastic efforts, is it still not

possible to simplify the evidence? If W-1895 was
collected with *in situ* artifacts of the variety found
at Hueyatlaco in beds where skeptical visitors could
remove more of the same, you would have no problem.
    Perhaps one reason I am mulish is that the Middle
Stone Age cultures in Africa in the 12,000 to 40,000
year time range have been abundantly dated by C-14.
If you are right in nailing down 20,000 year man in
Mexico, the implications are indeed astonishing—that
man should have got to Puebla so early without leaving any obvious evidence in the intensely studied
areas to the north. To disarm this objection will
require a very convincing exposure, one readily com-
prehended in one day by skeptical visitors. Do you
have it?
    Hopefully, Paul[18]

The letter offers insight to the U.S. archaeological mind. In the final paragraph Martin asks how it could possibly be the case that such early archaeology can exist in Mexico "without leaving any obvious evidence in the intensely studied areas to the north." In other words, *how could the early artifacts exist in Mexico and not in the United States?* Or, *It is absurd to think that the Mexicans are finding things down there that we are not finding up here.* There is a hint that Martin is actually insulted by the idea there are older artifacts in Mexico.

Any site that challenged the Clovis model had to be in a pristine context and possess a vestal nature if it was to succeed in busting the Clovis First paradigm. According to eminent archaeologist Dr. James Griffin, any contender must feature a clearly identifiable geological context with no possibility of intrusion or secondary deposition; this would be determined by several expert geologists. Further, there must be a range of tool forms and debris, well-preserved animal remains, pollen studies, macrobotanical materials, and human skeletal remains. Dating by radiocarbon and other methods was also required. To put it simply, the site that overthrew the Clovis paradigm had to be perfect.[19]

Looking back, what is remarkable about Martin's response was that he either ignored, forgot, or otherwise passed over the significance of the 21,850±850-year-old stone scraper from Caulapan. By itself, this *was* direct evidence for a 22,000y archaeology in Central Mexico, evidence that predated the Clovis hunters by 10,000 years! Maybe to him, Caulapan was a speck, an isolate. Martin's bias was devoted to the Clovis hunters as the first Americans. But he also seemed to ignore the other two excavated sites, the 80-plus kill sites around the shores, and the prospect that the entire region was rich with artifacts in hardened silts and sands.

Instead, at the moment the C14 dates were cast, he was on the defensive. Good scientist/bad scientist? Perhaps. Connecting the dots from Caulapan to Valsequillo was proving to be an ordeal. It would take interlocking support from geology, paleontology, soil, and geochemical relationships, and as many dates they could get.

ATOYATENCO
lake beds
XALNENE TUFF
AMOMOLOC
lake beds

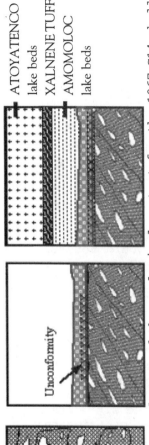

Unconformity

9,000y

22,000y

30,000y

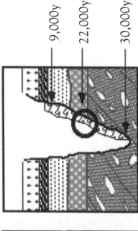

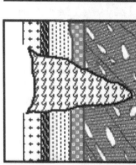

Xalnene
Tuff

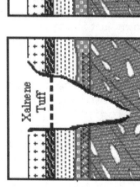

Formation of the Barranca de Caulapan and the geological context for the 1967 C14 shell dates 1. Balsas Group, a limestone conglomerate, deposited during early Tertiary Period (Eocene or Oligocene, ca. 65-40my). 2. Balsas Group deformed and eroded, followed by igneous and volcanic events (middle and late Tertiary). 3. Lake beds, with intercalated Xalnene basaltic tuff (late Tertiary or early Pleistocene), unconformable on older terrain. In 2004, the Xalnene Tuff would be dated by different techniques to either 40,000 years or 1,300,000 years. It is significant because footprints were announced with the younger dates.

4. Atoyatenco lake beds are eroded, followed by Valley cutting in the Pleistocene. 5. Valsequillo Gravels (alleged) deposited during Pleistocene. This is a classic "inset" scenario. 6. Gravels eroded. Circle approximates vertical location of flake tool, bone, and shells that were 21,880 years old.

A month later, the team received another memo from Dr. Malde summing up their concerns. Because of their central importance, only the comments on shell and bone dating are offered here, and prefaced by the memo's advisory on the need for secrecy.

Subject: Plans For Report On Valsequillo Radio-carbon Dates

January 3, 1967

As expected, each of you agreed that it is necessary to keep mum about the actual dates and to assign secretarial typing about this only to persons in whom we have confidence.

Shells

Irwin-Williams's concern about the dates echoed the suspicion of archaeologists that carbonate from shells is likely to be rich in dead carbon absorbed in a hard-water environment. Although this suspicion is verified by experiment (the measured age being as much as 3,000 years too old, and theoretically as much as a C-14 half-life too old—that is, 5,700 years), the applicable fudge factor would not substantially alter the astonishing date for shells in the middle part of Barranca Caulapan, which directly applies to an artifact. (Cynthia confirms that the artifact is "real" and was found *in situ*.) To please critics, the shell dates should be tested.

Various tests of the shell dates are possible, and Meyer has agreed to make them. One test will be a measurement on about 9 grams of modern snails that live along Barranca Caulapan in substantially the same environment as their fossil relatives. Although this sample is small and must be diluted with carbon of known activity, which will add to the experimental "standard error," these modern snails give the best available estimate of the amount of dead carbon possibly incorporated by the fossil shells.

Paul [Martin] suggested another test for the shell dates that might go even farther to allay fears from archaeologists. This will be a date on shells collected by William Minckley of Arizona State University, Tempe, from Monkey Spring, which is a hard-water environment analogous to Moctezuma's Well that yielded a 20,000-year date on living plants. So far, no shells have been dated from spring water in limestone areas.

Bone

Paul [Martin] pointed out that archaeologists will reject radiocarbon dates not actually at an archaeological site where the stratigraphy is unequivocally demonstrable. The only available material for this purpose is bone at Hueyatlaco, some of which according to Clayton [Ray] has no taxonomic value and could be sacrificed for radiocarbon dating. Clayton will contact Cynthia about the propriety of dissolving some of these bone scraps to determine the amount required to obtain sufficient material (that is, collagen, the "insoluble organic matter") for dating. According to M.A. Tamers and P.J. Pearson, Jr., bone collagen will yield only a minimum date (*Nature*, v. 208, p. 1053-1055; also Radiocarbon v. 8, p. 454-455). They list a turtle carapace at least 12,600 years old. As Libby [inventor of C14 technique] explained in his initial appraisal of this method, this may be close to the practical limit of bone dating, because collagen tends to disappear from bone with age. It is unlikely that enough collagen is present in bones as mineralized as those from Hueyatlaco, but this is the last hope we have to satisfy the most adamant critics.

Other samples

A few samples for radiocarbon dating have not yet been analyzed. One of these, shell sample 66 R 14 (site C), 2 meters above the base of Barranca Caulapan, has been cleaned by me and shipped to Meyer. It may yield a finite date and thus provide a basis for estimating the age of the lower part of the alluvium. Also from Barranca Caulapan, Cynthia has perhaps less than a gram of charcoal that was disseminated among the shells of sample 66 R 14 (site B), the lowest bed in the section. When received, I will forward this to Meyer.[20]

Malde and team agreed to keep this first date completely to themselves. Shell is not the best material for dating because it is subject to contamination that would make it 3,000 years younger, around 18,000 years—still the oldest date in the hemisphere. Under Malde's direction, more shell samples were collected up and down the Caulapan profile and from other local arroyos. Charcoal samples were taken from the flanks of La Malinche where the ash burned the ground cover.

Carbon 14 contamination of the dated shell was a big topic. Some believed that the Caulapan shell was likewise contaminated by an unknown source. To test the presence/absence of contaminating agents in the Caulapan sediments, Malde arranged to collect modern shells from living snails. If C14 tests returned dates for the modern shell, it would signal contamination. As it turned out, the modern shells could not be dated and contamination was ruled out. The profile of Caulapan's C14 dates worked out just as they should. The youngest dates were at the top of the column, the oldest were at the bottom—and an artifact was in between.

There were a number of hypotheses being tested, and many gaps that had to be filled and detailed. Was there a connection between the Caulapan beds and the artifact beds of Tetela? If so, where in the hundred-foot column of sediments did they fit? The ideas for the 35–40,000y antiquity of the sites came from multiple quarters. There was the thought that Hueyatlaco or El Horno might lie below the 22,000y artifact stratum at Caulapan. Also, an ash flow greater than 40,000y might overlie the three lower sites (Tecacaxco, El Mirador and El Horno). These were shocking estimates for the archaeologists.

The primary question still remained: Did the Caulapan column reflect the 15-meter deposit of sediments containing the reservoir sites? Was there a one-to-one association? Did it only partially overlap? The link was being suggested by circumstantial evidence, but not yet geologically proven. This assumed greater importance when the C14 dates became known.

Irwin-Williams knew it was going to be a tough sell. Dates from shell were always considered a poor type of material to date because of the error rates that can measure several thousand years. However, in this case, even if the maximum error was figured in, the dates would still be thousands of years older than the oldest Clovis sites. In an unpublished 1967 manuscripts she commented:

> Dates on shells from the Barranca Caulapan (W-1974, W-1896, W-1895, W-1975, W-1898, W-2189). Sample W-1895 yielded a date of 21,850±850 B.P. on shells recovered in association with a single man-made flake scraper. Other samples collected at the base of and near the top of the Caulapan section indicate that the Valsequillo deposition here began sometime before 35,000 years ago and ended about 9,000 years ago. Tentative geologic correlation indicated that the earliest archaeological site in the Tetela region (El Horno) may be about the same age as the basal deposits at Caulapan. The date collected near the top of the deposit provides a *terminus ante quem* for the Valsequillo Pleistocene.
>
> Commentary: Although shell dates were long considered "suspect", recent experimental data indicate that a maximum error of no more than ca.3,000 years is probable. The "modern" date on living snails (W-1974) indicates that present conditions at least do not produce significant deviation. In any case, the indications of man's presence in the Valsequillo region significantly before 12,000 years ago are not altered by a possible error of the magnitude of 3,000 years.[21]

The critical link was the 22,000y date for the Caulapan stone tool, and the associated dates from the geologic column. The top date of 9,000y was right at the transition from the Pleistocene to the Holocene, the modern era. The bottom had a 30,000-year-old date, and two that were "infinite dates": >29,000y and >35,000y. The dates should not be read: "29,000y or older." Rather, they indicate a date older than 29,000y. It could mean that the real date is 30,000y, 300,000y or 1.0ma. There is no way of telling without another dating method.

The majority of the column represented the final 20,000 years of the Ice Age, roughly 9,000y–30,000y. The lowest part of the column hovered at the limits of C14. Malde's geological instincts estimated a fairly old date of 40,000y or older, based in part on the archaeological designation of the tools as modern.

Irwin-Williams balked at the notion. She was willing to consider 30,000y, perhaps 35,000y for El Horno, but only grudgingly. A 40,000y date was too close to the dawn of modern humans.

The Announcement

Irwin-Williams made her first official presentation of the findings in 1966 during a symposium on Pleistocene Extinctions. Paul Martin and others championed this theory about hordes of adept, bloodthirsty Clovis hunters pouring out of the north and killing everything in sight. Her summary paper on Valsequillo was included in the resulting volume, published in 1967, but the new dates were withheld. It was decided that they would make the announcement at the 1967 Society of American Archaeology (SAA) meeting. This was considered the appropriate venue for a discovery of this magnitude. At least, that was the plan. A few weeks before the meetings, on April 10, 1967, Malde wrote the team.

> Rumors about the Valsequillo radiocarbon dates, presumably emanating from the Peabody Museum where Jo Brew spilled the beans, are now beginning to move around the country. To quell misleading tales that may reach Mexico, Cynthia and I agree that our present best course is to prepare an informal statement for quick printing as a newsletter by the Peabody Museum. Obviously, this is not the path to publication we would ordinarily choose, but it seems to be required by circumstances.[22]

The press spread the story throughout the nation. The emphasis on the 40,000y date was something of an embarrassment to Irwin-Williams, who realized she would be "up against it" at the national meetings. The date of 40,000y was synonymous with the first modern humans. A 40,000y presence in the Americas would mean that modern folks appeared in the New World at the same time they first appeared in the Old World. It would spell trouble. She was pissed. It was not supposed to go down this way.

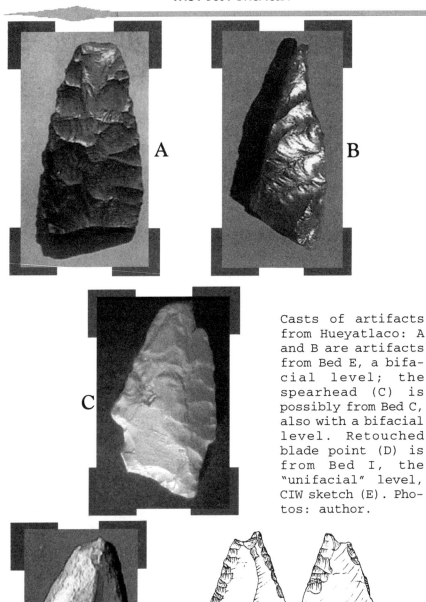

Casts of artifacts from Hueyatlaco: A and B are artifacts from Bed E, a bifacial level; the spearhead (C) is possibly from Bed C, also with a bifacial level. Retouched blade point (D) is from Bed I, the "unifacial" level, CIW sketch (E). Photos: author.

Malde and Irwin-Williams submitted a preliminary report to the Peabody Museum containing a general summary, and then discussed the relevance of the C14 data to the still-undated Tetela sites. Key paragraphs are included here:

Preliminary Report On Radiocarbon Dates From The Valsequillo Area, Puebla, Mexico, by Harold E. Malde, Geologist and Cynthia Irwin-Williams, Archaeologist. (For release by Peabody Museum of Archaeology and Ethnology, Harvard University)

April 18, 1967

A field party of Harvard's Peabody Museum, working with the University of Puebla during the last three years at the Valsequillo archaeological sites in the Puebla Valley of Mexico, has used various indirect geologic methods for dating, which suggest that these sites may represent the earliest known signs of man in the New World. The sites cluster around the northern shore of the Valsequillo Reservoir south of Puebla. Although the only artifact directly dated is in a 22,000-year-old alluvial layer in a tributary north of the reservoir, some of the sites near Tetela may be at least 40,000 years old.

In 1962 Armenta and Cynthia Irwin-Williams, representing the Peabody Museum of Harvard University and supported by the American Philosophical Society, located and tested four sites near Tetela which contained unquestionable artifacts in direct association with extinct vertebrates in the Valsequillo Gravel. With subsequent support from the National Science Foundation, work continued in 1964 and 1966 at Hueyatlaco, the youngest of these sites, which is situated ten meters below the top of the Valsequillo Gravel....Even this youngest site at Tetela may be in part more than 40,000 years old.

First of all, radiocarbon dates for the snails and clams provide rough limits of age for the Valsequillo Gravel, the formation in which evidence of man is found. These dates indicate that the lowest deposits are at least 35,000 years old and that the highest beds are about 9,000 years old. Unhappily such fossils are not preserved in the sites at Tetela. They have been found only in Valsequillo Gravel in three tributary barrancas (deep arroyos) graded to the main body of Valsequillo from the north. Snails and clams in the lowest beds of these barranca deposits, at the localities known as Rio Atepetzingo, Barranca de Xochiac (directly east of the village of Zacachimalpa), and Barranca de Caulapan, are all older than 35,000 years, according to determinations made by Meyer Rubin at the U.S. Geological Survey Radiocarbon Laboratory (samples W-1899, W-1901, and W-1898, respectively). A shell collection two meters above the base of Valsequillo Gravel at Caulapan is dated at more than 29,000 years (sample W-1975). The flake scraper previously mentioned was removed from a bed ten meters higher at Caulapan, in the middle of the barranca deposit where gravel begins to give way to succeeding finer-grained alluvium. Shells from the site of this artifact are dated 21,850±850 years (sample W-1895). Considering the lack of fossil shells in the main body of the Valsequillo Gravel, and the paucity of artifacts in the barranca deposits, it is indeed fortunate that an artifact could be directly dated in this way. Finally, close to the top of Valsequillo Gravel in Barranca de Caulapan, twenty-four meters above the base, the highest collection of shells is dated, 9150±500 years (sample W-1896).

On the chance that these fossil snails and clams may have incorporated some radioactively "dead" carbonate in their shells, thus giving dates that are incorrectly too old, some living shell snails from Caulapan were dated in the same way and were shown to be indeed "modern" (sample W-1974). With this possible source of error ruled out, the dates for the fossil shells are presumed to be accurate.

Summary

The potential significance of these radiocarbon dates for American archaeology cannot be overestimated. In the perspective of man's long history in Europe, Asia, and Africa, where his time or origin is reckoned in millions of years, such ages at Valsequillo do not seem especially old; but the heretofore accepted ages for man in this hemisphere extend back no more than about 12,000 years. (A few somewhat older dates have been accepted by some archaeologists.) If the indirect evidence for the apparent ages at Valsequillo can survive the test of scholarly scrutiny, including further laboratory work by the project members, present hypotheses about man's arrival in North American will have to be revised. For instance, many archaeologists believe that migration from Asia through Alaska and Canada was impossible until about

Hueyatlaco projectile point technologies. All specimens covered with metallic powder to emphasize flaking patterns. Top left: The only specimen noticed so far that seems to exhibit pressure flaking. Top right: A bifacial spearhead with clear flake scars suggesting a percussion technology.

Bottom left: A blade point from Bed I and right, sketches of both faces. Generally, the "unifacial level" contained blade points that were retouched on one side only. In this case, both sides were retouched. Photos: CIW Collection.

12,000 years ago, when a barrier imposed by Pleistocene ice sheets began to melt away, and that man's entrance at that time accounts for the sudden subsequent extinction of many Pleistocene animals which were exploited as food. The evidence at Valsequillo suggests that man's role as predator began much earlier.[23]

For the time being, the 22,000y dated artifact would stand both as a reference point and as a harbinger for Valsequillo's antiquity. It was only one artifact and, similar to the single date, it was not enough to halt the momentum of Clovis First. Other than the absence of direct dates, the sites and their context satisfied Dr. Griffins's list of requirements: The artifacts and bones were gently buried by sands and silts in their primary context with no later additions, intrusions, and no redeposition. All three excavated sites fit the bill. Hueyatlaco fit the bill in spades because it contained a technological sequence from blades to bifaces.

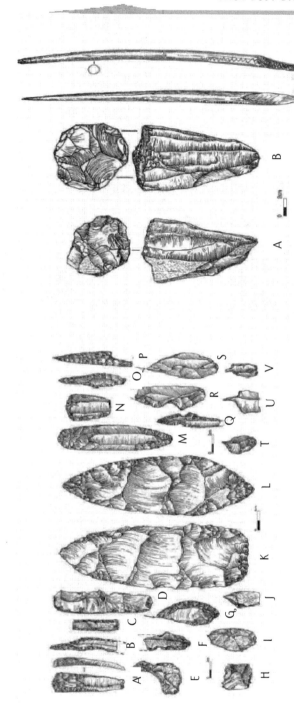

Figure 1. Clovis and Solutrean tools. a–k: Clovis; l–v: Solutrean; a, m–n: end scrapers on blades; b, o: borers; c: retouched bladelet; d: retouched blade; p: shouldered point; e,f,r: notches; g,s: burins; h–j, t–v: gravers. (a: Gault Site; b, c, j: Bostrum site; d, e: Simon Cache; f, g, i: Murray Springs; h: Blackwater Draw Locality 1; k: Fenn Cache; l: Solutre; m, q: Fourneau-du-Diable; n, r, s, t, u: Laugerie-Haute Quest; o: Qulen; p: La Placard; v: La Riera.)

Figure 2: Solutrean and Clovis artifacts. a: Solutrean blade core from Les Maitreaux; b: Clovis blade core from Gault; e: Solutrean sagai from Grotte des Harpons; d: Clovis sagai from Aueilla River.

Comparing New World Clovis technology and Old World Solutrean technology. The Valsequillo technology uncovered by Irwin-Williams would fit comfortably as an earlier technology stage for either assemblage. Photo: World Archaeology.

Stratigraphic Sequence	Typology	Technology
Upper Hueyatlaco Unit C		Well-made bifacially worked artifacts: projectile points, knives, percussion and pressure flaking; burins, scrapers, wedges, knives on flakes and blades; prepared striking platforms.
Upper Hueyatlaco Unit E		
Lower Hueyatlaco Unit I		Edge retouched artifacts: projectile points, scrapers made on blades and flakes with prepared striking platforms.
Tecacaxco		Edge retouched artifacts: scrapers, knives; blades and flakes with prepared striking platforms.
El Mirador		Single edge retouched projectile point made on blade with prepared striking platform.
El Horno		Edge retouched flake tools: projectile points (?), scrapers, burins; prepared striking platforms; no blades.

Irwin-Williams's chart from the 1978 paper depicting the technological evolution at play at Valsequillo. She writes:"An unconformity at Hueyatlaco between units I and E coincides with a change in the artiacts: from simple edge-retouched tools...to sophisticated bifacially worked tools (above) which were made in a variety of forms." "Nowhere in the New World had there been such an exquisite, stratigraphically-supported case for paleo technological evolution. It was what everyone was looking for. However, the 22,000y C14 dates from Caulapan changed all that. Now her sites were more on par with the Upper Paleolithic revolution in Eurasia, a full 10,000 years earlier than Clovis. Photo: CIW Collection.

Chapter 2.5

Lorenzo's Wrath

Early Man a Hoax

Jose L. Lorenzo, in an article in the INAH *Boletin* 289 J(une 1967, pp. 48–51), said that the "evidence" for a 40,000-year-old man at Valsequillo, Puebla, Mexico, was "planted" by the workers who wished to keep their well-paying jobs. He also contends that there is no stratigraphy, that the field notes were kept by the workers themselves, that the scientists supposedly in charge of the dig were seldom present, and that responsibilities were left in the hands of a foreman who frequently had up to 58 workers in charge at three different digs. We are greatly disturbed by all of this. Prof. Lorenzo, head of Monumentos Prehispanicos, is a thoroughly responsible scholar and we must believe his statements, which, incidentally, are documented and notarized. As Prof. Lorenzo says, this is a real blow to Mesoamerican archaeology and must be a severe embarrassment to highly placed U.S. anthropologists and foundations. Moreover, this will give aid and comfort to the "latter-day Hrdlickas" who have their own "Oriental Exclusion Act." In the light of this article we understand clearly the statements which we published earlier that the "materials seem too sophisticated for the date attributed."[24]

This nugget was in the same issue of the newsletter that announced a new Valsequillo grant from the National Science Foundation. It was a double-whammy—good news and bad news all in the same publication. *Dear World, Valsequillo research is going big time thanks to the NSF, and by the way, it was a hoax.* Although the editor, Carl B. Compton, thought Lorenzo's piece would be published before his newsletter, the June 1967 issue of INAH's *Boletin* did not surface until late September because of production delays.[25]

According to Lorenzo, he had just entered one of his Hueyatlaco trenches a couple days after the Peabody's press release. Hueyatlaco was now *his* site and he was continuing the massive trenching operations. On an upper ledge he noticed one or more stone artifacts, which was strange because he knew that those sediments were completely sterile.

Three of the workers allegedly confessed and signed affidavits in front of armed guards. They told him how the artifacts were planted; They pushed them into the floors of units.

One of the most intriguing statements to come out of Lorenzo's snow job was that not all artifacts were planted—just some. However, according to Lorenzo, now that they were all mixed together, and presumably due to the poor memories and trustworthiness of the guilty laborers, it would be impossible to separate the real from the planted. Of course, this was nonsense. Irwin-Williams knew how to take notes and how to take pictures. She had thousands, not the hundreds you see in the archives. The NSF report she was going to work on with Malde was going to include about 2,000 photos from the work.

(Of the thousand or so close-up artifact photos taken during excavation prior to collection, maybe a dozen are in the archives. They were already missing when Virginia Steen-McIntyre checked the archives in Portales, New Mexico, before they were shipped off to the National Anthropological Archives in 1997. Because they are not in the archives, I hope whoever has them steps forward. Maybe there is another set in Mexico.)

Regardless of anything else this affair brought to the surface, an important point shines forth. Amidst all the fireworks, at least there is the admission by Lorenzo that there were Pleistocene artifacts at Valsequillo because he admitted that not all of them were planted. Over time, at least in the United States, many professionals seem to have gradually lumped this "several" into "every."

Armenta's Daughter Speaks Out

Armenta's daughter, Celine, recounted the story she heard from museum workers about the time that armed individuals followed Lorenzo onto the Hueyatlaco site. They were there to terrorize the 50-plus workers while Lorenzo told all of them to sign the affidavits. Only three did. It was a matter of pride for Celine that only three out of 50 stepped forward; the others remained silent. According to Celine, Irwin-Williams was in Puebla at the time getting ready to catch a flight to the States. A museum staffer passed along the news.

```
      The  scientific  authorities  sent  some  men  with
   pistols  to  try  to  scare  the  workers  at  the  field.
   There  were  about  60  workers.  But  three  of  them
```

accepted that the fossils were planted. And only these three people signed the paper, saying, "yes we planted, and the scientists planted the fossils." The other workers never accepted. They were very honest."[26]

A fairly newsworthy incident centering on the Hueyatlaco site, the Irwin-Williams archives contained no accounts asking, *Why was my site raided by Lorenzo's army?*

In Irwin-Williams's mind, there was every assurance that she would be coming back for years and years. *An American in Puebla*. It would probably become her second home. At this point, she was looking at a handsome two-year NSF grant, 20,000y dates, and five out of five Pleistocene sites. She was batting a thousand. She was on top of her game and the whole world was watching. Now she knew her work at Valsequillo was over.

News of the nightmare article reached the Peabody Museum by mid-summer. Lorenzo's charges came out of the blue. As paleontologist Clayton Ray told me, "Everybody just ran for cover." It was a huge shock. Allegations of this nature cannot only destroy projects and careers, they can destroy international relations. An announcement such as this would place the entire network of U.S.–Mexico archaeological relations in jeopardy, especially the projects under Lorenzo's extensive permit-signing domain.

From John Paddock
University of the Americas
July 15, 1967

Dear Dr. Brew:
    The other day I was interviewing Jose Luis Lorenzo to get some material for the Current Research section of *American Antiquity*. Inevitably we came to the topic of the early man work in Puebla, and Lorenzo clearly didn't know what to say. After some hesitation, he swore me to secrecy and then got out some papers for me to read. They were the manuscript of an article he is publishing in the next issue of the *Boletin* of the Instituto Nacional de Antropologia e Historia, and some relevant affidavits. He said he was sending you these documents, and an English version as soon as it can be made. I agreed with him that this is not material for Current Research, but preferably for [the] Facts and Comments [section], where an interchange of views can take place.
    Realizing that you are responsible only in a legalist sense, and that other esteemed colleagues are likewise involved without having had real control over the events, Lorenzo has written his account in a tone that I found very fortunate: restrained, friendly,

almost light; but clear and firm at the same time. Often in circumstances of misunderstanding no graver than these in Mexico and elsewhere, there have been scorching denunciations. These impede communication within the profession, and it seems to me that science is strangled by lack of communication. I do hope that the serene and judicious language used by Lorenzo may be maintained in the inevitable and necessary rejoinders. Keeping it all secret would only lead to rumors, always exaggerated. Ventilating it calmly will hurt those involved less than rumors, and will help orient all those planning to come here from other countries to work in the future.

Perhaps I should note that I do not know any of the principals, nor have I ever visited any of the sites concerned. The reason I presume to write you is simple; I have a selfish interest in good Mexican-U.S. relations. And I know that your Mexican friends are likely to be somewhat too politely reticent in a case like this, whereas painful candor comes easier to us northerners. Please don't think I make an exception of myself; see *America Indigena* XVIII:1, pp. 73–75, for one incident in which I learned the hard way.

No doubt a field archeologist of your experience knows that the attitudes of one's workmen, their state of education, their poverty, their tiny local problems all are highly meaningful to our work, and may be ignored only at the cost of incidents like that of Valsequillo. But there probably are some pertinent factors that may not occur to you. For example, you may not be aware of all the many incidents of various kinds of misunderstandings with foreigners working here in recent years (and we *gringos* are a large majority of all the foreigners). The Oscar Lewis scandal affected us. Dumping of cotton by the U.S.; setting sugar quotas; the bracero problem; and many other even less clearly related factors affect any archeologist working here, whether in his relations with officials, the press, villagers, or all of them. In a country whose very selfhood is symbolically (if not in reality) threatened by the inescapable colossal presence on the north, the patience being shown is encouraging. They could make some political hay by striking chauvinistic attitudes, but they have not done so.

> Both in this case and in general, I am aware that I have much to learn. Skillfully handled, the Valsequillo case can be a useful experience for all of us.
>
> With utter sincerity, then, I wish you well in fielding this hot potato.
>
> Yours cordially,
>
> John Paddock
>
> cc: Jose Luis Lorenzo[27]

Politics were in full swing, diplomacy was imperative, and careers were at stake. Paddock's bottom line: *Tell Cynthia to be nice.*

Lorenzo had sent an English translation of his *Boletin* article to *American Antiquity*, the first and last word for New World archaeologists. The president of the SAA, Dr. Gordon Willey, wrote *American Antiquity*'s editor to discuss what to do.

> Gordon Willey to R.E. Bell (Editor, *American Antiquity*) 24/July/1967
>
> I have been in touch with J.O. Brew and know about the Lorenzo correspondence concerning Valsequillo.
>
> As you perhaps know, Lorenzo has always been dead-set against the very early claims made for Valsequillo —even back when Armenta was running it alone, before Cynthia Irwin-Williams came into the picture. It looks as though he is working overtime to discredit the claims for Antiquity. The question is still up in the air—and he may be right—but I don't have a very high opinion of affidavits signed by Mexican workmen. Why is it that every time we move up on this question of how old man is in the Americas the record has to be muddled up so that we can never be sure?
>
> Anyway, Jo, the Peabody Museum, and I, in an advisory capacity as President of the SAA, have no objection to [Lorenzo's allegations] being published in *American Antiquity;* however, if it is published it would be only fair to let Brew, Irwin-Williams, or both have equal space, in the same issue, for a rebuttal or whatever statement they may care to make. I think you will agree that this is the proper course. With all best wishes[28]

Bell wrote Lorenzo and told him they would publish his paper followed by a rebuttal from the team members. Lorenzo backed down. It would only be published in the *Boletin*. Still, what was his motive?

Tlapacoya

A little more than a month later, in early December, the next issue of INAH's *Boletín* loudly announced the discovery of the "earliest site in the Americas" by Lorenzo's prize student Lorena Mirambell. Located 30 kilometers south east of Mexico City, Tlapacoya was a site with extinct mammal bones and artifacts. Mirambell's article was backed up with a report by C. Vance Haynes about Tlapacoya's multiple C14 dates ranging from 22,000y to 24,000y. Tlapacoya was a tad older than the Caulapan artifact. Tlapacoya's sediments would also be contemporaneous with Caulapan's mid-section. Lorenzo had a lot of respect for Haynes and he asked the geoarchaeologist to collect the charcoal samples to run dates at the Tucson radiocarbon lab.

When Tlapacoya was published in the following *Boletín* issue in December, it may have given a clue to Lorenzo's intentions. First, he would stain the competition at Valsequillo, and then champion his own candidate for "The Oldest Site In The Americas" trophy. (In a paper he wrote in 1978 on pre-Clovis contenders, Lorenzo's Tlapacoya is labeled 24,000 years old, still the oldest, while Valsequillo's dates are shown as 22,000y.)[29]

This was a critical juncture in the history of archaeology, and little if any evidence has been divulged on either side—the gringos or the Mexicans. It has laid dormant, way beneath the surface. In 2001, the planting scenario was still the official scenario, which had made it okay to ignore the Valsequillo region. Asking Lorenzo if you could work Valsequillo would be similar to asking Vance Haynes to support your work at Calico. Not a good career move.

In September 1967, Malde let fly a letter to Mexican geologist Guillermo P. Salas, a colleague in Mexico who served as liaison to the geology side of the project.

```
Ing. Guillermo P. Salas
Instituto de Geologia,
Ciudad Universitaria
Mexico 20, D. F.
September 29, 1967


Dear Ing. Salas:
    I have the unpleasant task to inform you that Jose
Luis Lorenzo has again become hostile toward the
Valsequillo Project. You will recall that, in March
1966, Lorenzo required that Juan Armenta and Mario
Pichardo could not collect fossil vertebrates in the
Valsequillo region, and he further insisted that our
collecting of vertebrate fossils could be done only
with his permission. Lorenzo's requirements hampered
our work in Pleistocene paleontology.
```

Now, by a manuscript submitted to the Society for American Archaeology for publication in American Antiquity, Lorenzo makes the fantastic allegation that artifacts recovered in 1962-1966 by Cynthia Irwin-Williams and Armenta from the Valsequillo Gravels were "planted" by local workmen. To support his charge, Lorenzo has obtained notarized statements from three of the workmen. We understand that Lorenzo will also seek to publish his allegation in a Mexican journal, probably the Boletin of the Instituto Nacional de Antropologia e Historia.

Lorenzo's manuscript and the statements by the workmen are full of inconsistencies, inaccuracies, and lies, which are easily refuted by verifiable field records. Cynthia Irwin-Williams has prepared a detailed reply that she hopes to publish simultaneously with Lorenzo's allegation, both in Mexico and the United States. If you wish, I can send you a copy of her response.

Lorenzo's behavior in this affair borders on paranoia. I write to you about his peculiar (not to say, unprofessional) activity so that you can be on guard in future official matters in which he has a part. I regret, wholeheartedly, that the present deplorable situation makes this necessary.

Sincerely yours,
Harold E. Malde[30]

Dueling Archaeologists

After going through the Irwin-Williams archives, I can only wonder about the letters related to this incident are stuck in other archives from the central players on both sides of the borders. But it was Irwin-Williams's call, and Compton agreed that Irwin-Williams could reply to the November piece in the December newsletter. She fired back with both barrels.

Valsequillo Finds Well-Documented "Hoax" Was a Hoax

Dr. C. Irwin-Williams wishes to express regret that the Instituto Interamericano saw fit to print and apparently approve without attempt at verification of the irresponsible and false statements of J.L. Lorenzo concerning the archaeological work of Harvard University and the University of Puebla at Valsequillo, Puebla. A full detailed rejoinder to these statements should appear in the literature in the near future. A few brief comments, all subject to verification, are appropriate at this time.

Lorenzo's nearly pathological opposition to the Valsequillo work for nearly ten years is a matter of record. It has led him to commit several extraordinarily unethical actions, (details available), of which this is simply the latest. The so-called documentation of Lorenzo's allegation consists entirely of statements elicited from three native workmen who were and are entirely under his control. (Two subsequently received lucrative jobs and one was saved from legal prosecution for crudely planting an artifact in one of Lorenzo's trenches on our principal site, which Lorenzo had taken over.) The statements themselves are so filled with internal inconsistencies and clumsy verifiable falsehoods as to be ludicrous.

On the other side of the coin, in point of fact the Valsequillo work was actually purposely excessively well documented because of its potentially controversial nature. A few verifiable facts of the matter are as follows:

1. The matrix of the Valsequillo is much too hard to permit indistinguishable "planting" (the local people build their houses out of blocks of it).

2. No artifact or flake was ever excavated by a workman; all were excavated and fully documented by a professional archaeologist (95 percent by myself personally).

3. In several instances, close associations of artifacts and extinct fauna were removed in blocks and preserved. These exhibits were seen by several Early Man specialists in 1962. They were destroyed by Lorenzo in 1963.

4. More than 1,000 closeup photographs minutely documenting each find are available.

5. The statement about one foreman for 58 workers and high wages is simply nonsense, and records already on file in the granting institutions and at Harvard University document this.

6. Workers' notes were kept only to supplement my own full and detailed records and to promote accuracy on the part of the workmen.

7. A professional archaeologist was almost always at the sites that I myself was present at, except when writing up field reports.

8. If the stratigraphic situation is unclear to Lorenzo, it is because he has failed to read or comprehend my three detailed annual reports to the Instituto Nacional de Antropologia e Historia.

9. For accuracy, the Instituto Interamericano should have checked my statements on the relation between the uppermost sophisticated materials from Valsequillo, and the 40,000-plus date. Nowhere do I state that I accept this age.

Before accepting Lorenzo as a serious scholar whose opinions should be given credence, I suggest that members of the Instituto Interamericano:

1. Observe first hand some of his own field techniques (I will be happy to loan photographs of these);

2. Search the literature for a single monograph by Lorenzo on a major site.

3. Interview Middle American specialists (Mexican and foreign) concerning their knowledge of the increased difficulties surrounding field research in Mexico and the deterioration of international relations, which have accompanied Lorenzo's term in office.

Dr. C. Irwin-Williams[31]

By attacking her methodology, Lorenzo was attacking her personally. In a paradigm-busting case such as this, methodology was everything. If you can tarnish the method, you can tarnish the discoverer, and thus the discoveries. This is what Lorenzo did, along with blaming her for local economic instability.

In effect, it created a chasm between the gringo version of the discoveries and the Mexican version, versions that persisted up to 2001. The Mexican officials I worked with were all told the artifacts had been planted. The Smithsonian's Dennis Stanford told me that there was never any doubt in the States regarding the archaeology because they never had a doubt about Irwin-Williams's mastery in the field. The 3,000 photos didn't hurt either. *Where are they?*

A Case of Gringo Disrespect?

Up until now, I have tried to emphasize the intra-Mexican case of academic "jealousy" that scuttled Juan Armenta Camacho, because Armenta felt Lorenzo's breath from the get-go. But now it became an "international incident." Lorenzo held all the cards that mattered, the ones with his signature on them. I do not know how many gringa projects relied on that signature, but I suspect quite a few. If things got nasty, gringos doing research in Mexico could indirectly suffer.

Was the only reason for this outrage because Lorenzo wanted top-billing for Tlapacoya? When the permits were signed, there was a stipulation that any announcement of a discovery go through Lorenzo's office. When J.O. Brew sent out the press release in April of that year, Lorenzo and INAH must have felt slighted. It was an international affront to Lorenzo, his office, INAH, and the Mexican nation in general.

The press release from Director Brew took place just days before Lorenzo found the "planted artifacts." After the release, Lorenzo contacted Director Brew at the Peabody complaining that the contract signed with INAH explicitly stated that *INAH* would be in charge of any announcements of significant finds in Mexico. He had a point. The gringos had shown disrespect for the Mexican nation.

Lorenzo learned of the announcement when everyone else learned about it—in the morning papers or at work. Nobody—no gringo nor Pueblan—contacted him. This oversight probably infuriated him. This was the biggest news to hit Paleo America since Dr. Figgins announced the Folsom discoveries! And to make matters worse, there was Armenta on the front page again alongside Irwin-Williams for a photo op.

Within a week of the announcement, he discovered the "planted" artifact(s) perched on a ledge inside the trench, in the open. It is here that the planting theory has its beginning, just days after the gringos went public. Circumstantial? Sure.

The Tempe Meeting

Before the Boletin article was even in the mail, Marie Wormington arranged for an invitation-only meeting in late October at the Arizona State University in Tempe. This included key paleo-archaeologists from around the nation. It took a single afternoon of slides and presentations to demonstrate that the Valsequillo data was concrete, and that Lorenzo was out of his mind. It also made the news. George Turner wrote a fine summary of the discoveries, also noting the problems with Lorenzo, in the *Amarillo Sunday News-Globe*, on December 3, 1967.

> Team of U.S. and Mexican scientists soon will publish evidence suggesting that man existed on this continent far earlier than had been previously known—possibly as long ago as 35,000 or 40,000 years.
> The first stone artifacts were found nearly 30 feet below the surface of the formation include knives, scrapers, stemmed points and perforators. They are strikingly sophisticated in manufacture, featuring bifacial work of a high order and the use of basal thinning.

At a somewhat lower strata they encountered arti-facts of a still earlier period, also of a high technical quality. These include bifaced tools and a large, leaf-shaped point [found next to a] horse.

Below the second group of artifacts is a strati-graphic break - a "missing" period of indeterminate duration. Below this the scientists found, to their amazement, four more assemblages of artifacts, the lowest of which was at the very bottom of the forma-tion [El Horno], nearly 100 feet below the surface!

On Oct. 27, a symposium was held at Arizona State University at Tempe, where a number of the nation's most distinguished scientists gathered to study the Valsequillo evidence. The consequences of these find-ings may shatter some long-cherished theories. Dr. Marie Wormington, curator of archaeology at the Den-ver Museum of Natural History, told the symposium that the finds represent "our earliest known traces of man in the Americas."

"There is an intelligent climate for accepting earlier dates in the New World," [she said].

A newly developed method of dating by Thorium-Uranium measurement is being applied now to the or-ganic material. The results should be known by late in December and may do much to dispel the controversy.[32]

The Thorium-Uranium dating would dispel the controversy about as much as gas dissipates fire.

Part III

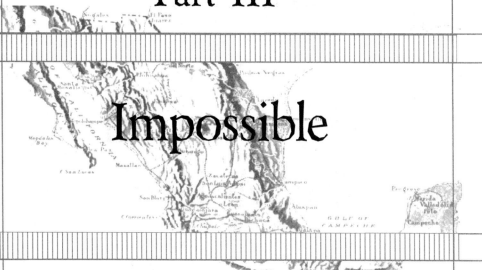

Impossible

Chapter 3.1

An African in the Mojave

Louis Leakey must have felt right at home when he visited the Mojave Desert. He could visualize savannahs and mountain forests nourished by deep, flowing rivers, intersected by lakes and about 30 inches of rain a year. He was looking at thousands of square miles, millions of birds, elephant herds, camels, horses, big cats, and canine carnivores. The Mojave Desert during the Pleistocene would have been a lot like home.

He saw vast stone workshops set into desert pavements, and tight windblown mosaics of small lithic survivors nestled together by deflation, and protected for thousands of years by a fragile crust. Cores and flakes and occasional tools littered the mosaics, sometimes on top, sometimes enmeshed.

The Calico Hills belong to a huge alluvial fan complex: sedimentary erosional aprons that build up around the base of desert mountains. The Calico Hills were part of an alluvial fan that was cut off from its source by earthquakes. It was no longer building up, but eroding and sending out its own mini-aprons instead.

Dr. Leakey was on the hill overlooking Pleistocene Lake Manix, a huge dry lake in the middle of the desert (one of many nourished by the Mojave River from the southwest and the Owens River from the northwest, both draining into Death Valley). These rivers actually made a circle of lakes, making the Mojave a wildlife wonderland with 30 inches of rain a year during the glacial periods (pluvials). During interglacials, such as now, it would revert back to a desert.

The African gravitated toward very old sites, so this was nothing new for him. He probably never collected a C14 sample in his life. For Leakey, 40,000y was yesterday, no big deal. Add another zero and he might be interested.

For Leakey, Calico would have been a paradise for early man. The beautiful cherts meant it would be a paradise for archaeologists, too. The Calico Early Man Site was born. It was 1964. So began Dr. Leakey's only New World dig. He would succeed if he found anything that was more than 12,000 years old. The artifact he saw in a nearby bulldozer cut had already assured that.

The hill excavations were next to a county dump just north of Yermo, a desert hamlet sharing the monstrous sky, searing heat, and blasting winds. Located east of Barstow, California, between Los Angeles and Las Vegas, the Calico Hills was best known for its "ghost town," a wild west attraction. For rock hunters it was known for its agates, jaspers, and fossils. For miners there was copper and bentonite, an industrial clay.

Leakey had long believed that Asian tribes could have migrated down the Pacific Coast earlier than Clovis. Lowered sea levels, as much as 300 feet, would have extended the coastline another 10 miles west. And that's where most of the best early American evidence would be: underwater.

Above: Master Pit I showing the nature of the Yermo Formation and grid units. In the upper right is the witness column left as a check on pit stratigraphy. Page 136, top: Louis Leakey removing an object left in place on the floor of a Calico Master Pit. Important objects were preserved *in situ* for Dr. Leakey to inspect before their extraction. Page 136, bottom: The superstructure that protects the Master Pits. Photos: Dan Griffin, courtesy of the Friends of Calico.

He had heard of the 30,000-year-old sites on Santa Rosa Island off Santa Barbara. Phil Orr found roasted remains of pygmy mammoths, and he even collected artifacts. Similar to the pebblefacts from San Diego collected by George Carter during the '50s, the specimens were all condemned as geofacts—Nature's mimicry of intentional fractures. What made the Calico venture superior to other pre-Clovis candidates was the rock: cherts and agates. Similar to flint, these rock types make it much easier to separate Nature's mimicries from the real McCoys. Experience also came in handy, and Leakey knew early tools as good as anyone alive. And good rock made all the difference in discerning intent, a human thing. The Lake Manix cherts and agates, besides gorgeous, clearly captured the flake scars and platforms that evidenced human activity.[1]

At the time, Leakey wasn't exactly sure how old New World cultures would date, but he figured at least 50–60,000 years. At the same time, 20,000-year dates were coming out of Australia, the official index for Pleistocene seafaring. It could only be reached by water. It had never been connected to southern Asia, or else those lovable marsupials would have disappeared into the bellies of Asia's felines in short order. It was indeed an island continent. Not even the New World held that honor since it was connected to Asia off and on for millions of years. Because Australia could only be colonized by boat, the date for the First Australians was also regarded as the index date for the First Pleistocene Seafarers. Currently, the earliest sites Down Under are more than 60,000 years old.[2]

Dee Simpson

Ruth DeEtte "Dee" Simpson, of the San Bernardino County Museum (SBCM), had caught Leakey's attention a few years before with some stone artifacts from Pleistocene Lake Manix. The stone was generic flint: chalcedony, chert, jasper, agate, and petrified palm. (For geologists, frustrated by archaeologists demanding exact identifications, they are often clumped together as cryptocrystalline silicates or siliceous rock.) These were highly valued materials, the kind used to make the best spearheads and arrowheads.

And that's what caught her attention! There were no traces of projectile points, whole or fragmented, among the thousands of surface artifacts she walked over. However, there were plenty of cores, and handaxe-types, and other more primitive looking tools. As she surveyed the higher, older lakeshores of Pleistocene Lake Manix, the tools were more sand-blasted, and more patinated than the artifacts on the lower shores—indications that the higher artifacts were older still.

At first, Dee thought the ovate bifaces ("handaxes") were initial preforms or roughouts for spearheads. During the early stages of point manufacture, the biface material is tested for flaws. If it is pure, the points are roughed out into basic triangular or oval shapes, sometimes to be finished as spearheads at the quarry sites, and sometimes packed up and finished at the village. Invariably, bifacial preforms are broken during the operations and are tossed. Dee saw no sign of spearheads or even preforms in the Calico Hills. Neither did Leakey.

Supported by the National Geographic Society (NGS), the Calico Hills became the Calico Early Man Site. There was a little grumbling among the gringo paleoarchaeologist clan, but they were totally eclipsed by the giant NGS public relations machine. Leakey was becoming a household name and he was there to solve the great mystery of the First Americans. There was plenty of fanfare, excitement, specials, news, and interviews.

The Academy had not invited Leakey, and he was not sponsored by the Society for American Archaeology (SAA). Instead, he had been invited by one of their own, behind their back and without their blessing. Dee Simpson was now a turncoat, an outcast.

Dee earned her Master's degree in anthropology at University of Southern California in 1944. Early on, she hadn't seen any pre-Clovis evidence either. She knew George Carter and had seen his "Carterfacts," and she had long thoughts about the so-called "pre-projectile point horizons" being reported around the state and the nation. Then she happened across her own patch of preprojectile point artifacts.[3]

Reports of such artifacts were rarely made of such high-grade material. Generally, pre-projectile point assemblages are equated with pebble and cobble industries where quartzite and other intractable materials dominate. The square miles of high-grade cherts changed everything. She showed Leakey some of the Manix surface artifacts, and that was pretty much that. Good rock is good rock, regardless of where you are in the world.

The cherts around Calico were rarely rounded cobbles or pebbles. Some were boulder-sized, but many were squared off, already fractured, and then eroded some more by the fierce sandy winds. The 15–20ma Miocene limestones were the source of the siliceous rocks that mysteriously form as geochemical precipitates inside the stone. Sometimes they formed into hollow geodes with their interior crystal wonderlands. Look closer at the geode's edge and you find layered agates and cherts. The chunks and pieces eventually eroded out onto the surface. Later, they became part of the alluvial fans of the region. This type of stone quarry is known as "float."

The Calico excavations took place in a small area of a huge fan that was no longer connected to its mountain source. The flat stratigraphy inside the pits meant that the mud, rocks, and artifacts were deposited on level ground, and subsequently buried by another level deposit of mud, rocks, and artifacts—maybe 11 deposits in all. Once the fan had been cut off from its source, perhaps by an earthquake, there were no more depositions. After that, the fan remnant entered into its present stage of erosion. During all this, the mud sediments became very, very hard, harder than those at Valsequillo.

On the surface of "the hill," and for square miles around it, there were countless artifacts catching the sun's rays for more than 12,000 years—possibly double or triple that—but there was no way to date them. On the bumpy and eroding fan surfaces, there were likely instances where surface artifacts could have been reburied as sediments from higher ground sloughed down the slopes. But for the tens of thousands of artifacts trapped 20 feet below the surface in cemented deposits, they were put there when the fan was still "alive," still attached to its mountain source, still building.

The Calico artifacts were going to be old, very old, and that was going to be a practical problem, as well as theoretical. No organic material for C14 was available.

Even though it was probably going to be more than 40,000 years old anyway, it still would have been nice to find something (anything) with carbon. The subsurface artifacts were extremely suggestive of human workmanship and they were trapped in natural cement. But the artifacts were just strange enough (non-Clovis enough) to arouse catcalls by the orthodox geofactsters. *The geology of the site was going to be so old, there's no way these could be artifacts regardless of what they look like.*

By 1968, Calico achieved the status of a true American wonder. The PR machine at NGS made sure of that. For the first time in U.S. history, a full-blown archaeological expedition was excavating a Pleistocene alluvial fan. Among the more orthodox archaeologists there was a lot of doubt. Calico had become both a site and a non-site to most archaeologists. All agreed there were artifacts on the surfaces of the Calico Hills, but it was the subsurface finds that were being disputed by the geofactsters. Because there was no available carbon to date, the Clovis Firsters remained unmoved by all the hoopla.

Leakey and Simpson understood what Wormington and Irwin-Williams understood: They had to find artifacts *in situ* under the surface. They had to dig. Between 1964 and 1967, Calico produced dozens of good artifacts and hundreds of waste flakes amidst plenty of naturally fragmented float.

One of the things that many pros do not know or comfortably forget is that several test pits were excavated away from the excavations to see if the same artifact densities occurred elsewhere in the alluvial fan. They turned up virtually nothing, a comparison of maybe two or three possible artifacts versus the average of at least a thousand per unit down at the master pits. But hey, if the Firsters were already of mind to ignore the likes of superstars Francois Bordes and Mary Leakey, who both agreed with Louis Leakey that these were indeed artifacts, then this rather dramatic presence-absence pattern was not going to phase them either.

A Preprojectile Point Horizon?

In 1960, when word of Armenta's art was announced, Dee Simpson immediately took notice. In 1962, she traveled with a team of enthusiastic luminaries to the Valsequillo sites and the feature blocks first hand, *before* Lorenzo destroyed them. Back in 1962, Dee was still respected by the Paleo professionals. By 1968, she was a renegade.

In that year, Irwin-Williams requested from Dee, and others, a short testimonial to support her rebuttal to Lorenzo. Aware of her less-than-cherished status among the *American Antiquity* crowd, the journal printing the rebuttal, Dee declined because her reputation might have done more harm than good to Cynthia's cause. She wrote back.

```
March 5, 1968
Dear Cynthia,
    I have your letter of February 22 regarding your
continuing problems with the Valsequillo work. I am
amazed that there can be problems related to the
```

block material. By its very destruction it is evident
that the material was in it, not loose or just in
association. I should think that Prof. Armenta would
have the proof in photographs.

Looking back to 1962, this is what took place: I
arrived in Mexico City for the Congress and found
messages from Dr. Krieger saying that I should get to
Puebla and see this material. I tried to find Marie
but she had gone down already. There was one free day
between the Congress sessions and the field trips I
was to take. On that day, Dr. Carl Schuster, Dr.
Charles Rozaire, Dr. Krieger, Dr. Muller-Beck and I
drove to Puebla, were met by Dr. Armenta and his
student and first visited the site. The block material had already been removed. We then returned to
Puebla and saw the block material.

I did not actually handle the matrix or specimens
as I would not have wished visitors to handle such
material had I found it. However, I am fairly certain
that Dr. Krieger did.

Cynthia, in view of my involvement with this highly
exciting and controversial project [Calico], I suspect that any comment I might make would bring more
fire down upon you and the Valsequillo work. I suggest that you contact Dr. Krieger at the University
of Washington, Seattle, or Dr. Charles Rozaire at the
Los Angeles County Museum and get a statement from
one or both of them. So far as I know, Dr. Schuster
can be reached through the American Museum of Natural
History. I do not know where Dr. Muller-Beck might
be. I suggest you get a statement from one of these
(or more) and then, if you wish, note that I was also
in the party and did see the site and did see the
block material in Puebla.[4]

Dee was concerned that her association with the "controversial" Calico project might diminish Cynthia's attempts to restore the integrity of the Valsequillo discoveries. It shows the career pressure Dee was under for taking a risk and asking Leakey for help. She knew the stalwarts of the Academy would not support a non-Clovis look for early man. She stepped out of line and invited a "foreigner" in to help—an act that forever disassociated her from the archaeological main stream.

Others were also involved in treading the pre-Clovis/non-Clovis waters, but without the entourage that followed Leakey. A few months earlier, Irwin-Williams received another letter from Alabama. Pre-projectile point assemblages were turning up outside California, and looked primitive and crude compared to the slick Clovis technology. Its friendly tone turns into frustration when the discussion turns to pebble tools that are not receiving serious attention.

From: Dan Josselyn
Alabama Archaeological Society
University of Alabama

To: Dr. Cynthia lrwin-Williams
Eastern New Mexico University
Portales, How Mexico 88130
Dec. 21, 1967
Dear Dr. Cynthia:
Thanks for your comments in full on Lorenzo's allegations. But you have no cause for worry—this affair will get you tremendous publicity which people will read! And it will be good for archaeology too—a dash of pepper. I'll run a third and final item on it in our Feb. newsletter.

We who "hope to have readers" are quite grateful for this exchange. Archaeology can get a bit dull.

Your reputation is of course secure. Only yesterday, as it happens, I wrote the Denver Museum asking the price on [your] "Excavations at Magic Mountain." I want to give it a more than average review, recommending it to all archaeologists, especially those struggling with the problem of lithic taxonomy. As a retired science writer, I am particularly interested to see good archaeological reporting.

I've had my own problems of misrepresentation, misunderstanding, etc. For eight years I've been running an annual fund drive...to finance highly select summer excavations by the Univ. of Alabama. This began as a search for a good Paleo site—we have fluted points by the actual thousands, in many varieties. Then, with the discovery of really classic "pebble tools," by the tons and with a broad tool assemblage, I turned to promoting interest in this direction.

I was obliged to publish privately to get what I wanted, some 300 illustrations and 20,000 words (mimeographed), it is most "preliminary" but I'll send you a complimentary copy as soon as the seasonal load of mail lightens.

The pebble tool picture has proliferated amazingly since I began the vigorous agitation. How on earth we overlooked them so long, I shall never understand—though our American "thin biface eye" no doubt contributed largely. I ran a second drive in

1965 to finance professional exploration for a pebble tool site worth excavating, resulting in the 1966 excavation of a high terrace site and a shelter. I am now in the delightful throes of classifying the thousands of artifacts, and hope to heaven I can finance a major publication.

I'm accused of "theories"—which I detest. My only point is that we have overlooked an amazing and abundant lithic technology—let's <u>see what it means!</u> I wish all archaeologists could see the ton of "crude stuff" spread all over my tables, floors, spare beds. Wormington, Krieger, Desmond Clark, Dragoo, Vertes, Bordes, Leakey, Muller-Beck, Stirling, etc., agree with me that we <u>must</u> investigate this matter thoroughly.[5] (Emphasis in original.)

In Josselyn's last paragraph we find that just asking questions about early assemblages brought a lot of heat, regardless of the luminaries who felt the same way. This heat came from the dogmatic Clovis First folks. By merely acting on his interest and curiosity, Josselyn was accused of "theories." "Theories," specified in this way, resemble the modern accusation of conspiracy theories.

In the "you're with us or against us" world of Clovis-Isolationism, every question, no matter how innocent, was regarded as an allegation against the Brahmin, who would then turn around and let you have it. When they accused Josselyn of "theories," it was his thinking abilities that were being attacked. It carries the notion that you suffer from a gullibility toward the fantastic, that you cannot discern science from fantasy. The fact that he lists so many others sharing the same curiosity strengthens Josselyn's position. His frustration was evident, but he was not alone. In the end, it did not matter one bit. Clovis First was just too entrenched to let *facts* get in the way.

Why were pebble tool industries such a sensitive issue in 1967? For one reason, there was something nonsequitur between the glorious Clovis and Folsom technologies, and the relatively crude and primitive broken pebble assemblages found on the west coast, the south, and north into Canada.

If Clovis was first, how could such a crude, primitive, expedient, simple technology be derived almost immediately from the Clovis-Folsom technologies—two of the most exquisite hi-tech traditions that ever graced the prehistoric stage?

❋ Were the pebble tool traditions derived directly from the Clovis culture?

❋ Did the pebble tool traditions represent Clovis progeny adapting to Holocene conditions?

❋ Did the primitive pebble industries represent the way the Clovis-Folsom flintknappers worked with pebble and cobble rock sources?

❋ Were the pebble industries linked to Clovis industries?

❋ Were the pebble industries the proto-Clovis stage out of which Clovis technology evolved?

✳ Did they belong to a contemporary non-Clovis culture?

✳ Did they represent the vestiges of an earlier arrival?

These were questions worth asking. Alex Krieger brought attention to pre-projectile point assemblages in 1961 while he was going through Juan Armenta Camacho's pebble and flake specimens prior to the fieldwork. Even today, the pre-projectile point category is used in modern California archaeology, yet no attempt has been made to rectify its obvious conflicts with the Clovis First framework.

The Clovis arrived with a full-blown spearhead tradition and a range of high-tech Pleistocene skills. If they, and their super spearheads, were first, how can you argue for a pre-projectile point horizon and not at the same time infer a pre-Clovis horizon? How do you go from ultra-sleek sophistication to ultra-primitive cores and flakes in an archaeological blink of an eye? Did something happen that made the immediate offspring of Clovis-Folsom suddenly forget how to make the fancy stuff? Or was it how they dealt with cobblestone—same people, different kinds of rock?

Pebble and cobble artifacts of quartzite and basalt and other tough rocks are often regarded as "crude," "primitive," "simple," "core and flake industries," and "expedient." Quickly made and disposable tools are the name of this game. Ancient stone worker's wisdom ruled the day: "There is nothing sharper than the fresh edge of a new flake." The clean edge is an instant knife. Whack a flake from an obsidian core and you have the sharpest knife on earth; only a laser is sharper. Whack off a flint flake and you have a knife harder than steel. A quartzite flake, also harder than steel, had the added advantage of a naturally serrated edge, similar to a steak knife. Retouch is generally used to make the edge stronger and to shape it, not to sharpen it. When it dulls, then it can be resharpened.

There was another reason to wonder about the old pebble tools in the Americas. Everyone had agreed that Native Americans came from Asia. And what do you find in Ice Age sites in eastern Asia? You find pebble tool assemblages up and down the coast. Pebble tools are everywhere. They go back more than a million years in East Asia. In outback regions like New Guinea and other island jungles, they are probably still being used.[6]

You would think then that pebble tool assemblages would be a natural specialty for New World archaeologists. Yet, the idea that their makers came before Clovis was something never seriously considered (by anyone who mattered). Given the weight of technological progress in evolution and archaeological circles, you would think someone would have asked: Who ever heard of such a highly complex technology suddenly devolving into something so primitive and cruddy? Though it contradicted our sense of progress, it just didn't fit the Clovis framework, so it wasn't talked about much. If you considered early pebble technologies as something older than the Clovis hunting technology, you too might have been accused of "theories."

Some discoverers of pebble tools lost their jobs, and, in one case, the boss of a discoverer, a museum director, lost his job, too.

Sheguiandah

Sheguiandah, a site near Lake Huron in Canada, cost the director of the National Museum of Canada his job. Dr. Thomas Lee had uncovered stone tools that geologists dated at up to 120,000 years old. After discussing the matter with a trusted friend, Lee reported a date of greater than 30,000 years to make it more palpable. The Clovis Firsters would not be denied. Dr. Lee wrote in the *Anthropological Journal of Canada*:

> The site's discoverer was hounded from his Civil Service position into prolonged unemployment; publication outlets were cut off; the evidence was misrepresented by several prominent authors among the Brahmins [Clovis Firsters]; the tons of artifacts vanished into storage bins of the National Museum of Canada; for refusing to fire the discoverer, the Director of the National Museum, who had proposed having a monograph on the site published, was himself fired and driven into exile.… Sheguiandah would have forced embarrassing admissions that the Brahmins did not know everything. It would have forced the rewriting of almost every book in the business. It had to be killed. It was killed.[7]

Texas Street and George Carter

George Carter is one of the most conspicuous mavericks in American archaeology. He even had a whole class of artifacts named just for him: Carterfacts. Even though his doctorate was in geography, he had a strong archaeological background from his Berkeley graduate days and hooked a job at San Diego's Museum of Man as a curator. His 1957 *Pleistocene Man In San Diego*—and later his 1980 *Earlier Than You Think*—tore apart the Clovis First arguments by citing Southern California artifacts that were clearly in sediments dating back before the Wisconsin Ice Age. He found many examples of tools belonging to early Asian cultures, including skreblos (a type of chopper) and large scrapers, in San Diego sediments he dated to at least 50–100,000 years.

Ideas such as this were strictly taboo. It would mean that people were here before they were human (officially 40,000y). The archaeological academy would not stand for it, and neither did San Diego's Museum of Man. Carter was kicked out on the spot and took off for Johns Hopkins University, later ending up at Texas A&M University, teaching geography and continuing to buck the orthodoxy for the rest of his life. His 1950s exile from San Diego's Museum of Man was legend—a successful sacrificial warning for all wannabe pre-Clovis explorers. It didn't matter; it probably steeled his resolve to spend the rest of his life figuring out new recipes for sacred cows.

Carter had taken on the two taboos: *Thou shalt not exist before Clovis*, and verily, *Thou shalt not sail the ocean blue before Columbus*. Everything you need to know about the last 50 years of gringo prehistoric research is wrapped up in these axioms. Carter found evidence for all sorts of New World plants that mysteriously turned up in Asia, and vice versa, without explanation. As with all such mavericks in 20th-century archaeology, he was resoundingly ignored, and in some quarters even despised.

His current work is an attempt to answer a variant of the old question, "Why did the chicken cross the road?" For Carter, he wanted to know how chickens crossed the Pacific. *How did Asian chickens get here before Columbus? And while we're at it, how come Mesoamerican corn is accurately illustrated in 12th-and-13th century East Indian art?* He had no shame.[8]

One of Carter's great legacies was that he was the first to seriously introduce bipolar flaking as a counter to all of the geofact-happy assignments being given to his artifacts. Bipolar flaking is a technique to break cobbles and pebbles similar to breaking a walnut by laying it on a rock and smashing it with another rock. A pebble or small cobble is held vertically on a large stable boulder (anvil), and then struck from above with a large hammerstone (maul). This process generates fracture forces from opposite points, often meeting in the middle of the core. It generates a huge and varied (chaotic?) range of shapes and fragments. Its strength is that it supplies a lot of edge per core and lots of different kind of edges, such as steep and thin, convex and concave.

Bipolar flaking was one of the first technologies identified among Gona, Ethiopia's 2.6 million-year-old artifacts. Chimps use it to break nuts. It also appears to have been used by hunters for breaking open long bones for their marrow, and for cutting edges. Late Prehistoric Pueblo and Moundbuilder societies commonly used this technique to make quick, sharp edges for expedient tools. Bipolar flaking has always been around, and with pebbles and cobbles it was always an option for tool making. Sadly, it has been virtually ignored by all but a few flintknappers and other experimental-minded archaeologists, and for no good reason except that you cannot control it, which is not a good reason either.[9]

Had more students and professors just tried it out, to see what happens when you break a rock as you would a nut between two rocks, we would be in a much better position to deal with lithic assemblages, old and new. This is not brain science, but it might be a study in chaos theory. Altogether, it is a powerful, if haphazard, but eminently useful pebble breaking technique. You might not be able to predict what you would get, but it sure gives you a lot of edge types and choices. Had the mainstream experienced what bipolar flaking was all about, they might have thought twice about Carter's claims. It was a tragic and costly oversight.

Bipolar flaking became associated with geofacts, aka "Carterfacts," and the traditional desert taxon for questionable artifacts, "leverites." If you mentioned bipolar flaking as a viable technology, at least on the West Coast, you could be accused of giving oxygen to Carter's theories, or actually endorsing them, and not even know it. A guilt by association thing? If so, it was just silly. If you don't know bipolar, you don't know the full range of intentional fracture types nor their context. Period.

Lithic analysis has come a fair distance since a few centuries ago when lithic scatters on the English countryside were thought to be caused by exploding witches. The lithic universe of the archaeological mission will not be complete until it deals with bipolar flaking, which might actually be worse than exploding witches, but I will leave it to material scientists to make that determination.

An Early Man Death Sentence

In my first upper division archaeology class at San Diego State in 1973, my professor warned us all not to visit Carter's Texas Street site. Carter had apparently returned to do some more excavations at his infamous site, and my professor must have feared we might be "infected" with his madness if we got too close. The professor made a point of not telling us where the site was. His final words: *If you visit the Texas Street site, you will be kicked out of the department.* This was essentially a death sentence for any aspiring California archaeologist...if you got caught. It meant your curiosity would never be tamed, disciplined, nor aligned with the scientifically credible. It meant you had a yen for the incredulous. Such interests would only tarnish the good name of archaeology in the future.

None of us had ever heard of Carter or his infamous Texas Street excavations, and a few of us walked out of class that day in a bit of a fog. *What was that all about?* We didn't know, but it gave us a mission: *Get a six-pack and find the site.* It turned out to be only a few miles from campus, but we managed to miss it anyway. That lecture *did*, however, fill our heads with suspicions that there was more drama than we thought to American archaeology, but it was something we'd have to find out about on our own. Valsequillo nor Sheguiandah were ever mentioned in class, and Calico was always considered an official joke.[10]

The Middle Way

Everyone realized that if you crossed the line into the pre-Clovis school, you had better be right. In 1966, nobody worth listening to was. By the end of 1967, the Tetela sites stood front and center. Valsequillo was anything but a pre-projectile point assemblage. It had plenty of points. That's what made it stand out, along with the art. The Valsequillo artifacts were at least 10,000 years older than Clovis, and they were fairly sophisticated. There were also the pebble tools that Juan Armenta Camacho sent to Dr. Krieger and Irwin-Williams in 1961. Could they be older still?

The group of archaeologists supporting Valsequillo were not Clovis First fanatics, nor did they believe in Carter's and Leakey's 100,000y-plus Pleistocene Man ideas. They were somewhere in the middle, and not immediately dismissive of the pebble tools *per se*. They remained devoted to the idea that modern humans, *but only modern humans*, were capable of making the overland trip from Asia. Theoretically, they were ready to accept immigration scenarios as old as 35–40,000 years, the same antiquity as modern man. They had suspicions that there was more to the origins of American prehistory than a virgin world culturally impregnated by a single (Clovis) culture. Valsequillo was proving their suspicions correct.

When Dr. Wormington told the ASU symposium in October 1967 that Valsequillo represents "our earliest known traces of man in the Americas," she also opined that, "there is an intelligent climate for accepting earlier dates in the New World." Her statement was a direct communication to the Clovis Firsters to put on their seatbelts. The perfect proof for pre-Clovis presence in the New World had been found, and it was at least 22,000 years old.

Chapter 3.2

Valsequillo:
Coming of Age

During the mid-1960s, Louis Leakey had his hands full with another matter back in Africa. In 1961, "Zinj" had been dated by a new technique called Potassium-Argon, or K/Ar. Certain types of lava and ash can be dated with this technique. K/Ar gauges the radioactive decay of an isotope of potassium to produce argon gas. The switch to argon can be clocked, but minimum dates do not kick in for hundreds of thousands of years. (The technique had been suggested for dating volcanic ash layers at Hueyatlaco, but the mineralogy was wrong.)

The stratigraphy of Olduvai Gorge, similar to Valsequillo, was interspersed with ash beds. In 1961, K/Ar tested an ash bed above the spot where his wife found Zinj. Mary Leakey also happened across another set of bones as old as Zinj, but they were modern enough to qualify as *Homo habilis*, or "handy man." For the world, it was the oldest member of the genus *Homo*. The K/Ar dates would apply to both species. Prior to this, nobody imagined it would be older than 300–600,000 years. When the results were announced, everyone choked: Zinj and *Homo habilis* were 1.8 million years old.

The two hominids were 1.8ma, according to a new dating technique. Trusting the date depended on your trust in the technique. Not surprisingly, suspicion fell on the K/Ar dating technique like a pile of bricks. *It had to be wrong! It's impossible! This is crazy.* Suspicions lingered. Even in the Olduvai camp there was doubt, but then, what if....*Have a beer, mate. Let's talk about this.*

In the time it took to read the results, the secure foundations of human evolution theory crumbled to dust. (Imagine finding out in your 40s that you were adopted.) It meant a total restructuring of the accepted academic framework that sanctioned and approved Ph.D. dissertations and grant requests. Entire research programs would need to be revised. All textbooks would have to be rewritten. For those with careers invested in the mainstream theories, it was a suckerpunch. For students not yet shackled by the old dogma, it was sheer joy. *We just got a lot older and there's a whole other continent to look at!*

The human legacy had increased by a million years. The backwoods, incidental role assigned to Africa was replaced with superstar status. Other than Leakey, most anthropologists figured the roots of mankind were in Asia or Europe. Finding Zinj in Africa was a huge surprise. Finding Zinj to be 1.8ma was mind-blowing. Africa, the Leakeys, and the roots of humanity would forever be entwined in the annals of anthropology and science—like it or not.[11]

The Olduvai debunkers consoled themselves: *What do geochemists know about evolution anyway?* K/Ar was a single technique and its track record was short.

Nevertheless, the Olduvai dates were now on the table. Some chose to believe them; others did not. Deep down nobody knew what to believe. Any degree of certainty would have to wait until they could somehow double-check the K/Ar dates.

Bitten by the insatiable bug, others began gearing up to explore the rift valley's buried secrets even though the doubt about the Zinj date lingered. It was *not* the kind of doubt that throws the baby out with the bathwater. The doubts surrounding Zinj were questioning "certainty." *How can we be certain the K/Ar dates are this old? How can we be certain the dating technique really works? What other dating technique could check the K/Ar results?*

This type of doubt did not ignore the fact that, whatever the dates, the region was hominid rich. Africa was now fair game.

Dating Discrepancies

C14 dating was going through its own series of checks during the 1960s. Minze Stuiver at the University of Washington came up with the bright idea of dating tree rings with C14. Tree ring analysis, *dendrochronology*, counts years by annual rings. It is by far the most accurate dating technique, but the oldest trees were around 6,000 years old. Beyond that, C14 was on its own.

Because you know the age of a tree ring, why not date the tree ring with C14 and see if it jives with the tree ring age? It was a test of C14's accuracy. If there was always a constant amount of C14 in the atmosphere as had been assumed, the C14 dates should coincide with known tree ring dates. Generally, these tests found that there was close agreement between the carbon dates and tree ring dates. But in some cases, the C14 dates were way off. Conclusion: The assumed atmospheric constants used in the C14 formula were not always constant. All previous dates falling into the problematic temporal zones had to be recalibrated to derive the adjusted "real" dates. This turnabout did not adversely affect prehistoric reconstructions in the Americas; in terms of the Old World, prehistorians were sent scrambling.

> Back at 3000 B.C. the necessary change is as much as 800 years. These changes bring with them a whole series of alarming reversals in chronological relationships. The megalithic tombs of western Europe now become older than the Pyramids or the round tombs of Crete, their supposed predecessors. The early metal-using cultures of the Balkans antedate Troy and the early bronze age Aegean, from which they were supposedly derived. And in Britain, the final structure of Stonehenge, once thought to be the inspiration of Mycenaean architectural expertise, was complete well before the Mycenaean civilization began.[12]

Flip-flop. The traditional timeline of sophisticated technologies was put on its head. What came before is now after. What was thought to be the cultural source of Stonehenge may have actually been the recipient. The country bumpkin megaliths of western Europe predated Mediterranean civilization by a millennia, forcing folks to consider: Did Stonehenge culture beget the Mediterranean, or did the two regions grow independently? For Classical archaeologists in love with the romance of the eastern Mediterranean and the Near East, it came as a slap in the face, but one they had to get used to. They finally had to accept this science thing about changing amounts of carbon in the atmosphere.

The Whole World in His Hands

Simultaneously, the Leakey discoveries in Olduvai and at Calico were threatening another flip-flop in the prehistoric evolutionary realm. He was taking on both the Old and New World arenas. If both Calico and Olduvai were true, they would combine to toss out the rule books for the Old and New Worlds. The whole world would be a whole new game. Olduvai succeeded in rewriting the books in the Old World, but Calico continues to be demonized and ridiculed, largely because Leakey died before the matter could be settled. Nobody with gravitas came forward, probably because while the artifacts may have been convincing, the age was beginning to look similar to 500,000 years old, maybe more. Oh my!

A classic example of these frail confidences can be found in a couple letters from the Smithsonian, the first congratulating Dee Simpson on her Calico artifacts, the second to tell her she should have kept the first letter confidential. Dr. Allan D. Griesemer, former director of San Bernardino County Museum, and old friend of Dee Simpson, recounts the incident.

> As an example of the paranoia that existed within the profession in North America at the time, when 37 casts of some of the best artifacts were sent to the Smithsonian in 1969, Dee received a glowing letter about their authenticity, a portion of which said: "We are delighted to see the specimens for they look so much like the kind of chipped artifacts that come from sites in southern Brazil, northern Argentina, and Uruguay and other parts of South America. Anyone who doubts these are artifacts is making a grave error." But when Leakey made pubic mention of their reaction, their enthusiasm rapidly diminished. They sent another letter to Dee stating that those words were written "in confidence."[13]

Salvaging the self-esteem of New World archaeology meant total war on Leakey by the geofactsters. A similar battle had happened a decade earlier with Tom Lee's Sheguiandah and George Carter's distressing 100,000y pronouncements for San Diego's Texas Street. The orthodoxy had successfully stripped them of credibility. But if Leakey's Calico "artifacts" were accepted publicly, then you could bet your bottom dollar that Carter and his Carterites would reemerge from exile and *that* battle would flare up again as well. (It did anyway in 1979, during an Early Man conference at the San Diego Museum of Man. It was a great show-and-tell featuring non-Clovis and often extremely weathered artifacts from San Diego to West Texas. It ended the same way other attempts to extend the Clovis boundary ended: *No skull, no dice.*)

For Leakey, then, on the world stage he was 50/50: Olduvai, yes; Calico, no. In truth, he was 100 percent right about Calico's artifacts. Francois Bordes and Mary Leakey concurred. Calico has every Middle Pleistocene tool in the book and then some. And if they weren't artifacts, then there was a genuine miracle in the Mojave, because nowhere else on earth is there another such "geofactual" parade of types and subtypes. Being right doesn't always work, though. Academic fear can be a fierce and unreasonable opponent.

Calico's historical demise was due to Vance Haynes's hatchet job in *Science* a year after Leakey died. Bottom line: Each and every one of the 60,000-plus artifacts were geofacts. No, that's wrong. This was not established. Rather, it was more a hypothetical conclusion built on shady innuendoes that each and every one of them *must* be geofacts because they were *too old*. It was a huge difference because it did not matter what they looked like or how many there were. It was clearly a case of "a nod's as good as a wink to a blind horse," so Haynes got away with it. How *Science* peer reviewers ever permitted such skewed reasoning in their pages should be a scandal; instead, the community at large regarded the article as Calico's guillotine. They still do. They are still wrong.[14]

Glass Fission Track Dating at Olduvai

At Olduvai Gorge, another "new" uranium technique called Glass Fission Track dating was being tested. Using a different set of principles, Fission Track dating came up with similar dates of 1.8–2.0 ma. The results were printed in *Science*. Two dating techniques based on different principles produced similar dates. The agreement of the two dating techniques substantiated the enormous antiquity of Zinj and *habilis*. Evolutionists—physical anthropologists, archaeologists, paleontologists, biologists—were stunned. Now they had to deal with it.[15]

To their credit, the experts came around to accepting the dates *and* the dating techniques. There was little choice because the science was sound. The more they understood the local geology and the animal remains, the more the dates made sense. They adjusted. This is what real scientists do. In 1974 and 1980, two papers were published showing how additional Fission Track dating agreed with the first results. The Olduvai hominids were the oldest on Earth. The new isotopic techniques had successfully withstood the cross-checks; they would become popular methods used around the world for charting distant time. Also, as all archaeologists will attest, reliance on multiple dating techniques is always preferred: the more the merrier, especially for dates beyond 40,000y.

The great antiquity of humans in the Old World requires techniques that can measure past the 40,000y mark. New World archaeologists, on the other hand, certain of the recent nature of human occupation, figured that C14 would be the only dating technique they would ever need to date the earliest Americans. Valsequillo changed all that.

Coming of Age

Between the 40,000y limits of C14 and the earliest dates available from K/Ar, there was about a 700,000 year gap. This Middle Pleistocene gap coincided with the time that *Homo erectus* evolved into *Homo sapiens sapiens*, the most critical—and still the most mysterious—transition period that scientists quest to expose.

Attempts to date the final stretch of human evolution relied on relative geological and paleontological reconstructions. In Europe, glaciers had flowed and receded several times leaving footprints of their comings and goings. General sequences of geological deposits could be relatively plotted and dated to one of the four known ice ages. Elsewhere, certain extinct species gave you a ballpark time period. Glaciers never passed over the Olduvai Gorge during the Pleistocene, nor did they pass over Valsequillo. And in central Mexico, the extinct animal record was still open, because species closer to the glaciers in El Norte may have gone extinct while they thrived further south, such as the four-tusked gomphothere on Armenta's art piece.

The quandary of how to directly date the Tetela sites continued to haunt the Valsequillo team. Then came one of Hal Malde's USGS cronies, geochemist Barney Szabo. On May 15, 1967, another day of infamy, Malde gave a talk about Valsequillo to the Colorado Scientific Society. Szabo, who was present in the audience, approached Malde asking if he could be of help. He had been working on a technique called Uranium Series Disequilibrium (U-Series). One of its advantages was that it had a range of around 10,000 to 400,000, overlapping with the 40,000 range of C14. It could also date bone directly. Hueyatlaco, Tecacaxco, and El Horno—the Tetela sites—had plenty of bone.

The mineralized quality of the bone meant it could not be dated by the C14 technique. Did this mean the bones were older than C14's 40,000 limit? Not necessarily. The local geochemistry may have quickly mineralized the Valsequillo bones. It was only a guess, but it made people cautious about leaping to conclusions. The bones may have looked "real old" but there was no way to prove it objectively.

After the May 1967 announcement of the 22,000y dates, and throughout the rest of the year, the team was dogged by complaints that they had not yet demonstrated a geological or temporal connection between Caulapan and the Tetela sites. For Hal, Szabo's invitation sounded like a good idea. *What could it hurt?*

As it was politely described to me, uranium decay can be metaphorically understood if we recall the watches with radium dials. Elements on the watchface would glow in the dark and we could tell the time at night. Over time, the glow would diminish and fade, and it would be time to buy a new watch. The period it took for the glowing elements to fade was predictable and measurable; the decay of the glow was something you could clock.

U-Series dating measures a process of uranium decay whereby the uranium gives birth to daughter elements, thorium and protactinium. The ratios of these elements to uranium in a sample can be measured and dated. If valid, it would effectively close the undatable gap between *H. Sapiens sapiens* and *H. Erectus*. It was still regarded an experimental technique, and there was still some doubt about the most recent periods it could date. Could you date things that were 10,000y? 5,000y? 3,000y? Nobody knew.

For Malde and the rest, Szabo's Uranium Series technique might add some light on a number of unresolved issues:

❋ The ambiguous C14 infinite dates for lower Caulapan and the other arroyos.

❋ The undatable condition of bone at the Valsequillo sites.

❋ The growing call for greater proof that the Caulapan sediments were contemporaneous with the Tetela sites.

❋ Nothing else on the market could be applied to this time frame.

The team decided to use the U-Series technique to date the same places the C14 technique had dated to check one against the other, such as Caulapan and a couple other barrancas. They would also date bone from Hueyatlaco, the highest site in the Tetela column, and El Horno, the lowest (older). If the new dates coincided with the earlier C14 dates, then there was greater reason to accept the "stand alone" Tetela dates where C14 could not be applied.

By the end of 1967, the bone had been collected from the sites and the arduous process of obtaining the U-Series dates had begun.

Malde wrote letters to archaeologist Jean Brunet of Puebla and to paleontology grad student Mario Pichardo. Both letters requested additional samples of shell and bone for Dr. Szabo's tests. Malde had hoped to use the U-series technique to date shell from Caulapan that had been dated by C14. It would serve as an effective one-to-one comparison of the two techniques. Shell could not be found, so they had to content themselves with bone.

Bone samples for the U-series tests were collected from two barrancas, Caulapan and Atepitzingo, and the Tetela sites. The bones from Barranca de Caulapan were both proboscidean (elephant). A vertebrae fragment was collected from "Unit E," the same stratum containing the chert artifact that was shell dated by C14 at 22,000y. A tusk fragment was collected near the base of Caulapan's stratified column, previously dated to 30,600y±1000. From Barranca de Atepitzingo—the source of two other mineralized engraved bones—a horse footbone (metapoidial) was collected from a stratum previously dated to greater than (>) 35,000y.

At Hueyatlaco, a camel pelvis fragment was taken from Stratum/Unit C, the youngest (highest) Pleistocene stratum that contained bifacial artifacts. From El Horno, representing the lowest (oldest) archaeological stratum, a cheek tooth from a butchered mastodon was selected; according to Hal, Irwin-Williams insisted that this specimen was itself an artifact (modified).

Two samples from previously dated Colorado sites were included as additional checks for U-Series accuracy. An extinct Bison anklebone (astragalus) was collected from the 10,780-year-old Folsom horizon of the Lindenmeier Paleoindian site. From Fremont County, a skull and horn fragment of a giant bison was taken from sediments previously estimated as Sangamon to Illinoian in age, or about 80–250,000 years old.

The results of the U-Series tests were mailed to Malde in June 1968. According to Szabo, the thorium (th-234) dates and the protractinium (pa) dates were derived by independent methods. This means that the U-series dating technique includes a "self-checking" component. If the two date ranges do not overlap, there could be problems. If the ranges coincide or overlap, the dates are probably accurate, or at least "consistent."

Caulapan Uranium Series dates

(U-series: th=thorium; pa=protactinium)

Middle Caulapan (artifact stratum, "Unit E"):
C14 shell dates: 21,850±850
U-series, th: 20,000±1500
U-series, pa: 22,000±2,000

Lower Caulapan (base stratum)
C14 shell dates: 30,600±1000
U-series, th: 19,000±1500
U-series, pa: 18,000±1500[16]

The U-series dates for the Caulapan artifact stratum, "Unit E," matched the Carbon 14 results. The U-Series dates of 20,000 (±1500) and 22,000 (±2,000) overlapped with the radiocarbon dates. This was an incredible hit, because two very different dating techniques came up with virtually the same dates. From a scientific perspective, a securely dated, 22,000-year-old utilized flake alone should have substantiated the argument for a pre-Clovis antiquity in the New World.

The news was not so good for the second set of dates from the bottom of the Caulapan column. The U-series technique dated a tusk fragment from the basal strata at 19,000 years, at least 10,000 years younger than the radiocarbon dates (>29,000y, >35,000y, and a newer shell date of 30,600y±1000). It was also 3,000 years younger than the 22,000y artifact dates meters previously mentioned. When dates fall out of sync this way, it is called a "reversal," bringing up the specter of contamination or some other anomaly.

Later, it was determined that the tusk had not been excavated from the basal strata, but was collected from the surface near the base—it could have dropped out of the cliff face above. The semi-good news was that the date still registered in the Late Pleistocene ballpark.

The dates from the Valsequillo bones were something else altogether.

Valsequillo Uranium Series Dates

Hueyatlaco (youngest Tetela site)
245,000 yrs±40,000 (th)
>180,000 yrs (pa)
245,000 yrs±40,000 (open system)

El Horno (oldest Tetela site)
>280,000 yrs (th)
>165,000 yrs (pa)
>280,000 yrs (open system)

Atepitzingo (barranca) Dates
340,000±100,000 (th)
> 180,000 (pa)
260,000±60,000 (open system)

It was here that Team Valsequillo officially entered the Twilight Zone—literally. Instead of 20,000 or 35,000 or even 40,000 dates, the U-Series dates indicated that the Tetela Peninsula artifacts were in the neighborhood of a quarter million years old!

It was another bombshell, and compared to the other bombshells—the 22,000y C14 dates and the charges of planted artifacts—the Valsequillo U-Series dates were positively nuclear. In the words of Irwin-Williams, the Valsequillo dates "were crazy." The dates were a surprise to everybody and brought up an immediate dilemma: Either the dating technique was bogus or the final phases of human evolution were in need of a total rewrite. For the archaeologists, Valsequillo had graduated to a world-class pain in the ass—way worse than Olduvai.

Time charts show the great magnitudes of time at stake. The 22,000 year Caulapan dates almost doubled the 12,000 cellar of the Clovis Americans. The Tetela sites, averaging 250,000, were 20 times older than the Clovis dates and a full 10 times older than the Caulapan dates.

Using the cellar metaphor, the present time is the floor of your house. The 12,000 year-old Clovis First cellar is a cellar 12 feet deep, a thousand years per foot. You step in an elevator and head down smoothly to the 12th subfloor, the Clovis level. When the 22,000y Caulapan C14 dates were announced, visualize yourself in an elevator free falling 10 feet. It's a jolt but you survive. This would be the new Caulapan cellar, the 22nd subfloor level. From an evolutionary perspective, this early date would not be considered impossible because it is fully within the time frame of modern man.

Now imagine a 200-foot drop. The U-Series dates meant that there was at least a 200th subfloor to American antiquity. At this depth, Dr. Irwin-Williams would be shaking hands with Mr. Erectus. It was a nightmare.

1969

Clovis 10,000 B.C.

Caulapan 20,000 B.C.

First Humans 40,000 B.C.

Valsequillo 200,000 B.C.±

A depiction of the archaeological chasm that opened up with the announcement of the Uranium Series dates from the Tetela sites in the Valsequillo basin.

Chapter 3.3

A Fork in the Road: Archaeology Versus Science

A date determined for bone associated with an artifact (Caulapan sample M-B-6) agrees with a radiocarbon date for fossil mollusks in the same bed and indicates man's presence more than 20,000 years ago. However, some of these bone dates exceed 200,000 years. Because such dates for man in North America conflict with all prior archaeological evidence here and abroad, we are confronted by a dilemma - either to defend the dates against an onslaught of archaeological thought, or to abandon the uranium method in this application as being so much wasted effort. Faced with these equally undesirable alternatives, and unable to decide where the onus fairly lies (if a choice must be made), we give the uranium-series dates as a possible stimulus for further mutual work in isotopic dating of archaeological material.[17]

—Abstract: Szabo, Malde, and Irwin-Williams, 1969

It was the summer of 1968—a week since Robert Kennedy was gunned down in Los Angeles, two months since Martin Luther King, Jr., was murdered in Memphis. The presidential primaries were over, and the conventions were on the horizon. If 1967 is remembered for its Summer of Love, 1968 was the Summer of Revolution.

The future and the past were quickly expanding out of the present. The whole world was watching as NASA was readying for the first moonwalk. Leakey's Olduvai Gorge was adding more than a million years to the human legacy, his Calico site was threatening to add a hundred thousand years to American prehistory, and now Valsequillo was knocking on the door.

A Fork in the Road: Archaeology Versus Science

The sophisticated artifacts dated to more than 200,000y, and were as socially charged as the 1.8my dates at Olduvai. Though not as old as Olduvai, the scale of difference between scientific expectation and scientific result *was* comparable. For New World archaeologists the discoveries implied that *Homo erectus* or very early Neanderthals had settled in Valsequillo a quarter million years ago. And if that was not enough, the paleo hunters of Valsequillo had mastered a stone technology that Eurasians would not dream up for another 160,000-plus years. The archaeological consensus of this scenario was: *Fat chance. Sheer nonsense.*

The most visible premodern contender was Leakey's Calico site, but it was highly contentious. Here was an Old World superstar up against a bunch of aspiring New World superstars who had very little experience with Early and Middle Paleolithic artifacts. It would be one thing for gringo archaeologists to swallow a 10- or 20-thousand-year error. But a 100- to 200,000-year error? *This old guy from Africa is coming over here, throwing his National Geographic Society weight around, and in less than a year he is lecturing to all of us that we have overlooked an extra 90,000 years of prehistory? Who does he think we are, a bunch of idiots?*

There would be another reason for corporate displeasure if Calico turned out to be "real." After ridiculing and scorning and virtually outlawing both Carter and Leakey from the gringo classroom, it would be a terribly bitter pill to swallow if the mavericks turned out to be right. This could not be allowed to happen—not without some awfully good evidence to back it up.

That brings us back to Valsequillo. It was not just one site, but four, with dozens of others waiting in the wings. Valsequillo was an entire region! Three sites had been excavated and analyzed by experts—some of the same experts who dismissed Leakey and Carter. The Valsequillo archaeology was not in doubt; it was never in doubt. It was a textbook case of primary deposits with artifacts and bones: a terrific context for a paradigm-busting discovery. It only had to be older than 12,000 years, and the Caulapan dates had already clocked in at 22,000y.

But then the geologists had to go ruin the whole thing by insisting on dates when only *Homo erectus* and Neanderthals roamed the earth. The certainty of a dating error was based on the most sacred archaeological canons of the day:

✳️ *Homo erectus* and Neanderthal were not intellectually capable of adapting to the arctic rigors of the trip from Asia.

✳️ Even if they did somehow make it across from Asia, they would not be capable of making the sophisticated stone tools for another 160,000y or so, which is the earliest they turned up in the Old World.

Nothing added up. The Valsequillo dates were simply impossible. Conclusion: The dating technique must be faulty. Dates on an order of 200,000y had to be wrong, and not just wrong by a little bit, but wrong by a whole bunch, maybe a factor of 10. The Hueyatlaco and El Horno dates should have been 20,000y as with Caulapan, not 200,000y-plus. All doubt and suspicion focused on the "messenger," the experimental Uranium Series technique. *Szabo better check his numbers again! We're not buying this for a minute.*

Hal Malde and Barney Szabo knew from the start that the U-Series dates from Hueyatlaco and El Horno would upset the archaeologists. They were also wise in the way that science sometimes works, recalling the atmospherics after the first Olduvai dates. In that case, science ultimately prevailed. But that was the Old World.

The New World archaeologists would not be so easily swayed. If some archaeologists were willing to cry "bloody murder" when the 22,000 year dates were announced, coronaries were predicted for the 200,000-year announcements. Indeed, U-Series dating was still being refined, but did that mean it could be rejected wholesale? There may have been slight errors, but there was no reason to throw the baby out with the bathwater; yet, that is exactly what the gringo archaeology community did. In fact, they ended up throwing out the entire tub, the Valsequillo basin.

The archaeologists, geologists, and paleontologists who had worked together as an integrated team had reached a fork in the road. Either the geochemists were completely wrong, or the archaeologists were completely wrong. Who was it going to be?

"Completely Wild!"/"Rolling in the Aisles"

The letters and memos that follow were never written for the public, but as a means of figuring out how best to present the "crazy" dates to a curious public. These behind-the-scenes communications between the central players contain language you would never see in the peer-reviewed literature, and it exposes what was *really* on their minds, such as the off-the-cuff, gut-level wisdoms you hear in bars during archaeology conferences.

The results of the U-series dates arrived in Malde's mail in mid-June. Irwin-Williams was directing fieldwork at the Clovis site of Blackwater Draw, and would not hear a word until August. On June 11, 1968, Malde reported the dates in a letter to paleontologist Clayton Ray.

> I understand that the Th-234 and Pa methods are independent, in the same sense that fission-track and K-Ar [Potassium-Argon] are independent. The analyst, Barney Szabo, therefore is encouraged by the concordant results. He thinks they could be correct. He is further delighted by the agreement between C14, Th-234, and Pa for Middle Caulapan. I, of course, am fighting against my instantaneous disbelief. Apart from archaeology, we should be able to appraise the feasibility of these results....The very old dates from Hueyatlaco, Atepetzingo, and El Horno shatter my imagination, but I know of nothing from geology to reject them categorically....What worries Barney is that, if two of the dates (Lindenmeier and Caulapan) are reasonable, the other concordant dates cannot be ruled out.[18]

Atepetzingo was the arroyo where Armenta found two other engraved bone artifacts. The C14 shell date for the arroyo (W-1889) had measured ">35,000," meaning only that the shells were older than 35,000 and could theoretically be 36,000y or 360,000y. When the 260,000 year date was established for the arroyo's bones, it lined up with El Horno and Hueyatlaco, the vicinity of Armenta's other engraved art pieces.

In a June 21st letter to dating specialist Meyer Rubin, Malde said that "Barney likes the concordant dates," and that the Middle Caulapan date for the artifact agrees with the C14 shell date. The U-Series test has built-in cross checks. Each date concluded through an independent method. If the two dates are concordant (meaning they overlap each other), it adds validity to the acquired dates. If the dates do not overlap, then it probably denotes a problem. Szabo's dates were largely concordant. From that vantage point there was credibility in Szabo's findings.

```
    If some of the dates are correct, we can't cat-
egorically reject the older numbers. Geology and
paleontology can't disprove them. I haven't yet heard
from Cynthia, but may soon hear a loud explosion from
New Mexico. No archaeologist is going to accept those
numbers.[19]
```

Concordance was also applied to the C14 dates, and here the U-Series dates did not fare so well. Or did they? The best example was the direct hit with the 22,000-year date for the shell/artifact/bone stratum at Caulapan. On the other hand, Szabo's Lower Caulapan date of 18–19,000 was at least 10,000 years *younger* than the 30,000(+) C14 shell dates. Malde was also skittish about the archaeological reaction to the 4,000-year-old U-Series date for the Lindenmeier bison. C14 tests show a 10,780 B.P. age. This was almost a 7,000-year error. But it is precisely here that the geological perspective differs from the archaeological. Question: How do you define "ballpark"?

Geological ballparks are measured in much greater scales than archaeological ballparks. Where an archaeologist might work with time in terms of centuries and millennia, a geologist commonly juggles with 100,000y to 10,000,000y chunks of time. What the geological side considers a valid ballpark date might be way out of line for archaeologists. Lower Caulapan's 19,000 U-Series date signified a reversal to the archaeologists. According to the C14 dates, it should have been 10,000 years older than the flake tool in the previous picture. For an archaeologist, that's not a ballpark—it's a galaxy! The same criticism was levied against the Lindenmeir date that was 5,000 years too young. *Is that another one of your ballpark concordances?*

For the geologist, it was precisely that. A 10,000-year variance with a C14 date may indeed be considered "close" or "a hit" in the sense that it was not a 100,000- or 200,000-year variance. In that sense, that relative sense, the C14 dates *are* fairly concordant with the U-Series dates. If that kind of give-and-take between dating techniques is permitted, then the geologists *would* have a case. After all, a 6,000 to 10,000 year error is not a 200,000y error. A date of 19,000y within the 9,000–30,000 range of Caulapan dates could be considered a ballpark hit. The same could be said for the Lindenmeier specimen.

The First American

What is the minimum age U-Series can detect? This was one of the unknowns that made Szabo choose the Lindenmeier bone in the first place. The 5,000-year variance could mean that they were reaching the technique's minimum limits. Its maximum range might reach as far back as half a million years, but what were the youngest, most recent dates it could detect? It was considerations such as these that convinced Malde and the other geologists that they could not dismiss the results outright.

Malde understood that the tremors from archaeologists would be strong and loud. His own first impressions, phrases such as, *my instantaneous disbelief* and *shatter my imagination*, would never be used in print, yet they deftly provide a real sense of Malde's shock in trying to reconcile the archaeology, not to mention his own geological estimates for a greater-than-40,000y estimate for the Valsequillo sites. He could only guess how Irwin-Williams would react when she found out. *If 40,000y made her nervous, how is she going to handle a 250,000y date?*

> Hal Malde to Cynthia Irwin-Williams, August 2, 1968
>
> Dear Cynthia,
> Barney wants to go ahead and publish these results. He has encouragement from Clayton and me. However, the numbers are meaningless without explanation of the context of the samples. Also, there should be comment on archaeology, geology, and paleontology. The most direct approach is a single report with all of us as joint authors each contributing our bit. The main pitch for archaeology would be that these results support a 20,000-year age for man at middle Caulapan (illustrate flake scraper). Further, the results open the possibility of man at Valsequillo at least 250,000 years ago (more illustrations).
> If you shun so direct a tie with these numbers, we could write an adjoining report with you saying the results are crazy—or what have you. Barney needs to know your thoughts, as I do also.[20]

Irwin-Williams's responses on the U-Series dates ranged widely depending on who she was talking to. In an exchange of short memos with Marie Wormington in August 1968, both shared a complete disbelief and a deep concern about how their peers will react to the announcement.

> Irwin-Williams to Wormington, August 1968
>
> Dear Marie,
> I recently got a letter from Hal with some (completely wild!) uranium dates on the Valsequillo

material. I don't see how he can take them seriously
since they conflict with the archaeology, with his
own geologic correlations, and with a couple of C14
dates. However, God help us, he wants to publish
right away. I am enclosing a copy of Hal's letter and
my reply. Needless to say any restraint you can
exercise on him would be greatly appreciated. All we
need to do at this point is to put that stuff in
print, and every reputable prehistorian in the country will be rolling in the aisles.[21]

Wormington's reply to Irwin-Williams soon after:

Dear Cynthia:
Your letter, fortunately, caught up with me before I took off. I have been unable to reach Hal, who
is probably in Idaho. If he persists in publishing
those dates, or if there is any probability that he
will, I would strongly suggest that the article in
American Antiquity be withdrawn. We're all going to
look like absolute fools.* Obviously, no one would
ever believe that the Lerma point wasn't planted.
Even Leakey, who is still sold on a 100,000 plus date
for man at Calico, wouldn't buy that.
*Including Bell [editor of *American Antiquity*],
who will never forgive you if he is criticized for
publishing this article.[22]

Wormington was referring to Irwin-Williams's January 1969 article in *American Antiquity* that rebuts Lorenzo's planting scenario; the article had been submitted in April 1968 before the U-Series dates were known.

The "Lerma-like" point was the rounded stem spearhead that resembled a well-known Paleoindian style, c. 9,000–11,000y. The idea that this artifact, or for that matter any of the other bifaces, could be more than 200,000 years old was way out of line. It did not make sense. It could not make sense. It would never make sense. This technological sophistication of the Valsequillo artifacts versus the outrageous U-Series dates would remain a primary point of contention for the rest of both of their lives. A resolution would not come until the eve of the new millennium.

Archaeological psychologies are not beyond "guilt by association" tendencies, and by merely reporting these humongous dates, Irwin-Williams knew that she could be pegged as a loony. Once in print, it's permanent. She knew she could never accept the dates, but maybe that wouldn't sink in among the readership; maybe it was enough that she dug the sites. What seemed a remarkable start to a professional career now became a huge albatross around her neck. For the good of the community at large, and for her own peace of mind, she countered this foul turn of events with a Joan of Arc assault against the "crazy" dates.

Irwin-Williams quickly realized that she was not going to get any help in disputing the dates from her Valsequillo colleagues. Even Armenta sided with the geologists. And the idea that Szabo was in a hurry to publish the dates in *Science* or *Nature* did not help matters. *They simply did not realize the ludicrous nature of what they were proposing!*

Irwin-Williams's reply to Hal Malde, August 14, 1968.

Sorry for the delay in commenting on your news concerning the uranium decay dates; the field season has been even more hectic than usual.

Concerning you and Mr. Szabo's desire to publish this material right now: After some thought, I am afraid I am firmly opposed to this for the following reasons:

I think (as you thought I might) that the dates are a bit "crazy." However to substantiate this in print I would need more time and more information. Some of my initial reactions are:

a) If correct, these dates in connection with even one flake recovered in place (and as you know, they all were), would conflict with practically every bit of data available on the prehistory of the Old and New Worlds.

b) If the date at Hueyatlaco were correct, there would presumably be a period of c. 220,000 years between the archaeological level and the overlying ash deposit [indirectly] dated at 25,000 B.P. This to me does not seem very likely.

c) If the El Horno date were correct, what has happened to your initial correlations with the Caulapan sequence?

d) If the Atepitzingo date were correct, what happens to your initial correlations of the barranca sequences and what about the possible conflict with the basal C 14 dates there?

None of these comments by themselves constitute proof of the invalidity of the uranium dates. However I think that for us to suddenly alter your correlations and/or to conflict so completely with the archaeological evidence in order to accept them (or for me even to tacitly accept them by lack of informed contradiction) is at this point unwise. In this line, I feel now that the leakage and the premature publicity for the radiocarbon dates a year ago was unfortunate, and did our case no good.

... This does not mean that I am simply opposed to publication of the dates. However I would like to know more about a number of aspects—for example the amount of previous research on uranium dating in a volcanic region. Since we are all hopefully planning to get together a major manuscript on Valsequillo this winter, could Mr. Szabo be persuaded to present his data in this? It certainly seems to me that this would be the best outlet since we could deal with the problem as fully as possible and leave nothing either hastily and incompletely done (as my comments would be now), or open to any misconstruction.

You might talk to Marie about the problem—she can certainly give you what the reaction of other professional archaeologists will be. (In my own opinion. there is not one reputable prehistorian who could treat these dates seriously.)[23]

This was how the controversy began. For Irwin-Williams and Wormington, the Valsequillo discoveries had become an archaeology of the impossible. Knowing the brevity of space allowed by most science journals, Irwin-Williams suggested that the "crazy" dates best be published in the project's official report. This would allow enough space and time to discuss this unimagined turn of events in detail, *and* give her time to get second opinions about the U-Series technique from other authorities. She was not a loony, and was never going to become a loony. She had worked too hard and was not about to betray her profession or her credibility. Szabo and Malde, on the other hand, were thinking about submitting a brief, concise article in a lead journal such as *Science* as soon as possible.

Such an announcement would cripple the discoveries more than Lorenzo's lies could ever do. After all the pains she and Wormington went through in late 1967 to defend her work against Lorenzo's allegations, they ended up convincing everyone who mattered that the sites were indeed genuine and that, yes, Lorenzo was indeed nuts.

Lorenzo was nuts for about a year. Once the huge dates came out, more than a few began to think that maybe Lorenzo was on to something. *Maybe the artifacts were planted after all.* Planting all of a sudden became much easier to stomach than *Homo erectus* blades and bifaces. How else do you explain 20,000y spearheads in a 200,000y geological context? The answer was easy: You don't. You just don't.

For some it was too late. Everyone at the 1967 Tempe meeting, who previously agreed that the data was good, all of a sudden found themselves in an immediate bind. If everything was methodologically copasetic, how do you explain the monster dates?

The top gringos found themselves in a pickle and Lorenzo must have had a great laugh. *I told them the deposits were too old for archaeology.* All of the elites had been assured that the sites were legit, but the new dates upset that conviction. The Uranium-Series dates instantly transformed Valsequillo from a cutting-edge paradigm buster into a career killer from the ultra-fringe. Soon, in the United States and Mexico, Lorenzo's "unknown number of planted specimens" graduated into *all of the specimens*. And one of archaeology's greatest urban legends was born.

For the archaeologists who were certain of the archaeology, there was only one reasonable explanation: *There's something wrong with the U-Series technique*.

Writing to Szabo, Irwin-Williams's sense of politique is in full gear.

Irwin-Williams (ENMU) to Barney Szabo (USGS Denver), 10-10-68

I have recently received a copy of a letter to you from Hal Malde reporting the results of our recent discussion concerning the advisability of immediate publication of your uranium dates on bones and teeth from Valsequillo, Puebla. First let me express my gratitude to you and the U.S. Geological Survey for your efforts in our behalf.

From Hal's letter it seems to me that I should clarify my position in the matter, since it would seem from this account that archaeologists generally are more than necessarily suspicious and obstructionist. This is doubtless one aspect of the problem, but by no means the only one. My basic position with regard to the matter was expressed in correspondence with Hal last August and remains essentially the same.

First the problem of the antiquity of man in the Western Hemisphere is perhaps the most controversial single subject in New World prehistory today. (Estimates range from 12,000–40,000 years ago). It seems to me that any new data on the subject should be dealt with as thoroughly as possible with sufficient discussion of all aspects (archaeological, geological, geophysical, etc.), by various specialists including individuals not directly associated with the Valsequillo project. Incomplete or premature treatment of any controversial matter seems to me unfortunate and may be at worst disastrous.

Second, on the basis of every scrap of data now available on both Old World and New World prehistory (a not inconsiderable weight of evidence), certain of the dates (>100,000 years) would seem to be essentially impossible, and neither I nor any other reputable prehistorian could accept them. Those of my colleagues who do not have intimate knowledge of the field situation (the direct association of man-made artifacts with the bones, etc.) have the choice of disbelieving either the dates or the archaeology. For myself and those colleagues who do possess detailed knowledge of these associations, there is no choice but to examine closely the dating problem. Since few archaeologists possess an extensive background in nuclear physics this involves considerable familiarization with the dating methodology, its strengths and weaknesses. I feel at present somewhat better able to appreciate the situation than I did in August, but obviously no really complete background is possible to the nonspecialist. In any case, I plan to be in Denver later this year and would welcome and very much appreciate the opportunity to discuss the problem with you.

Meanwhile, concerning your publication of your results, please do not consider our restraint as obstructionist. We believe that precipitancy in controversial matters is unwise and would in this case seriously impair the value of the Valsequillo data to archaeology. It is for this reason, and because presumably your interest in immediate publication is in communicating with other specialists that we requested Hal and request you that these results appear in a journal which will not directly affect the archaeological problem nor archaeologists involved in it. We would very much appreciate your help and cooperation in this.

Finally, despite the immediate dilemma created by these dates, you and your colleagues working on these new dating methods have the heartiest congratulations and thanks of myself and my colleagues in archaeology, particularly those of us who are working beyond the range of Carbon 14 dating.[24]

Regards

Barney Szabo's reply to Irwin-Williams:

BRANCH OF ISOTOPE GEOLOGY
USGS FEDERAL CENTER. DENVER, CO.
October 28, 1968
Dear Dr. Irwin-Williams:

I appreciated very much to hear from you and hope that you will visit Denver soon so that some of these problems can be discussed. In the meantime, a preprint is enclosed in which the bone dates from Valsequillo are discussed as I see it. Please consider it as a first draft.

I understand your hesitation concerning the obtained dates and their implication and I am hoping that you will be able to participate in this report. The main problem facing us is that the rejection of our data means the rejection of a potential dating method of the Late Pleistocene. There must be a way to rationalize the results and perhaps you can help us to find a solution.

Yours Sincerely,

Barney Szabo[25]

Irwin-Williams's to Barney Szabo (USGS Denver):

October 30, 1968

Dear Mr. Szabo:

Thank you for your letter and for the preprint of your work on uranium-series dating of the Valsequillo specimens. I have a number of comments, which I will deal with as briefly as possible.

First, I definitely do not reject the use of uranium-series dating as a potential source of Pleistocene chronology. However, although I am a specialist in another field, I have been able to communicate with enough individuals in isotopic dating to realize that the method as applied to dry-land studies is new, and still somewhat experimental. Accordingly, as in the case of the early radiocarbon studies, a number of unknown variables may and probably do still exist.

As I have already noted in correspondence, my purpose in this matter is simply to avoid the extremely detrimental affects of sensationalism or premature conclusions on the problem of early man in the New world, and particularly on the Valsequillo project. Indeed the sensationalist treatment of the early radiocarbon dates by the press last year did no end of harm. Therefore, my position has been that I would have preferred to hold off publishing the uranium dates until the full monograph so that a thorough discussion of the method and the archaeological situation, etc., could be made, and so that we might also include a selected commentary by other specialists in isotopic dating and in archaeology.

Since you prefer to publish the information now, you have of course every right to do so. However, I must insist as originator and director of the Valsequillo research project, that it be done so that it is not in any way detrimental to the project, and particularly to the archaeological aspect of it. Accordingly with regard to your current article I would like to comment and request the following: (1) I will contribute a paragraph or so at the end of the article. It will I'm afraid be negative, since an antiquity of 300,000 years for man in the New World is an archaeological absurdity (it is roughly comparable to telling Hal in the face of more than a century of geological evidence and chronology that the Pleistocene is sixty million years old [as opposed to its established 2ma timeframe]). (2) However, since the article essentially concerns isotope dating, methodology, and geology and is written largely by specialists in those fields, I must insist that the archaeological terms and references in the title and text be omitted, and that commentary on the archaeological implications of the data be confined to that section which I, as a specialist in archaeology, contribute. In the same way that I would hesitate as a responsible researcher in archaeology to draw conclusions in isotopic-dating, I feel that commentary on the archaeological situation should be handled by the appropriate specialist.

My apologies if the above commentary seems very firm; however, there are moments when straight forwardness is the best policy. I will be seeing Hal within the next week in Mexico and will discuss the matter with him. I will also make a direct commentary on the text, and contribute a few comments on the archaeology as soon as possible, and send them to you. Meanwhile, I understand that you plan to publish this material in a specialized journal, and would appreciate your letting me know which one you have in mind.

Yours Sincerely,

Dr. Cynthia Irwin-Williams

Department of Anthropology

Eastern New Mexico University[26]

The dilemma is mapped out by both Irwin-Williams and Szabo in the letters. On the one hand, the dates were in total disagreement with everything that New World and Old World archaeologists knew (or thought they knew) about human evolution and the evolution of stone technologies. (They still are, kind of.) The dates also disagreed with Malde's own geological time frame for the artifact sites. On the other hand, as Malde admitted to Szabo, there was *nothing that categorically disproved* that the geology could indeed be 200,000y; rather, Malde had estimated the younger view on the basis of the archaeology. A vicious circle.

To his credit, Szabo fully understood Irwin-Williams's concerns. He, too, was extremely surprised at the Hueyatlaco and El Horno dates, but the science told him they were accurate. He realized the dates presented a concrete dilemma: Either the dates were valid, or the dating technique was faulty. If faulty, it meant the science underlying the technique was also faulty. And for Szabo, it would take more than furious archaeologists to trash a century's worth of hard science devoted to uranium decay. He also felt it was his academic duty to share the results soon, so that his new dating technique could receive the attention he felt it merited.

The result: The fields of archaeology and geochemistry separated, as though oil and water. The breach remains as I write; it was never resolved.

Tucson Pow-Wow

Early in October 1968, there had been a private gathering for Paleoindian specialists, archaeologists, and geologists during the annual *Friends of the Pleistocene* meeting in Tucson. The issue: How can we publish the dates without destroying Valsequillo's integrity and validity in the eyes of the archaeological community?

Szabo did not attend, but Malde sent him a summary of the discussions. It is a discussion that would never find its way into a peer-reviewed journal, but it shows what the experts were thinking about when their backs were against the theoretical wall. How could both the 200,000y dates and human evolution theory be correct? Was there any way to compromise the two? The conclusion: apparently not. So the main thrust of the pow-wow seems to have been how to disguise the article by giving it an ambiguous title, and placing it in an obscure peer-reviewed journal.

Though humorous on one level, it demonstrates the fear and concern about how the archaeological community at large would react. Valsequillo was a high-profile case, and so there were suggestions to "hide" the new information in a second-tier journal, preferably one that did not attract archaeologists.

```
October 2, 1968
Dear Barney:
     During the Friends of the Pleistocene field con-
ference a week ago at Tucson, I had opportunity to
discuss publication of your uranium-series dates on
Valsequillo bone with Cynthia Irwin-Williams, H. Marie
Wormington, and Dwight W. Taylor. Also present were
```

C. Vance Haynes, Peter H. Mehringer, and Larry D. Agenbroad—all of whom have done work with archaeologists.

At this tête-á-tête, I argued that progress in science is enhanced by a free exchange of results (i.e., rapid publication) and that none of us can ethically urge you to procrastinate. Cynthia and Marie, however, as well as some of the others who were present, are understandably concerned that most (practically all) archaeologists will immediately assume that something is phony about the Valsequillo archaeology—unless the dating results are accompanied by a lengthy discourse on the archaeology and its apparent conflict with the dates. I fail to grasp why archaeologists will not equally distrust the dates, but I accept the informed opinion of Cynthia and Marie about their colleagues. Even with a lengthy archaeological rebuttal, many archaeologists will persist in evil thoughts. On this, Dwight remarked "You can't make an omelet without breaking a few eggs."

The solution to this dilemma was proposed by Marie, namely for you to publish the dates in a specialty journal read by others in your field but not by archaeologists. This would exclude *Science*, *Nature*, and all journals indexed in *Readers Guide to Periodical Literature* where archaeologists commonly search for new titles. Pete, in jest, suggested an artfully disguised title: "Preliminary results of isotope dating on certain North American fossil bones." Whatever journal is selected, Cynthia chooses to participate as joint author by contributing about 200 words to affirm that the dates are "All wrong!" and to explain that a detailed analysis of the archaeology is being prepared separately.

I send you this letter so that you may know my understanding of the conclusion of this discussion. If any of the others listed below understand differently, I trust that they will let you know.[27]

Sincerely
Harold E. Malde
cc: Cynthia Irwin-Williams
H. Marie Wormington
Dwight W. Taylor

"Dilemma Posed By Uranium-Series Dates On Archaeologically Significant Bones From Valsequillo, Puebla, Mexico," *Earth And Planetary Science Letters* 6 (1969): 237–244
"*Preliminary results of isotope dating on certain North American fossil bones.*" Mehringer's satiric title is hilarious in its construction. A title such as this *would* pass under the archaeological radar. The *Reader's Guide* is indexed so that scholars can quickly find articles of interest. Mehringer's title has no indication and no key words signaling archaeological content, with the result that archaeologists would likely pass right by it. The Uranium Series information would be noted by geophysicists, geologists, and paleontologists, but bypass archaeologists—that was the idea. While humorous, it speaks volumes of the effect the U-Series dates had on the circle of experts familiar with the Valsequillo discoveries: *Make sure archaeologists do not get wind of the article*, at least until the official Valsequillo report is published, and all its aspects will be treated in depth.

In November 1968, a field trip to Hueyatlaco and some of the geological sites was planned in conjunction with the annual meeting of the Geological Society of America (GSA). Malde gave a paper on the Valsequillo work, but opted out of announcing the new U-series dates.

The Publication

The Valsequillo U-Series article appeared in a small science journal, authored by Szabo, Malde, and Irwin-Williams. To their credit, the title contained the word "archaeologically," which *would* show up in the *Reader's Guide*.

By the time the paper was submitted in June 1969, a lot of hemming and hawing passed under the bridge. As she promised, Irwin-Williams emphasized the experimental nature of the U-Series dating process, and even found a paper by some scientists who doubted its accuracy. For Irwin-Williams, experimental meant faulty. Out front she was the politician: "You and your colleagues working on these new dating methods have the heartiest congratulations and thanks of myself and my colleagues in archaeology..." Telepathically you would have heard, *I wish I had never heard of Uranium Series!*

Irwin-Williams's statements were curtailed a bit in the final version, but they are fully contained in the following copy she sent to Malde and Szabo. It is what she wanted to say, and how she wanted to represent her case to the archaeological community. It is the clearest surviving statement of her mindset when confronted with the "impossible" dates.

Brief Commentary Concerning Uranium Series Dating from the Valsequillo Region and Their Archaeological Implications.

Cynthia Irwin-Williams, February 1969.

New developments in isotopic dating continue to hold considerable promise for the construction of an exact chronology for very early archaeological and geological deposits. Barney Szabo in cooperation with Harold E. Malde has here reported on several uranium-series dates on bone samples from localities in the Valsequillo region. Two of these analyses yielded indications of *spectacular antiquity* of potential relevance to certain of the archaeological sites. However it is Irwin-Williams's opinion that the results cannot at present be considered to be an accurate basis for an exact chronology of the Valsequillo deposits for the following reasons:

1. Sample M-B-3 was recovered from the site of Hueyatlaco, from the same stratum and in close proximity to an archaeological assemblage characterized by sophisticated bifacially worked tanged projectile points, knives, scrapers, burins, etc. Therefore the great antiquity (245,000±40,000 years) assigned to the Hueyatlaco sample would postulate the existence of sophisticated bifacially worked tanged projectile points in the New World nearly one-quarter of a million years before their appearance in the Old World and indeed over 150,000 years before the generally accepted appearance of the large brained technologically competent *Homo sapiens* species on earth.

2. Sample M-B-8 from the El Horno site was a cheek tooth from a mastodon known to have been butchered by man, and was intimately associated with an assemblage characterized by simple but technologically excellent tools (burins, scrapers, knives, etc.). The even greater antiquity assigned to El Horno (280,000 years) would postulate the appearance of such technologically excellent tools in the New World over 200,000 years before their appearance in the Old World and as noted above long before the appearance of *Homo sapiens.*

3. The Old World has produced a complete sequence of evolutionary development of Homo Sapiens from more primitive hominids and from a long line of the higher primates. The New World has never produced any evidence whatever of early hominoid (pongid or hominid) development. To postulate a separate New World origin for man and advanced human technology is essentially impossible. To derive that technology from the Old World hundreds of thousands of years before it existed there is patently impossible. To postulate a sudden New World development of sophisticated technology by biologically primitive beings, completely unparalleled in the well known and populated Old World, is equally impossible.

4. The uranium-series-dating method as applied to dry-land studies and relatively young samples is new and still experimental. Accordingly, as in the case of the earliest radiocarbon studies, a number of unknown variables undoubtedly still exist. Particularly serious may be the effect of differential chemical leaching and/or deposition of the various elements involved in the uranium decay series. Indeed the chemistries of uranium and its daughters are such that one might expect them to be even more labile in typical geochemical environments than is carbon in materials normally used for C14 dating.

In the face of the weight of evidence incompatible with an extravagantly early age for man in the New World, the burden of proof lies heavily with the uranium-series method as applied to the Valsequillo samples. It is Irwin-Williams's opinion that the method is still too new and studies too incomplete to provide convincing evidence of great antiquity, and that the dates here are best interpreted as an example of the potential for order of magnitude errors in uranium-series dates even when internal consistency exists.[28] (Emphasis in original.)

In other words, the U-series dating technique was okay if you could live with dates that are sometimes 10 times older than they should be—for gringo archaeologists, such a lack of control made the technique meaningless. It was a terrible indictment of the dating technique, and a good enough argument for archaeologists to dismiss the dates.

Any dating technique that delivers dates in a 200,000y "ballpark" for artifacts in the 20,000y "ballpark" needs fixing.

Irwin-Williams was confident that srchaeology had already uncovered the "complete sequence of evolutionary development of *Homo sapiens*." It was a classic case of professional hubris. It suggested that, in 1969, we knew all about the evolution of our species—at least enough to know that a 200,000y modern(?) man in the New World was impossible. Based on their absolute confidence and professional loyalty, Irwin-Williams, Marie Wormington, and the rest of the community flatly refused the U-Series method even though it produced dates in virtual agreement with Caulapan's radiocarbon dates.

The geologists were a bit perplexed with her attitude. Although she had no end of bad things to say about the uranium dates, she never presented one shred of proof to dismiss them—except to say they were wrong. Circular arguments do not make for good science. And what about the matching C14 and U-Series dates at Caulapan? Be that as it may, the argument made perfect sense for the archaeologists.

The "impossible" U-series dates, along with the war concerning INAH's Sr. Lorenzo, effectively ended all Pleistocene archaeological investigations in and around the Valsequillo Reservoir. It would not be until 2001 that there would be another archaeological assault on Valsequillo. But the archaeology was not in question. More than enough had been collected, recorded, and photographed to prove the archaeology beyond any doubt. What the archaeologists doubted were the scientific interpretations by the geochemists. The archaeologists were more than convinced that they had done their part, but the geologists still had to get their act together.

For several years there was a stalemate. The plans to write the final, "official," Valsequillo report was put on hold. Irwin-Williams began receiving letters from pre-Clovis believers hoping they had found a new champion for their own ridiculed sites. She would have none of it. She championed the Caulapan C14 dates and decried the wild Uranium dates. The geologists had little reason to negate them.

Chapter 3.4

The Dirt on Archaeology

I do not know what is wrong with Malde. I feel so sorry for Cynthia. That wretched site has been a nightmare for her from the beginning to end. I still think that some of the material is possibly the oldest yet found in the New World, perhaps some 25–30,000 years old, but the whole thing is now so thoroughly botched up that it seems unlikely that it can ever win full acceptance. [29]

—Marie Wormington, 1973

In 1973, Hal Malde asked Sr. Lorenzo if he could dig a geological trench at Hueyatlaco. Lorenzo hemmed and hawed, but finally gave the go-ahead on the condition that no archaeology was carried out; *P.S.: Don't bring Irwin-Williams*. The plan was to dig a cross-trench perpendicular to the archaeologist's south wall, and extend it up the slope to cross-cut Lorenzo's old trenches. Everyone wanted to be sure about the exact stratigraphic position of the artifact beds. Could it be that the sediments were not part of the basin's structure as had been thought, but actually deposited much later *on top of a series of much older deposits?* If so, that would mean that the artifact beds were "insets." A trench would reveal the truth.

Irwin-Williams tested this possibility in 1964. In the western half of Hueyatlaco, she cut a small trench south into the slope. At the time she tentatively concluded that the creek beds with artifacts continued underneath the lake bed layers above. She had planned a much longer trench into the slope in 1966, but Lorenzo's huge trenches changed her mind. From all accounts, she was satisfied that the artifact beds did indeed lie underneath several meters of clay and an intercalated volcanic bed 1 meter thick: the Hueyatlaco Ash.

HUEYATLACO ASH

MARIO'S CORNER

ARTIFACTS

Hueyatlaco, 1973.
Photo: Hal Malde.

Top: Virginia Steen-McIntyre
cleaning up a monolith prior
to removal. "Monoliths" are
thin vertical sections cut from
the trench wall so that strata
can be studied up close and
personal back in the lab, such
as archaeological feature
blocks.
Below right: The Man Who Could
Read Dirt, master stratigrapher
Roald Fryxell. The 1973 expedition revolved around this
man, the inventor of the monolith collecting. Fryxell was
simply the best person for the
job, but a fatal auto accident
the next year robbed the world
of this geological maestro.
Photos: R. Fryxell

Virginia Steen-McIntyre would attempt to identify and match Hueyatlaco's ash lenses to specific volcanic eruptions, and assess their ages. Roald Fryxell, who was highly regarded for his research on archaeological sites in the Pacific Northwest, and who had worked with Francois Bordes in France, would do a detailed study of the stratigraphy. During a discussion with Virginia, she recalled, "My husband reminded me that Fryx was chosen by NASA to be one of the very few scientists allowed to work on the lunar samples. He taught the astronauts how to collect samples of the lunar regolith, helped design their sampling equipment, and studied the samples when they were returned." In 1977, the Society for American Archaeology named an award after him. From Wikipedia:

> He died due to a car accident, and his family chose to honor his memory by endowing the Fryxell Award for Interdisciplinary Research, given annually by the Society for American Archaeology in recognition of interdisciplinary excellence by a scientist. The SAA also holds a Fryxell Symposium during their meetings. An overlook shelter at the Palouse Falls is also named after him, as is the Roald H. Fryxell Memorial Scholarship at Augustana.[30]

Fryxell's job, besides drawing a minutely accurate profile of the exposed stratigraphy, would be to collect large columnar sections from the trench walls—a task for which he was uniquely qualified. They would also submit samples of Hueyatlaco Ash and the Tetela Brown Mud to Dr. Charles Naeser, a geochemist specializing in another kind of isotopic dating technique known as Fission Track dating, and a veteran of teams dating Olduvai Gorge.

Geologically, the impossible dates forced everyone to rethink their original assumptions. Were the artifact-laden creek beds akin to new icing on an old cake: separate and only draped on top of much older lake deposits? Irwin-Williams thought she was certain that the artifact/creek bed layers followed underneath the higher beds, but now she was not so sure. No one was sure. For Irwin-Williams, her real doubts focused on the validity and integrity of the U-Series dates themselves, not the geology.

Malde's trench spanned the entire slope linking the east-west trenches sunk by Lorenzo and the southern edge of Irwin-Williams's excavations. "We started by cleaning up the western part of the INAH trenches, exposing the beds below the Tetela Brown Mud (including the Hueyatlaco Ash), and then dug the connecting trench to the CIW excavation."[31]

Once connected, the geology would tell archaeologists and geologists whether:

1. The artifact beds were laid down earlier than the lake beds, the Hueyatlaco Ash, and the Tetela Brown Mud.
2. The artifacts beds were laid down on top of the higher beds (that is, insets), and separated by an unconformity.

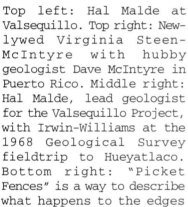

Top left: Hal Malde at Valsequillo. Top right: Newlywed Virginia Steen-McIntyre with hubby geologist Dave McIntyre in Puerto Rico. Middle right: Hal Malde, lead geologist for the Valsequillo Project, with Irwin-Williams at the 1968 Geological Survey fieldtrip to Hueyatlaco. Bottom right: "Picket Fences" is a way to describe what happens to the edges of glass (obsidian) particles as they get older and older. These particles from Hueyatlaco indicate an antiquity of about 200–300ky. Photos: courtesy of Hal Malde and Virginia Steen-McIntyre.

This second possibility does happen now and again in nature. For example, newer creek or stream channels can cut into older beds and fill the channels up with newer sediments. Known as "cut and fill," the team encountered an excellent example at Caulapan that was drawn out for me by Virginia. Cut-and-fill events are always associated with an unconformity, and are fairly obvious when you know what to look for.

The findings were clear to the trained eye. The artifact beds were part of the main body of the Valsequillo Gravels. They were not redeposited. They were not laid down later. There was no unconformity. They were creek and stream beds criss-crossing each other for a long period of time, and later buried by the younger lake clays above them.

After the lake clays had accumulated on top of the artifact beds, a meter or more of the Hueyatlaco Ash fell from the air, probably from Popocatépetl. Above the Hueyatlaco Ash several more meters of clay had built up. On top of these clays was the Tetela Brown Mud, a slurry of mud, 1 to 2 meters thick, crowded with lumps of pumice, that was laid down widely on the Valsequillo alluvium. Finally, the Brown Mud was capped by a surficial volcanic layer named the Buena Vista lapilli, which is preserved only in scattered outcrops

The artifact beds were underneath all that.

For the archaeologists it was very hard to stomach. No unconformity was present. The artifact beds were not late additions. They were not recent "icing" on an ancient layer cake. The artifact beds were a part of the cake itself.

The creeks and streams that had crisscrossed the area gently buried the archaeological features and bones. Later, according to Malde, the immediate region became a tranquil flood plain.

> Because of the fine-grained nature of these deposits and their limited outcrops, the actual environmental conditions of the upper Valsequillo deposits are still somewhat undefined. The important thing...is that there was a build up of 15 meters of alluvial material above the lowest artifact bed, and that there are volcanic layers that can be dated by suitable analysis.[32]

Stratigraphically, everything was in order and fairly straight forward.

Picket Fences and Tephra Hydration

Steen-McIntyre studied ash flows and ash particles from Hueyatlaco and compared them to Tlapacoya, Lorenzo's own "earliest site in America." Tlapacoya had been solidly dated to about 24,000y. This age made it contemporary with the 21,000y Caulapan site. With techniques she developed, the Hueyatlaco volcanic deposits proved to be much more weathered than those at Tlapacoya. In particular, given time, mineral crystals in volcanic ash can become partly dissolved and take on a "picket fence" appearance.

At Hueyatlaco the "picket fence" development was quite advanced. By contrast, crystals of the same mineral in the Tlapacoya ash were still relatively smooth and unaffected by weathering.

In another, even more definitive test, she measured the degree of hydration in small shards of volcanic glass, or chilled bits of magma thrown out by volcanic eruptions. She compared samples from Hueyatlaco, Tlapacoya, and several other volcanic eruptions of known age in western North America.

The microscopic beads of natural glass in the ash take on water over long periods of time. The water penetrates and partly (or completely) fills bubble cavities in the glass shards. Steen-McIntyre called this process tephra hydration. The hydration for Hueyatlaco was advanced, and the only comparable ash being sampled had erupted from Yellowstone National Park around 250,000y. The degree of hydration in a volcanic ash from Saskatchewan dated at 600,000 years was somewhat greater, and the hydration of other samples less than 40,000 years old was quite small.

At this point the geological indicators—the stratigraphy and weathering—were lining up on the side of the Uranium Series dates, but there was still another test to be done: Fission Track dating.

Fission Track Dating Results

News of dating Olduvai Gorge with the Fission Track technique reached the Valsequillo team. Spontaneous fission of Uranium-238 occurs when the nucleus of one parent uranium atom splits in two with such a force that it leaves a trail (track) of damage in a mineral crystal, preferably zircons. This phenomena was predicted in 1940, but it was not until 1960 when it was actually observed. The technique can be applied to materials that were once heated, such as ash flows, glass (natural and manufactured), hearthstones, boiling stones, and fired ceramics.[33]

At Olduvai, Fission Track dating was used to test the validity of the "wild" 2ma Potassium-Argon dates. When the Fission Track dates matched the K/Ar results, it began to dawn on folks that there was indeed an extra million years of human evolution to work with. By 1974, a series of other tests ranged from 1.6 to 2.4y, and finally, with some fine tuning, the dates for Zinj hovered around 1.8my.

Because Valsequillo's U-Series dates had created a similar clamor among archaeologists, Fission Track dating was chosen for the same reason as it was at Olduvai, namely, to double-check the validity of the original dates.

Dr. Charles Naeser (USGS) was asked to use his Fission Track technique on Hueyatlaco's ash beds, the Hueyatlaco Ash, and the Tetela Brown Mud. Fission Track dating is a labor-intensive technique requiring multiple stages of analysis. In this case, only the initial stages were completed. The results were referred to as "quick dates" that generated large statistical errors. Nonetheless, the results would offer a general ballpark age for the ash beds above the artifact deposits.

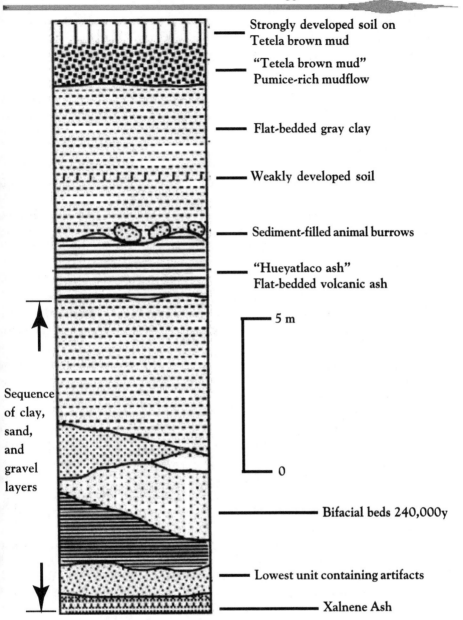

Strongly developed soil on
Tetela brown mud

"Tetela brown mud"
Pumice-rich mudflow

Flat-bedded gray clay

Weakly developed soil

Sediment-filled animal burrows

"Hueyatlaco ash"
Flat-bedded volcanic ash

5 m

Sequence
of clay,
sand,
and
gravel
layers

0

Bifacial beds 240,000y

Lowest unit containing artifacts

Xalnene Ash

Profile of the Hueyatlaco stratigraphic column. At the top
are datable ash features located on the surface of the
Tetela Peninsula, followed by lake beds interrupted by the
Hueyatlaco Ash bed. Below are are the sands, silts, and
gravels comprising the artifact beds. At the base is the
Xalnene Tuff. After Farley, Donelik, Dumitru 1998.

The Fission Track dates for the ash sediments equally startled and crushed the archaeologists, and Barney Szabo was waiting for an apology. He still is.

✴ Tetela Brown Mud: 600,000±340,000 years (260,000y–940,000y).

✴ Hueyatlaco Ash: 370,000±200,000 years (170,000y–570,000y).

✴ Had the Fission Track analysis been taken to further stages, it would have narrowed down the 200,000 and 340,000-plus/minus ranges, but it would not have changed the fundamental conclusion: *The fission track dates were in the same ballpark as Szabo's Uranium-Series dates.*

Everything the geologists threw at the sites came back old—real old. Too old.

The experimental status of these isotopic techniques were at the center of Irwin-Williams' slash-and-burn response. To Dr. Naeser, it was clear she was not familiar with the underlying science of the techniques. The term *experimental* did not mean that the date was questionable (or doubtful), only that the procedures used were in their relative infancy. For Naeser, despite the wide statistical limits of measurement, the results showed a 96 percent certainty that a sample was not younger than its minimum age.

Geologically, nothing disagreed with Szabo's original dates. This included Malde's estimate of great antiquity based on depth of burial and the extent of subsequent dissection. All of the different researches ended up in a ballpark that was more than 10 times older than any other dated site in the Americas. For archaeologists, it just compounded the madness.

It was a colossal difference of interpretation, and it remains one of the greatest interpretational differences in modern archaeological history. This chasm between geological science and archaeological theory has never been bridged. It was just ignored. It is still being ignored.

The Valsequillo problems were completely different from those that plagued Leakey's Calico site. Calico's new 200,000y U-Series dates were accepted and the geology was accepted, but it was the artifacts that were questioned. At Valsequillo, it was the artifacts that were accepted, but it was the dating techniques and the stubborn geologists that were faulty. For the archaeological community, it did not seem to matter that the U-Series technique was used at both Valsequillo and Calico's new 200,000y dates, nor that the Caulapan U-Series date jived with its C14 date.

Irwin-Williams was not comfortable reading dates with such excessive ranges—not with her site on the line! In the end she stuck by her guns, rejecting the geological findings. She just said no. She wished the geologists well, and silently hoped that someday they might further the archaeological mission—the erroneous dates surely indicated that day had not yet arrived.

Irwin-Williams, nor any other archaeologist or geologist, ever produced any evidence that scientifically disproved the geological findings. Nor was there a need to do so. All she had to say was, *Sorry Mac, we aren't buying it.* A few years later, in 1977, she was elected president of the SAA, so it is clear that her meager responses were accepted and respected by a majority of U.S. archaeologists.

A close-up looking at the artifact beds and the Hueyatlaco Ash. Barney Szabo's Uranium Series dating of Bed C produced bone dates of 240,000 years±40,000y. Fission Track dating of the Hueyatlaco Ash by Charles Naeser were 370,000±200,000 years. Photo: Roald Fryxell, CIW Collection.

The century-long tendency to view New World cultures as relative late-comers was beyond challenge by politically correct geologists as well as archaeologists. For Dr. Gordon Willey:

> The no-site-older-than date has changed, but the scenario has not. In the early 1900s Holmes and Hrdlicka set the date at 4000 years B.P. (Before Present) and declared all sites they visited as younger than that; they were educated, competent people and were often right about the sites they investigated; however, they had the effect of stifling research. Frank H.H. Roberts, a colleague of Hrdlicka's at the Smithsonian, admitted that "questions of early man in America became virtually taboo, and no anthropologist, or for that matter geologist or paleontologist, desirous of a successful career would tempt the fate of ostracism by intimating that he had discovered indications of a respectable antiquity for the Indian.[34]

The "no-site-older-than-4,000-years" policy imposed on early-20th-century prehistorians was replaced by a "no-site-older-than-12,000-years" policy based on C14-dated Clovis sites. Different antiquity, same stifling attitude. Amazingly, this 12,000-year boundary of antiquity lasted until 1999, the year Clovis First officially died.

The Bumpy Road to Publication

The published article that appeared in the *Journal of Quaternary Research* eight years later, in 1973, sounds almost apologetic for the coming emotional rollercoaster (that is, paradigm shift) that promised to carry the archaeologists to some forbidden place. The geologists themselves were still in the throes of their own world-shaking revolution (literally). Plate Tectonics had recently become the new geological reality after years of being vilified and ridiculed. Paleontologists were beginning to listen to ideas about warm-blooded dinosaurs. Now it looked as though the New World archaeologists had their own paradigm change to deal with.

The path to publication was rough. Conferences were attended and papers were given by members of the team. They expected their reports would be published in symposium editions. It didn't work out that way. Several years passed and nobody seemed interested in the incredibly old geology that contained the artifacts.

In 1974, a year after the geological study, Roald Fryxell died in a car crash. A few years after that, Hal Malde had to get busy with other projects.

This left Steen-McIntyre as the sole passion behind publishing the report in a peer-reviewed journal; it would be a key element for her Ph.D. dissertation, and she became lead author pretty much by default. Valsequillo would be her "career maker" because it was such an excellent subject for her innovative analyses of ash falls. Steen-McIntyre would not, could not, let it go. Beyond principle and stubbornness, she had faith and confidence in science.

Similar to Irwin-Williams, Steen-McIntyre was a graduate student when she came to Valsequillo. At the University of Idaho, she had developed several novel ways to match and date volcanic ash lenses, and the Valsequillo region was ideal. Things could not have looked brighter. She was applying her techniques to the critical question of human antiquity in the New World. Similar to Irwin-Williams's start, it seemed a perfect start to a budding career. In the end, however, the 250,000y challenge to the Clovis First Theory proved too much and began to scare her Geology chairman. The findings were becoming "too controversial." She would finally earn her Ph.D. by writing a manual for how to do tephrochronology. It would not include any Valsequillo data.

Steen-McIntyre did her damnedest to publish the findings, but met resistance at every turn. The paper would be either lost, put on hold, or outright rejected. In one instance, the sheepish editor at the Southwestern Anthropological Association told her that *"the paper had fallen between two filing cabinets where it remained for several years"* —an academic editor's equivalent of "the dog ate my homework."

Hal Malde convinced *Journal for Quaternary Research* editor Steve Porter to take a look at their joint report. The science was good, and he decided to publish it. In 1981, "Geologic Evidence for Age of Deposits at the Hueyatlaco Archeological Site, Valsequillo, Mexico," by Virginia Steen-McIntyre, Roald Fryxell, and Harold E. Malde became the second, the last, and the most important peer-reviewed article on the discoveries. The conclusion: *The geology really is that old.*[35]

An old friend sent a letter of congratulations.

> 28 Oct 1981
> Dear Ginger and Dear Hal:
> I received the copies of the magnificent work that you have finished on the geological antiquity of the Valsequillo zone, and I am very, very pleased with the concepts you have expressed to me.
> My human vanity is very gratified that my curiosity (and my obstinacy) have given fruitful results. But I recognize clearly that my work only represents an infinitesimal part of the final result; for if you had not intervened, with such strength, with such capability, and with such dedication, Valsequillo would be only a curious place for its old bones and used stones, without greater value for prehistory. You, and only you, have been the true discoverers of the scientific importance of this zone.
> Naturally, I don't cease to hope that all will recognize your success; there are many here who suffer a dirty disease called envy; others suffer mental myopia, and still others are incapable of understanding that scientific knowledge is valid only for one epoch and must be constantly renewed. No matter—the same has happened with other discoveries. Have patience. That which you have done will mark a new epoch for science.
> Please accept (both of you) the testimony of my appreciation and my profound gratitude.[36]
> /s/ Juan
> Juan Armenta Camacho

The geologists expected that the 1981 article would wow the world, that it would become a foundation for a new discussion on American antiquity. At least now there could be some closure to the professional tensions. Once the article was published, there would be a vast migration of archaeologists to Valsequillo. All textbooks would have to be rewritten. The mastodon art piece would be exhibited around the world, and hopefully Juan Armenta Camacho would get his job back....In a perfect world....

Reactions came in negative forms. At an archaeology conference party in San Diego, shortly after the paper's publication, Marie Wormington personally accused Steen-McIntyre of "ruining Cynthia's career!"—a reckless and damning accusation that Virginia has had to contend with for decades. This was hardball. If indeed Cynthia's career *was* ruined by valid, authenticated, and replicable geological facts, it was due to the intractable, implacable groupthink adopted by U.S. paleoarchaeologists. For Steen-McIntyre, "I was just doing science!"

Later On

From surviving notes, 1990 was the year Irwin-Williams hoped to complete the final Valsequillo report. In July 1990, she died in her Reno, Nevada home. After she died, no archaeologist raised a finger to resolve the scientific chasm that had opened up between the principles of geology and the human evolution theory. In Irwin-Williams's obituaries, Wormington and her Portales colleague George Agogino only included Valsequillo in passing. A similar deletion occurs in Wormington's archival summary at the National Anthropological Archives. Note the void between 1956 and 1966.

> In 1937–1938, she excavated rock shelters in Montrose County and, in 1938–1941 and again in 1947, worked at a Fremont village site in Grand County, Utah. In 1951–1952, she excavated rock shelters in Mesa County, Colorado, and in 1955–1956, she surveyed prehistoric migration routes of ancient hunters in the Province of Alberta, Canada. During 1966–1967, she worked at the Frazier Agate Basin site in Weld County, Colorado; and, in the following year, she joined Joe Ben Wheat at the Jurgens Cody site in the same county.[37]

From 1960 to 1968, Dr. Wormington was on the ride, then nightmare, of her life.

What the world was left with was sheer confusion, innuendo, and rumor. For Mexican archaeologists the discoveries were billed as a fake. For U.S. archaeologists they were now a nonentity. For those who looked closer, they only saw an impossible and irresolvable dialectic between geology and archaeology. For geochronologist Chuck Naeser, it was as if the whole thing drifted into a black hole.

The amnesia became so institutionalized that 20 years after Caulapan's 21,880y C14 dates, Dr. Paul Martin, who knew all about Valsequillo, wrote an article in *Natural History* magazine seeking to rename the Paleo New World, "Clovisia."[38]

The Valsequillo treasures would remain lodged in that black hole for years, until a single individual, a MIT engineer with means, was asked to make sense of it.

Where Things Stood

Regardless of the scientific weight that was screaming for a 200,000y ballpark for the Valsequillo sites, the archaeological community did the only thing they could: They flat-out ignored the science. From this time forward, archaeologists would never seriously entertain the findings of the Valsequillo geologists. No one sought to excavate the sites ever again. Instead, there seemed to be a mass denial that the whole affair had even happened. Gossip and speculation might have been spun around the water coolers, but it never made its way into print. They threw up their hands and let Irwin-Williams take care of it. It was her site, and she was entrusted with its official interpretation.

For the geologists, everything they found indicated a 200,000y-plus ballpark. If the geologists were correct, it would mean there were *Homo erectus* or Neanderthal brutes in Central Mexico making elegant spearheads a couple hundred thousand years before modern humans reinvented them in Eurasia. If the archaeologists were correct, it would mean that virtually everything that geologists thought they knew about Pleistocene landforms and isotopic dating was wrong. There was no in-between, no possible compromise.

ARCHAEOLOGIST: *You are asking us to believe that the sophisticated art and technology of the Upper Paleolithic was actually invented over 200,000 years ago in Central Mexico by Homo erectus? Ridiculous.*

GEOLOGIST: *You are asking us to believe that Science is off by a magnitude of 10? Ridiculous.* Charles Naeser explains.

> The question here is the relationship between the artifacts and the geology. All of the geologic evidence supports an old age for the artifact horizon. U-series, fission-track and U-Th/He dating as well as Sam's diatoms and Ginger's superhydration and mineral solution studies point to an age >200,000y. If the artifact bed is indeed younger there has to be geological field evidence that indicates it is younger, such as cut and fill. Then the problem becomes how to explain the U-series ages on bones from the artifact horizon. Someone could probably find something to question about each of the geologic indicators of a >200,000y age. The problem is that it would have to be something different for each technique. No single argument can reject all of the geologic data. That rapidly becomes a geologic impossibility.[39]

If the archaeologists considered their interpretation victorious over the geologists—and they did—it was through default. Because Irwin-Williams never published her findings in an official report, American archaeology could not be held to accountable for the anomalous ages. The only way she would work with the geologists was if they recanted the ridiculous dates. They couldn't so she wouldn't.

Put yourself in her position.

She found bifacial projectile points and/or knives exhibiting soft hammer percussion and maybe even pressure flaking. Lower down at Hueyatlaco, and at Tecacaxco and El Mirador, she found blades—purposely designed flakes that are twice as long as they are wide. Some were retouched into points. El Horno, the lowest site, had no bifaces or blades, just some flake tools, a small pebble chopper, and a mastodon. There were only three excavated sites, so it is unwarranted to demand a rigid conclusion about *in situ* technological evolution. But still, don't you think these discoveries were awesome enough to maintain just a teeny bit of professional curiosity among the community at large?

Ask the Clovis First guys if this is not exactly what they expected to find underneath a Clovis site: first, cruder bifaces, then blade tech. Clovis would be the natural apogee of that Pleistocene column. Progress. Evolution. Sophistication. Independent invention. Just as it happened in the Old World. And this is exactly what Irwin-Williams thought she had when she left the field in 1966: the roots of Clovis. Expectations were high that maybe the sites would date to 13,000y, and maybe, *dare I say it,* 15,000y? It would have been a perfect fit. Imagine what that must have felt like for her, and in a man's world.

Science then reared its ugly head. First there were 22,000y dates from Caulapan. In terms of the tender millennia that constituted the American paradigm, this was a kick in the stomach. Just a few years ago I had the pleasure of speaking with Alan Bryan, a longtime pre-Clovis advocate from Canada (in other words, he could get away with it). It was his position that the first real bifaces did not turn up until about 20,000y. The most skilled were the Solutrean of Western Europe, c. 14–21,000y. This was the going belief in 1966 as well.

For Irwin-Williams, the Caulapan dates meant it was no longer a question of Clovis technological evolution. Now it was about the world stage, the evolution of blades, and thinned bifaces in the Old World. Valsequillo was now on par with the first recognized blade-makers and bifacers of the Old World, a full 10,000 years older than the Clovis; and let's not forget Wormington's sense that it might go back to 40,000y. This was a case of contemporaneous independent invention on both sides of the world.

The transition from blades to bifaces paralleled the Old World model. It's been in the books for a century. This was the majesty of Valsequillo. It was old, but it was still modern humans. And there was every indication of an *in situ* technological evolution.

These were Irwin-Williams's prospects in the early summer of 1967:

❋ *In situ* technological evolution was in play, with another several dozen potential sites, all with mineralized bone, all within a short distance of each other, and all right next to one of the finest cities in Mexico. Not bad.

❋ All this was going on in Valsequillo around the same time the same technological evolution was going on in the Old World. Parallel evolution.

When others, such as Malde, Wormington, and Brew, voiced even older dates for the Tetela sites, such as 40,000y, she had to put on the brakes. Her extreme for the lowest site, El Horno, never went beyond 30–35,000y, and she never endorsed anything older, only younger. After all, you had to give them time to walk from Africa to Mexico, so it couldn't be too close to 40,000y. And it certainly could not be any older than 40,000y; otherwise, it just wouldn't fit the known world model for the paleolithic.[40]

The blast from the 250,000y U-Series dates punched a wormhole in the world model for the paleolithic. It became a riddle wrapped inside an enigma. The enigma was the great antiquity, an impossibility shared with Calico. But Valsequillo had "Upper Paleolithic" bifaces that were older than their Old World counterparts by a factor of 10. That's the riddle.

Interlude

A year before her death, Cynthia Irwin-Williams's was on a survey and seemed to have injured herself. Out of the experience came a celebration of life, and of her profession. It was sent to me by her close friend, Larry Baker (Salmon Ruins, New Mexico), one of many professionals who continue to celebrate her life. A few years later, Juan Armenta Camacho also passed away. He is shown in a 1978 photo holding Tetela 1. These were the last known photos of his priceless, now lost, Paleo masterpiece.

Coming Home From The Field

(Wilderness experience near Ely, Nevada, written May 29, Memorial Day, on my return from Reno)
What a Joyous Time—What a Rapture this has been.
In the physical reality, I am very lame and sore—my broken legs are swollen and painful; I am tired and sunburned; my eyes are puffed and windblown, and dusty and sticky with dust and tiny bits of cowdung.
And None of this is important at all! For there is another Reality.
I have been in these last three day overwhelmed
with a Renewing a Rebirthing of
The experience of Being, in the Field,
In the Wilderness, on the Quest to Explore and to Unlock
The Secrets of the Past
The Pure excitement of my Craft,
With its clarity of Purpose
Its mysteries, its hopes and dreams
The always novel and intriguing
Quest for the Unknown.
The sheer unbroken Beauty of the Upland Wilderness
With its own enormous, yet intimate, all encompassing Quality
Which Both overwhelms, and yet enlarges
The Individual Participant
In its Oneness, with the Cosmos and the Creator.
The incomparable joys of Comradeship

Of old friends and special trust,
 Sharing hopes and hardships; bad jokes and old
stories;
 Half-cooked camp food, in a cold wind full of
stinging sand,
 The clasp of a shoulder, a helping hand
 Chores and hardships gladly shared.
 Absurd and joyous, unselfconscious Fun
 Like lying for hours in the cold darkness
 On the bottom of a dry cattle tank, the only
windbreak
 With little eddies of dust and bits of cowdung
swirling past us,
 Telling the old stories, singing the old songs.
 What a Joy! What a Joy!
 This is part of My Song of Life
 It has always been so, but now,
 With the Experience and Enrichment, and Wisdom
 Of the last few years
 Of Growth, Depth and Breadth of emotions,
 The strength of fiber and clarity of Life
 Which comes as much from pain and suffering
 As from pleasure and triumph.
 All of this has made for a prolonged Rapture
 A quality of Joy, and a chorus of Gratitude
 Which is unique, perhaps, to these moments of my
Life;
 So much more glorious than the superficial, fe-
brile and uncertain
 Professional triumphs of my past.
 What a Wonder!
 That I have been given this chance
 To know the full glory of this Human Experience
 All my gratitude to You, Lord, for granting me
these days
 Of being fully alive, and in tune and harmony
 With your Creation.
 Freude, schoner, Gotterfunken Tochter aus Elysium
 (Oh Joy, Joy, Gift of God
 Daughter of the Heavens)
 (Schiller/ Beethoven)
 Cynthia Irwin-Williams
 May 29, 1989[41]

Juan Armenta Camacho in 1978 in a photo
series that were the last known pictures
of America's earliest art. This was the
same year he published his monograph on
his 30 years of Paleoamerican work in
Puebla and Valsequillo, which had gone
largely ignored by both INAH and U.S.
institutions. Photo: David Hiser.

Part IV

Valsequillo Rising

I don't see the logic of rejecting data just because they seem incredible.
— Astrophysicist Sir Fred Hoyle

Chapter 4.1

Raiders of
the Fringe

Never Say Die; Say "Action!"

Years passed. The U.S. archaeological community continued to fight over 14,000y and 19,000y sites, totally ignoring or ridiculing the Brazilian potboilers at Punta de Furada (50–100,000y) and Toca de Esperanca (250,000y), two sites that had been making Latin American headlines for more than a decade.

The ongoing debates about the 14,000y and 19,000y sites were nonetheless very important. Even though sites a couple thousand years older than Clovis may not sound like much, in an anti-sea migration paradigm such as Clovis First, an older-than-12,000y date would mean that folks were here before the ice-free corridor opened up. A 14,000y archaeology site would mean that whoever lived there was an ancestor of somebody who entered during a previous warm period. The last time the corridor was ice-free might have been about 25–35,000y. Therefore, a 14,000y site would automatically imply an archaeological cellar around 25–35,000y, because that was the last time Beringia was a land bridge, and people would hang out in Alaska until things warmed up enough to pass through the corridor. Then it would get cold again, the corridor would ice up, and they would be trapped in the virgin wilderness of the Western Hemisphere. This would be a reasonable implication for a 14,000y date in a boat-free paradigm.

For some reason, if you stepped across the line and suggested Pleistocene boat scenarios, or mostly any Precolumbian boat scenarios, aka. diffusionism, things got nasty really quick. Here's a taste.

> ...for Brian Fagan, an influential professor of anthropology at the University of California at Santa Barbara, diffusionism is exasperating. "Why do such lunatic ravings persist?" he asked in his book *The Great Journey: The Peopling of Ancient America* (1987). "To read the crank literature on the first Americans is to enter a fantasy world of strange, often obsessed, writers with a complex jargon of catchwords and 'scientific' data to support their ideas." The Colgate University astronomer and anthropologist Anthony Aveni tends to be more sympathetic, perhaps because the field of archaeo-astronomy, which he has helped to ennoble, was itself an academic pariah until recent years. Nevertheless, Aveni's sympathies go only so far. "I think there is, beneath all this dialogue about diffusionism, a will to believe in bizarre ideas," he says. "This is a romantic idea that we're talking about here, after all. These are bizarre tales of an imagined era in an imagined past. And like the occult beliefs they resemble, they're really just wishful thinking. It's a belief that we can wish into existence the universe we desire and deserve."[1]

Life was hard out there for a diffusionist.

Fagan's texts are standard archaeological fare in departments from coast to coast. You learn what to stay away from if you know what's good for you.

Some professionals *did* think about it, however, and they were angry at the iron fist of the Clovis Firsters.

> The story was so tidy that any skeletons that seemed to challenge this "Clovis model" were shoved back into the closet by the mandarins of American anthropology; any stone tools that seemed older than Clovis were dismissed as misdated. Clovis had American archeology in a stranglehold; James Adovasio of Mercyhurst College in Pennsylvania calls its defenders the "Clovis mafia."[2]

Meanwhile, folks continued to scratch their heads. Where were the proto-Clovis sites in Siberia? Where was the Clovis Trail? At the end of the Cold War, Dennis

Stanford was on one of the first planes to Siberia, where he expected to find traces of Clovis-like technology. He found none. Stanford and his fellow heretic-to-be, Dr. Bruce Bradley, had little alternative but to take a deep breath and begin looking across the Atlantic for a technological link.

Then fate, played by Charleton Heston, pulled a dirty trick on the archaeologists. On Sunday, February 25, 1996, NBC's, *The Mysterious Origins of Man*, boomed across the nation's airwaves. Inspired by hugely popular, though academically chastised (translation: "fringe") books such as Michael Cremo and Richard Thompsons's worldwide best-seller, *Forbidden Archaeology*, Graham Hancock's *Fingerprints of the Gods*, and Vine Deloria's *Red Earth, White Lies*, the *Origins* show was a two-hour prime time fringefest that showed Madison Avenue that fantastic archaeology *does* work on TV! The show used strange discoveries to assault the status quo—aka. Darwin's evolution, and most everything else that was held sacred by that evil cabal known as the National Science Foundation. Christian Creationists probably assembled house parties for the occasion.

I'm Back...

The Charleton Heston "shockumentary" was complete with cavemen riding dinosaurs, human fingers inside rocks tens of millions of years old, and other oddities that tried to show the public that anthropologists, historians, and scientists were pretty much wrong on just about everything, and...that they might even be hiding these oddities from the public.

For most academics, it was the usual poppycock craziness you see while waiting in a checkout line. You could almost hear the collective groan from anthropology departments across the land: *Here we go again. Another semester wasted wading through pointless questions about nonsense "facts" from undergraduates and public lecture audiences. Thanks, NBC! Thanks a lot!*

Then the surprise. There was Virginia walking along the margins of the Valsequillo Reservoir. The great discovery that had riveted the anthropology world during the 1960s was now reduced to a tabloid subject on a tabloid show. Personified, what was once archaeological royalty turned homeless derelict, was now all of a sudden wheeled out for another "15 minutes" by a bunch of marketing geniuses. For the New World archaeologists who knew better, it would be the only story in the bunch that made their neck hairs crawl.

The segment started off with Dr. Virginia Steen-McIntyre testing ash samples along the water's edge. Her summary was supplemented with recollections from Armenta's daughter, Celine, discussing her father's work, the excavations, sharing *LIFE Magazine's* photos of the engraved art, his savage treatment by Lorenzo, the armed guards, the extortion of signatures for prewritten depositions, and how all that misfortune tore Armenta up inside. It was the most interesting of all the show's segments, but then everyone loves a good tragedy, and, as archaeological tragedies go, this was probably the greatest the Western Hemisphere had to offer.

Rest in peace, Juan Armenta Camacho.

In the Beginning

The relation between the Creationists and the scholars previously mentioned is best described as apples and rocks. Cremo and Thompson, Hancock, Deloria, and others who write about phenomena that do not jibe with mainstream scenarios cannot be equated with the Christian Creationists one whit. Rather, when their investigations turn up findings that contradict, challenge, or otherwise embarrass the academic Brahmin, they often do it in a responsible and mature manner: with scads of references—the weapons of the trade. This made them much more dangerous. Quoting the Bible is one thing. Quoting peer-reviewed scientific journals is another.

The Christian Creationist extremists (a small, but very vocal minority of Christendom) love the controversies, only because they prove that scientists are not the Mr.-Know-It-Alls they pretend to be. Therefore, Earth is only 6,000 years old, and apeman evolution is right out. Their science is faith-based and assumes that secular scientists don't know what they are talking about. For the Christian extremists, the gist is that we are special—to the extent that even unbaptised babies go to Hell, and certainly not Heaven. Take Reagan's Secretary of the Interior James Watts, for example. He felt fine about trashing and polluting God's Creation (including His peoples) until the cows came home because Armageddon is going to trash everything pretty soon anyway. *Besides, we have been promised the good seats.* (Sometimes you hear the number of seats is about 144,000. When they all rush up to Heaven, what if they find only 143,000 seats? What happens next?)

The anthropological mainstream, of course, places all these folks in the same boat. Even though none of the previously mentioned scholarly authors are extreme Christian creationists, their contributions of difficult-to-explain artifacts give the Creationists ammunition. In essence, the non-orthodox scholars provided aid and comfort to the "enemy," along with being the enemy themselves—betrayers obsessed with the materially strange and exotic, rather than the more subdued (boatless) orthodox of the mainstream.

My own bigotry was evident in the way I viewed Cremo and Thompson's *Forbidden Archaeology*. It was not so much all the examples they shared that literally blew regular archaeology out of the water. I had grown up with books such as *Strangely Enough* and *Ripley's Believe It Or Not*, which had many of the same kinds of examples. So, it was not their buckshot presentation of the accumulated materials that bothered me. What I didn't like about *Forbidden Archaeology*, what was hard to shirk, was on the very first page: the publisher, Bhaktivedanta.

Radically unlike the 6,000 year old creation dates common to Christendom, Hindu orthodoxy holds that modern humans go back millions upon millions of years, unfathomable distances of time, and absolutely out of bounds in the anthropological playbooks of human evolution. Yugas and kaliyugas are immense temporal periods that become as equally offensive to anthropologists and scientists as the 6,000-year-old Biblical Creation. For anthropologists, whether humans appeared on the sixth day, or were born from Lotus blossoms a billion years ago, both sucked.

But none of this mattered to Virginia. Sure she was a Cremo "collaborator." She talked to anyone who would listen. Few have. *Isn't anyone going back?* She was right all along; she was right to be concerned. And this book would have been nowhere without her.

Bottom line: I knew that if I was ever going to try and make a case for early man in the New World, Cremo's *Forbidden Archaeology* would be the first book I would never use and never cite; to do so would destroy any chance of making a credible dent in the vox populi of professional archaeology. Guilt by association? You bet! Academic suicide should never be taken lightly. Besides there was already enough data out there, and it was all no-brainer stuff, such as, why did the Clovis Brahmin abandon, ignore, and vilify Valsequillo for a whole generation? They were prepared to abandon it forever; it would still be abandoned today had it not been for outsider and non-archaeologist Marshall Payn.

Thing is, this is the same way Virginia's work has been regarded by the same vox populi. Demonizing Virginia was far easier. Demonize her and you neutralize the importance of the findings by Fryxell, Malde, and Naeser, as well as Virgina. Four birds with one stone: that's a grand slam for the Clovis side. It was also a slam against science.

Cremo, as it turns out, had no role in Marshall's involvement, as Marshall stated to me in an April 2005 e-mail. George Carter had kept in touch with Virginia over the years. Then, in 1997, George got in touch with Marshall.

> To keep the record straight: George Carter called and asked me to take a look at Hueyatlaco. He had [Virginia] send me the geology report which I sent to three friends. The feedback prompted me to tell George I'd look into it which led to a trip to Puebla. As much as I respect Michael, his TV program had no effect on the project.[3]

Even so, it wouldn't matter. Virginia was responsible for Cremo's respectable treatment of Valsequillo's anomalies in his *Forbidden Archaeology*. This would be the ammo the critics were looking for, and they would use it. There was nothing anyone could do. Cremo was indisputably linked to modern Valsequillo research. In the end, he got it on TV. Son of a gun.

Valsequillo Rising

It was 1997. Marshall Payn had just hung up the phone. George Carter, a dear friend and partner in crime, had asked a favor: "Could you look into Valsequillo?" Marshall had said yes.

Marshall said he would follow up on some leads and that was that. He had never involved himself in the Early Man controversies before. Fantastic engineering accomplishments of the past were his specialty, along with pre-Columbian seafaring, transoceanic contact (diffusionism), and biblical archaeology. But Marshall would have done anything for this old lunatic geographer. Marshall would have walked a mile for Carter, which is saying a lot. When Marshall was 18, polio stole the use of his legs. Still, Marshall has probably been around the world more times than most of us get to go on vacation. Indefatigable curiosity runs through the veins of both explorers.

Partners in crime. George Carter (left) and Marshall Payn. Photo courtesy of Marshall Payn.

Marshall Payn, with degrees in engineering and business from MIT, knew how science worked and put it to use in his research of engineering and architectural marvels of the ancient world. His enchantment with the pyramids of Egypt led to the more general fascination with the rise of ancient sciences, such as astronomy, engineering, architecture, and—the key of keys—navigation and sea travel where it all needed to come together, if you wanted to survive. One of his great coups was developing a way to determine longitude using lunar eclipses, which was later picked up and used as Appendix 2 in the book *1421: The Year the Chinese Discovered the World*, by Gavin Menzies.[4]

Payn and Carter are Raiders of the Fringe, secure in the faith that the cutting edge is always in the fringe, by definition. The fringe is the place where all unexpected and unordained discoveries occur, and in 1997 it was heretical to argue that our ancestors figured out the ocean earlier than Columbus.

The Isolationist reply? Generally, silence punctuated by jeers from attack dogs yelling about "lunatic ravings" in the "crank literature." There was no room for a dialogue. Isolationism was an authoritarian paradigm. It had to be. One exception would threaten the floodgates for the crazy diffusionists. The Brahmin owed it to their profession to keep America pure. Think prime directive. Think "truthiness" (Google *Stephen Colbert, word-of-the-year, 2006*).

Having spent a couple decades in various academic battle zones, Marshall figured out how to negotiate "the impossible," those taboo propositions rejected by the orthodox crowd. How?

You just do it. Find and pay the best authorities in the field, and build a data set of the results. Sometimes it involved metallurgy, sometimes linguistics. This time it was all about geology and isotopic dates. I was at Valsequillo to record the events with a camcorder, and because I knew something about stone artifacts (lithics).

Just Doing It

Marshall had been involved in another scandal just before his involvement with Valsequillo. The Strange Case of Dr. Xu is a barn burner about scientific suppression; about a groupthink gone rotten and vindictive because it could. It's got everything.

Dr. Xu was not even an archaeologist or an anthropologist. He taught in Texas Christian University's department of Modern Languages and Literatures. Not having due appreciation of the dos and don'ts of gringo archaeology, he wrote about his intriguing discoveries; for his reward, TCU fired him on the spot.

He was examining artifacts from the Olmec Civilization, the sanctioned "mother culture" of Meso-American civilization starting around 1100 B.C. Dr. Xu found something amazing; he could read markings that previous scholars had written off as scratches and abstract symbols. For Dr. Xu, they uncannily resembled script from the Shang Dynasty of China, dated to 1500–1100 B.C. Other items of the material culture also had earmarks of Shang culture. To make sure, he needed to speak directly with Shang scholars in China. Marshall sponsored his trip.

The Chinese scholars, shocked, could read them, too. So he published a book describing the close linguistic and material culture similarities between the Shang Dynasty (1500–1100 B.C.) and the Olmec civilization (1100 B.C.). Then he was fired.[5]

Here was one man who innocently found himself on the cutting edge of science, and was tossed into the meatgrinder known as the Isolationist School. He was fired from his position, and subsequently he sued the university. With Marshall helping out with court costs, Dr. Xu was given back his office, but he could not teach classes.

Decades earlier, a few mainstream archaeologists had tried their hand at maritime diffusion. Back in the 1950s, the Smithsonian's Betty Meggars recognized Japanese Jomon-like pottery in 3000 B.C. Ecuador. Was Japan the cultural cause of New World ceramic technology 5,000 years ago?

The overriding consideration here was that, back in the 1950s and the 1980s, this stood as the oldest pottery dated in the New World, on the Valdivia Peninsula and nowhere else, and it looked similar to the Japanese Jomon pottery of the same vintage. A heck of a coincidence, but one that 99 percent of New World archaeologists were willing to believe was an excellent example of independent invention. Dr. Meggars was already professionally accepted—her Smithsonian appointment insured that—so the mainstream was stuck with her. They just ignored her Jomon ideas.

Decades later, Ecuadorian archaeologists excavated below this pottery horizon and found older, non-Jomon-like pottery, and everyone was able to breathe a sigh of relief. Even if a boatload of lost Jomon washed ashore along the Ecuadorian coast, bringing their strange pot styles to the culture there, earlier pottery and ceramic goods "proved" that ceramic technology was not introduced by an Old World source. Still, Meggars's work never received due notice from the Brahmin. There was no such thing as being a little bit diffusionist. It was all or none, and they decided none.[6]

What's a Couple Months?

Now Marshall was saddled with an early man site—one he had never heard of. And that's what hooked him. He had never heard of Valsequillo before, nor had he tread pre-Clovis waters before. *Heck, what's a couple months?* If there was nothing to it, he would report back to Carter and say, *Sorry buddy, I tried but it is not a viable site because of (fill in the blank).* He was ready to do exactly that if it turned out that way, but he also knew Carter's track record, and the old fox was rarely wrong. If Valsequillo was that good, how come it was canned?

Carter had been in touch with Steen-McIntyre before the wake of NBC's *Mysterious Origins of Man*. He knew that Valsequillo harbored the most significant pre-Clovis sites in the hemisphere. The fact that the excavations were directed by highly regarded mainstreamers was key. And even better, lead Clovis Firsters were also involved, such as C. Vance Haynes and Paul Martin, both of the University of Arizona. None of those involved with Valsequillo argued for premodern migrations to the New World; none of them bought the "Carterfacts," or the Calico dig.

But Valsequillo was way different. Valsequillo had spearheads and blades, and it was buried deep in a nonviolent Pleistocene column of silt and sand. Carter was approaching 90 years old, and knew it was time to request a favor from Marshall, the only person he knew who could afford the research.

Marshall had a few leads to follow up. He contacted Virginia to see what kind of data she had on hand, and sent her to Valsequillo to collect some ash samples to date. He would hunt down leading isotopic dating specialists and make sure they never talked to each other until *after* they dated the samples—this would insure against claims of bias in the dates.

And there was another person to contact: filmmaker Theodore "Ted" Timreck. Ted occasionally worked with Dennis Stanford. It was through Ted that Marshall met Stanford and learned about the Irwin-Williams archives still in Portales, New Mexico. He also got to see the artifact casts made by her mother during the 1960s.

The Shed

Stanford told Marshall that the Irwin-Williams materials—notes, sketches, files, and some photos—were going to be archived at the Smithsonian, including the Valsequillo data that survived. All of it was stored in Portales at the house of George Agogino, a professor at Eastern New Mexico University (ENMU), and that we were free to use the materials.

When Irwin-Williams died, he had collected her things from her Reno, Nevada, home. Stanford was planning to rent a van and drive it all back to Washington, D.C. He gave Marshall a few weeks to copy anything he might want while the files were still in Portales. The archives department was moving tons of archives to other sites. In all the commotion, once Irwin-Williams's files arrived, it might be a year or two before they were available. He told Marshall to use anything he wanted for film or publications, but to mention that they are all now stored at the National Anthropological Archives.

Marshall sent Virginia to Portales to peruse and copy what she thought was important. It may have been a mistake.

Over the years, Irwin-Williams had warned George Agogino not to show Virginia anything. There was bad blood between the two women since the 1981 article was published, and it may have extended beyond the grave. Steen-McIntyre copied hundreds of supplemental documents, letters, INAH reports, and some photos, but there was no sign of crucial primary data; there were none of Irwin-Williams's primary field notes, and there was the matter of the missing 3,000 photos. Virginia found about a hundred—many were washed-out black-and-whites, and only a few showed *in situ* artifacts. There were general overview photos of Hueyatlaco and some lecture slides featuring the artifacts, but only a couple for El Horno and Tecacaxco, and none for El Mirador nor of Caulapan. And there were only a few "official" photos featuring artifacts and/or features with a menu board detailing the provenience. Irwin-Williams took more than a thousand of these types of photos. Only a few were found.

These missing official photos are archaeological gold. With them, we might be able to reconstruct the site. One can only hope that another set was contractually submitted to INAH during the project. Who knows where they are? At least there might be a chance they were preserved in Mexico.

When Virginia asked Dr. Agogino about the missing data, he told her everything Irwin-Williams had in Reno and elsewhere had been collected; then he recalled something mysterious. Agogino told her a couple of officials from the Smithsonian had already gone through Irwin-Williams's material "a couple years ago," but he did not pay it much attention. Later, Dr. Stanford said no Smithsonian folks had been sent out. Who could they have been? Or was it a story to keep his promise?

Even without the primary data, there was still enough to begin reconstructing what happened down there. The Portales files were a treasure trove of materials that had never seen the light of day. They captured Irwin-Williams's certainty that the artifacts and bones had all been gently covered in place by the sands and silts of slow-moving streams.

She died before publishing her report. Officially or unofficially, it is at that point that the Society for American Archaeology (SAA) mentally buried Valsequillo as a nonentity, something fit for a pauper's unmarked grave.

They failed. The grave was too shallow.

Southern Connections

Down in Mexico, Marshall was planning fieldwork ideas with Mario Perez-Campa, an INAH archaeologist he had worked with for years. Mario and his assistant, Adrian Baker, had been charged with exposing the enigmatic "circular" pyramid of Cuicuilco, located at the southern edge of the Valley of Mexico, next to the Olympic Village. The Cuicuilco Pyramid was much older than the great city complex of Teotihuacan to the north, which benefited from Cuicuilco's demise under a lava flow. Teotihuacan soon fluoresced into the largest city in the Americas by A.D. 600, and one of the largest cities of the ancient world.

Marshall was trying to get an idea from Mario what it would take to open up Hueyatlaco for either an excavation, or for taking core samples. The permits? The estimated costs? The main problem turned out to be that Hueyatlaco was underwater for much of the year, and the dry seasons had not been too dry lately. They would have to catch the site whenever the reservoir was low. If they could not excavate outright, they could always drill and extract skinny cores from the site.

New Isotopic Dates

Marshall gave Virginia's Hueyatlaco samples to several of the best geochronologists in their field: Ken Farley, T.A. Dumitru, and Ray Donelik. The samples bore all the signatures of being a bit older, closer to 300–400,000y. A year later, all were interviewed on film and finished a professional paper slated for publication. The paper passed peer-review, but then one of the authors was warned off by some colleagues. The site was too controversial and he got cold feet.[7]

In May 2001, I got the call from Marshall. Mario and Pati were opening up Hueyatlaco.

Chapter 4.2

Southern Revelations

It was a beautiful first day at Hueyatlaco. Co-director Mario Pérez-Campa (INAH) picked up Virginia and me at the hotel in Puebla and took us out to the site. Patricia Ochoa-Castillo (co-director, INAH), paleontologist Joaquín Arroyo-Cabrales (INAH), and Ana Lillian Martín del Pozzo (geologist, principle investigator, UNAM) were the officials involved in the six-week field project. Adrian Baker, Sabrina Farias, and for a few weeks, Edgar Nebot were the archaeology assistants. Joaquin's assistant was Valeria Cruz-Muñoz. They were helped by locals who served as laborers. One of these gentlemen was Princiliano Garcia. Gentle, kind, and strong as an ox, he was a valued member of the original Peabody survey crew. In 1962, Princiliano spotted the first artifacts from Tecacaxco.

The crew had been there about a week, and Adrian was hard at work in Trench 1. Trench 1 ended up as Unit 1 because, when we arrived, Virginia told Ana Lillian that it was outside of the site area, where a lot of backfill was dumped. Adrian had to stop anyway because he came upon the Toluquillo Ash (which is also called the Xalnene Tuff), a layer of ash known throughout the entire region and at the reservoir.

The Xalnene Tuff separates two ancient Valsequillo lake stands. At Hueyatlaco, it was only in the western part of the site, and about a meter or so below the artifact beds. It represented the base of the Valsequillo Formation. Elsewhere, the ash layer turns up exposed on the surface. It was the same material mined by locals to build their houses. A few years later and a few miles away, another team would declare they discovered human footprints where the Tuff was exposed on the surface. If so, the footprints would be older than the Valsequillo artifacts.

The crew had rented a local house on the Tetela Peninsula, about a mile or two from the site. Virginia and I had brought down copies of articles, maps, notes, and photos to share, and one night after dinner we emptied everything on the floor. They had never seen any Valsequillo materials, so their interest was peaked. Not 10 minutes later:

"Oh my God!" blurted Mario.

All eyes fell on him. He was holding the 1973 photo showing Lorenzo's trenches.

"The trenches were still open?" Mario asked turning to Virginia. "Lorenzo's trenches were still open in 1973?"

Virginia casually nodded her head, saying they were in pretty good shape after eight years of exposure. "The Formation is so solid that Lorenzo didn't need shoring," she said. But that wasn't the point.

"Lorenzo always told us to fill in all trenches once the fieldwork was finished," Mario said. "If we did nothing else, we always backfilled the trenches. This was a primary rule."

This is not a neatness fetish. It is a true commandment of all responsible fieldwork. Open units and trenches must be filled back in; it is an archaeological universal. Open units and trenches can be hazards to livestock and people, and backfilling also preserves the integrity of the site. If left open and exposed to the elements, the sidewalls can collapse, combining artifacts and dirt from different levels, and making that part of the site virtually useless. What Irwin-Williams did back in the 1960s was the same thing the INAH crew did in 2001: before backfilling, line the trenches with plastic sheeting *and then* shovel in the backdirt. When future investigators come along, they will easily separate the dug from the undug.

Backfilling is a tradition of traditions in archaeology, which when done right, is always rewarded by fine, cold beer. In salvage archaeology there are times when the bulldozers and backhoes help out, sometimes free of charge when the clients want you gone a.s.a.p. Otherwise, grab a shovel and turn up the music, if you can't avoid it at all costs.

A few weeks later I walked over to Mario who was chiseling away in Trench 2. Shaking his head, he was bothered about something.

"What's the matter, Mario?"

"There's just no way. No possible way," he said.

"About what? What do you mean?"

Mario looked up still shaking his head. "There is no way the artifacts could have been planted in this stuff. It's too hard, too settled. Lorenzo told us about this place and how the artifacts were planted and it all made sense. Now that I am actually digging the site, well, there is just no way."

Any attempt to hammer artifacts into this matrix would have broken the artifacts. To dig a hole, then plant an artifact, and then cover it back up again—it would have been very obvious.

I saw a difficulty in Mario's eyes, adjusting to the idea that maybe Hueyatlaco was not as Lorenzo said. The compactness and appearance of the hardened sediments could not be hoaxed by the laborers. It was a revelation for him, and the other archaeologists, as well.

Sr. Lorenzo, however, had taught Mario, Pati, and hundreds of other students patience and close observation. It paid off. Their fieldwork seemed more akin to surgery than excavation. The trench lines were exact, and the walls and floors were so flat they resembled laid cement. Excavating in 2-inch levels, the bone fragments stood out as sore thumbs against the sandy silt matrix.

The Flood

When the water began to rise, Sabrina Farias and Adrian Baker were assigned to Trench 5, an undisturbed strip between two previous trenches that connected Irwin-Williams's Stations 1 and 2. The plan had been to strip the G Bed down to the Unifacial I Bed and then cover it with plastic to preserve the surface against the rising water and to separate it from the backfilled dirt. This would make it easy to find during the next field season.

Inevitably it happened. Valsequillo was indeed rising. Plastic was laid down to protect the undisturbed ground and the trenches were filled in.

The crew was fairly close and a joy to be around, with the only regret being that the time was too short. Mario is one of the luckiest guys in the world; his day to day equals the normal archaeologist's wildest dreams. Adrian's office is Cuicuilco. Pati has the whole world in her hands, a globe-trotter celebrating Mexico's incredible legacy. She has enough frequent flyer miles to vacation on Mars. And Sabrina had eyes that would shame an eagle. She unmasked several subtle features in the west end of the site, along with the old trenches. When Mario and Pati were not onsite, Sabrina was in charge. The main work was cutting the new trenches and watching out for bone, ferreting out obscure soil changes, discerning undisturbed ground versus rodent runs, and digging with picks, railroad picks, and dental tools.

It was with this group that I learned a very important lesson. One day, Adrian and I were having a chat and I said, "According to an American archaeologist"—and Adrian stopped me cold. "You see, that's what really bugs us," he said. "You folks think you are the only Americans. The only ones the name applies to. We are all Americans: north, south, Canada, South America. All of us. It's like you think you own the name or something."

I felt as if I'd been skinned. Sudden clarity dawned on a personal cultural deceit. *Busted!* He was right. I thought I was long free of the cultural vulgarities of nationalism and ethnocentrism. A wonderful lesson I will cherish, and the reason U.S. archaeologists are now gringos, and not the only "American" archaeologists on the block.

The Archaeology of Archaeology

When you dig up previous archaeology sites, you are practicing the archaeology of archaeology. Old trenches and units are your signposts. The more maps and data you have about the previous excavations, the better.

At Hueyatlaco, relocating the old trenches was fairly easy. The old backfill was still loose, full of trash, and very linear. Irwin-Williams also used plastic to separate trench walls from the backfill. Most trenches showed up on her map, but there was one, possibly two mystery trenches, probably Lorenzo's. It didn't matter. Shovels could easily determine the backfill from undisturbed matrix. (Remember the cartoon gag about hitting a petrified tree with an ax?)

Top: Hueyatlaco, 2001, looking south, toward the top of the Tetela Peninsula and the town of La Colonia Buena Vista Tetela. Left: Looking northeast, "Mario's Corner" (my nickname) with its namesake, Mario Perez de Campa, between two of CIW's trenches and where he later found the retouched flake.

Right: Looking northwest with Trenches 2 and 3 (in foreground), which followed the strata from artifact beds below to the Hueyatlaco Ash remnmant above; no evidence of insets were observed. Photos by author.

Clearing another trench wall, Sabrina found a squared vertical slot. It belonged to one of Roald Fryxell's monoliths removed in 1973. It extended down through the F, the G, the I (unifacial), and the J Beds. (The H Bed turned out to be an extremely local feature farther to the east.)

Soon, most of the old excavation surfaces had been cleaned up. The old walls had held up exceptionally well. Shifts in reservoir levels can harm, if not destroy, partly excavated archaeology sites; not at Valsequillo though.

We were in the right place and Virginia's memory was clicking on all cylinders. From now on, the surviving notes would guide us meter by meter. Now we could begin matching up Irwin-Williams's profile sketches with reality and see how accurate they were. They were spot-on.

Bob McKinney, who was still wondering what to do with the portable driller locked up in Nuevo Laredo, was down for a few days collecting samples from the Hueyatlaco Ash. It had been assumed that the Ash, which was sandwiched between two lake beds, had fallen on a lake. Later at his Houston lab, Bob looked at a cross-section and found that the Ash had been air-cooled, not water-cooled. The ash had cooled on a dry surface during a time when there was no water on the immediate floodplain. How could he tell? Bubbles. Hal Malde summarized for me:

> McKinney's finding of flattened bubble cavities in the Hueyatlaco Ash meant that it had fallen from the air and had cooled in place. That is, by ruling out a watery environment, none of the ash could have been later moved by water after it came to rest. And this meant that the zircons that had been dated by fission-track analysis were indigenous to the Ash, not something that might have been mixed in during later movement.[8]

As rising water filled up the lower regions, all work focused on the upper trenches, especially Trenches 2 and 3. Control Trench 6 to the southeast was also continuing. Trench 6 was at a higher elevation and the excavators had to go through about 2 meters of sterile (boring) lake clays. Now they were beginning to find clusters of bone in sandy beds resembling Trenches 2 and 3.

Trench Wogs

It was crucial that the correct geological facts be established at the beginning of INAH's renewed interest in the site. Trenches 2 and 3 were key. Ideas of insets and redeposited layers were on everyone's mind. Were 20–30,000y creek sediments cut into or laid down on top of 200,000y creek sediments? In 1973, insets tested in the western section of Hueyatlaco came up negative. This time we would test the idea in the site's eastern section.

Left: Trench 5 before the "flood," Sabrina (foreground), Adrian, and Mario quickly work to bring the level down to Bed I, the unifacial level, and then cover it before the water rises. A lot of bone fragments slowed the task.

Right: A day later, Pati and Sabrina work above and beyond the call, in boots in dangerous water, to recover as much bone as they can; in the foreground, Sam's diatom unit is now a bath.

Left: Standing next to Sabrina is Sr. Princiliano Garcia. He found the first artifacts at Tecacaxco in 1962 and helped out again in 2001.

At Trench 2, Sabrina and Adrian look on as Joaquin decides to sink an extension unit (the "bone pit") down on top of a bone extending into a side wall.
Photos by author.

The eastern part of the site had an untouched remnant of the exposed Gravels. Up the slope, there was the Hueyatlaco Ash. The idea was to connect the two strata with a couple trenches. Trench 2 ran southward through the Gravels outcrop beyond Irwin-Williams's Station 2, and up the slope. Trench 3 began as an exploratory unit adjacent to the remnant of Hueyatlaco Ash, dated in excess of 250,000y. It ran due east of the trench and intersected with the southern end of Trench 2. These cuts would expose the stratigraphic relation between the Valsequillo Gravels, the Hueyatlaco Ash, and any insets present.

Such a break in sediment continuity, called an unconformity, would be fairly visible and easily tested by assessing the geological make-up of the beds on each side of the unconformity. Also, legendary micro-fossil expert Sam VanLandingham was on site to check its diatom populations, which could also be used to compare different strata. From all accounts, no insets appeared.

A term that came up a lot, both in Spanish and English, was *facies changes*: sand and silts grading laterally into clays. When a stream overflows onto a flat flood plain, there is a characteristic lessening of energy. When a creek carrying sands and small gravels loses velocity by spilling over a flood plain, the creek continues on carrying only the lighter silts and clays in suspension, and then leaves the silts behind and continues with only the clay particles. *It is all one event.* And this is what was being described.

Adrian dug an exploratory unit next to the Hueyatlaco Ash. After about 5 feet of stubborn clays, the sediments turned coarse and sandy, similar to the artifact beds down the slope. Digging stopped and the decision was made to lengthen the unit into a trench. Intersecting with Trench 2, we could follow the stratigraphy from the Ash to Irwin-Williams's Station 2. If there was evidence of unconformities, it would show up in the sidewalls of the trenches. No natural unconformities were observed. It seemed fairly straightforward evidence that, yes, the creek sediments that contained artifacts did indeed run underneath the Hueyatlaco Ash. If correct, it would verify the findings in 1973. It would all be in the INAH-UNAM report.

There was a man-made unconformity in Trench 2, one of Lorenzo's trenches, probably excavated after Irwin-Williams left in 1966, because it was not on her map. Seeing the distinction in profile, however, gives an idea of what an unconformity is all about.

Naturally, we were all hoping to find additional artifacts, to witness for ourselves their presence in the cement-like beds. After a month none had turned up, not even a rock. Things were looking kind of bleak, and we had pretty much accepted the negative. It was already a site, so we weren't there to "prove" anything. The prime focus was on geological stratigraphy and bone collections when they turned up. After 30 years, any additional information would be regarded a plus, and the eastern end was already looking a lot different than the west.

Chapter 4.3

"Skull? What Skull?"

"You didn't know about that?" Virginia sounded puzzled.

A silent void met her voice at the end of the line.

A couple weeks before the fieldwork, I had been talking to Virginia about a whole bunch of things when this little nugget popped out about how and why Dr. Sam VanLandingham from Midland, Texas, was interested in Valsequillo.

"Gosh, I thought I sent you that," she said. "Anyhow, that's how I found out about Sam in the first place. The Dorenberg skull was named for the German/Austrian Ambassador to Mexico and was presented to him as a gift during the 1890s. There were extinct diatoms lining the inner surface of the skull. It was in the Leipzig Museum and reported destroyed during a WW2 bombing raid."

Thousands of questions began to form, clamoring at each other for immediate attention. There was only one thing to do—well four things, actually. I put her on hold, grabbed a bottle of wine, tore off the cork, took a big swig. This was going to take awhile. It did. Late in 2001, I asked her to send me a summary.

> We have evidence for a human skull from the Valsequillo area: the Dorenberg skull. The Dorenberg skull was collected in the area more than one hundred years ago. It was brought to Germany and put on display at a museum in Leipzig, where it remained for decades. It was destroyed during the bombing in World War II. We have been looking for a photo or illustration of it.

When the Dorenberg skull was examined in the 1890s, the sediment adhering to the skull was found to contain sediment rich in diatoms. The skull and the diatoms were briefly described in an article by Hugo Reichelt (1899) and a slide containing the diatoms is preserved at the California Academy of Sciences in San Francisco, where Sam VanLandingham discovered it in the mid 1970s. He noted the presence of several species [of diatoms] that became extinct before the end of the Sangamon interglacial, 80,000 years ago, and so inferred that the skull must therefore be older than that date. Recently, VanLandingham examined samples collected by Steen-McIntyre from the beds that contain bifacial tools at Hueyatlaco. He found the same suite of diatoms in these samples as was found by Reichelt with the Dorenberg skull.[9]

Growing up with *Ripley's Believe It Or Not,* strange skulls in the Americas was a popular topic. Some were really long, others looked squashed, and some had big, bony eye orbits similar to our ancestors. All of these mystery skulls had one tragic thing in common: They were gone. They were always *gone.* Missing. Lost. Stolen. Disappeared. Destroyed. Faked. Imagined. Translation: Unavailable. And here was another treasure, bombed in 1944. Sleuths continue to look for records of it, and hopefully any surviving pictures.

If it happens by some miracle that the Dorenberg Skull is found, or at least bits of it, there is a test we could submit it to. It is not a dating technique, but a geographic fingerprinter. Dr. Richard B. Firestone of the Lawrence Berkeley National Laboratory, has a gizmo that can verify an object's burial context. It is a non-destructive technique that can determine which sediments once contained a bone, such as a skull.

25 Mar 2002

The analysis technique you refer to is called Prompt Gamma-ray Activation Analysis or PGAA. It allows us to simultaneously measure the concentrations of all elements in a sample including many trace elements. PGAA is not a dating technique, but it may be useful in identifying the original context of an artifact. For example, if there are cemented sediments associated with an artifact found out of context, the analysis of these sediments could be compared with a nearby soil profile to determine the original position of the artifact. We found for example that hydrogen concentration decreased substantially with soil depth.

Richard B. Firestone

Lawrence Berkeley National Laboratory[10]

This test can be performed on any object collected from any site, preferably uncleaned. If any of Juan Armenta Camacho's original artifacts and art pieces are located, the PGAA will be waiting. Hopefully, Armenta's notes have survived as well.

For now, however, the diatoms taken from the Dorenberg Skull matched the same diatom patterns in samples taken from Hueyatlaco. Diatoms, similar to all creatures, go through changes over time. Genus and species are funny that way. Diatoms are used as environmental descriptors, and are not generally thought of as dating tools. Sam happened to know that many became extinct before the last glacial period, the Wisconsin ice age. Why not use extinct diatoms as pre-Wisconsin index fossils? If you find diatoms that went extinct by 80,000y, when the Sangamon warm period changed to the Wisconsin ice age, you have a valid temporal marker.

Thirty years ago, Sam happened to see a file and a sample from a skull collected from Puebla, Mexico. He was curious. Just a break in the action. Reichelt and Hustedt were legendary pioneers in diatoms and did a lot of work in the Americas. What did the diatoms say about the skull? It was real old, pre-Wisconsin, probably Sangamon, possibly the as old as the Illinoian ice age. In real time, this is what Sam was looking at.[11]

* Illinoian ice age: 500,000y–130,000y.
* Sangamon interglacial: 130,000 y–80,000y (peak 125ky).
* Wisconsin ice age: 80,000y–10,000y.
* Holocene interglacial: 10,000y–??? (tomorrow?).

At least these were the temporal periods up in the States. Was it the same down in Central Mexico? Sam figured he was looking at diatoms that were pretty old. Sam recalled the incident in a 2003 e-mail to me.

> While working at the California Academy of Sciences (CAS) in 1974, I first noticed that the type locality of the diatom *Navicula dorenbergi* was inside the Dorenberg Skull from Puebla, Mexico. At the time, I had thought that this diatom might be extinct, because there were no records of it in the living or extant state. I read Reichelt's original descriptions of the skull and its associated diatoms. Reichelt assigned a geological age of "Altdiluvial" (a rather loose term for a time "before the last ice age") to the deposits which encased the skull. Because the age of this skull was much older than any known human skulls from North America, I decided that it needed some further investigation. However, I was busy at the time with other projects and eventually forgot about the Dorenberg Skull and its diatoms.[12]

Krishna's Divine Intervention

For Sam, that was that for a quarter century. And then one day in 1999, Sam, now retired, got a call from a Midland cafe. A Hare Krishna guy peddling to Florida stopped in and a customer started up a conversation. The biker might be someone Sam would like to meet. Sam's also a yogi. Sam said he'd be right down. They talk for six or more hours, then it was time for the biker to be on his way. But he asked a favor. He was tired of carting that heavy book along and wanted to know if Sam wanted it. It was called *Forbidden Archaeology*—the large, heavy, expensive edition. Sam recalls:

> In 1999 I was reading Cremo & Thompson's *Forbidden Archeology* account of the Hueyatlaco/Valsequillo artifacts which were alleged to be older than the last ice age. As I looked at a map of Mexico to locate the Valsequillo area, which was a short distance south of Puebla, suddenly I remembered the Dorenberg Skull was from the Puebla region.
>
> An "Altdiluvial" age would make the Dorenberg Skull about the same age as the older dates for the Hueyatlaco artifacts. While I was compiling worldwide information on the "centric-paucity (C-P) zone* and published some articles about it in the late 1980's and early 1990's, I again by chance had encountered the Dorenberg Skull occurrences at Puebla because of its association with this zone. Since all known Pleistocene occurrences of the C-P zone are found in non-glaciated times, I realized the possible significance of the Dorenberg Skull and its diatoms: the skull would have to be older than the Wisconsinan Ice Age, because the diatoms in it are in the C-P zone! I did a detailed study of the Dorenberg Skull diatoms from an antique microscope slide from the CAS which was prepared by F. Hustedt (a close colleague of Reichelt) from Reichelt's original type locality for Navicula dorenbergi and the Dorenberg Skull. The diatoms indicated that the age of the skull was at least last interglacial (Sangamonian) as Reichelt had indicated.
>
> [*Centric paucity is a faunal zone characterized by an abundance of long, skinny diatom skeletons and a lack of round, chubby ones.][13]

He soon contacted Cremo, who got him in touch with Virginia, who was overjoyed. This would be a fantastic addition to the data pile. There was only one thing to do: collect more samples from Hueyatlaco and other locales to compare with the Dorenberg diatoms. Even better, bring him along to collect his *own* samples. Sam did better than that when he decided to bring along his trusted microscope to the site itself. It was a fascinating addition and everyone present learned about Hueyatlaco's diatoms throughout the day. Adrian and Sam worked together collecting samples.

Looking back, when Sam was first invited to head down to Valsequillo, he balked. He thought it would be a waste of time, that there would be precious few diatom deposits around the reservoir to justify his presence. Three weeks later, he left with about five year's worth of samples to look through. Valsequillo was a diatom bonanza! He quickly discovered that the Valsequillo sediments housed similar centric-paucity zones. He concluded that the geology was no younger than the Sangamon interstadial. It was at least 80,000 years old.[14]

Sam and Virginia continue to pursue information on the Dorenberg Skull. Some possible avenues have opened up in Germany, and, though there is precious little hope the Skull survived the bombs, there might be surviving photos and descriptions. We can only pray.

Dem Bones

The Hotel Colonial is situated a block away from the zocalo of Puebla, and adjacent to the University. During the 1960s it was ground zero for the gringos, and most visitors plunked their luggage down in the 19th-century lobby of this grand hotel. It was the hotel Virginia stayed at in 1966 and 1973. It was the same hotel that Irwin-Williams stayed at in 1958–59 when examining potsherds at the University next door. It was booked up in 2001 with language students, so we went there for dinner.

I was asking about Mario Pichardo del Barrio. He was the local paleontologist who was supposed to help the Smithsonian's Clayton Ray, but Lorenzo told Pichardo he could only collect road kills for modern collections.

Pichardo had maintained contact with Virginia and Hal over the years, especially during the 1990s, when he wrote a string of articles about the Valsequillo bones for German journals. German paleontologists had worked around the reservoir and apparently made a similar mistake in tying together the upper beds of Caulapan to the Tetela sediments.

For Pichardo, the bone beds had to date to about 20–30,000y. He had concluded that the beds were redeposited and that the U-Series dates were contaminated. With respect to the U-Series contamination, Pichardo was clearly speaking beyond his expertise, and, had he attempted to bring the subject up with either Barney Szabo or Chuck Naeser, he would have learned how improbable that really was.[15]

With respect to redeposition, well, Virginia had a few words to say about that in a 1999 letter response to Mario.

```
    Redeposited? Aw, come on, Mario! At El Horno, we're
talking about a butchered mastodon skeleton and associ-
ated stone tools in fine-grained lake or stream sedi-
ments, right? Show me what kind of a water current could
```

Bill McKinney with Virginia and Sam VanLandingham during a visit after the reservoir swallowed up the lower part of the site.

A couple days earlier, Sam had sampled the G, I, and J Beds that still included a slot from one of Fryxell's 1973 monoliths.

Sam set up shop onsite and schooled us in what was meant by Centric Paucity Zones (page 216). Photos by author.

Artifact Beds at Hueyatlaco are Centric Paucity Zones. Based on extinct species and extant diatom species found, the Beds conform best to the Sangamonian Interglacial period.

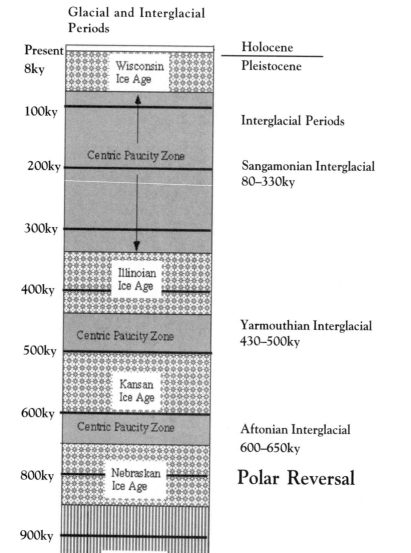

Glacial and Interglacial Periods

(after VanLandingham 2002)

deposit gigantic bones, small stone tools and fine sands, silts, and clays all at the same time! Ditto for the articulated, butchered camel pelvis and associated bifacial stone tools at Hueyatlaco. And between the unifacial and bifacial tool bearing sediments at Hueyatlaco there were sterile layers with no artifacts of any kind.

As for contamination, Szabo's ratios checked for that (see his 1969 paper). The fact that his Caulapan bone date agreed with a 14C date on associated shell showed that the [U-series] method was working at the younger end of its range...where U-series and 14C dating methods overlapped. The fact that Szabo's bone/tooth dates for Hueyatlaco and El Horno agreed roughly with Naeser's fission-track dates on zircon phenocrysts from overlying [ash] layers gives added confidence for the 250k dates. I believe that later modification in the U-series dating methods would suggest that, if the series dates are wrong, they err in being too *young*.

We thought [the 1981 geology paper] would be published quickly—it was to be a preliminary report on the geology—and that a major paper with Cynthia would soon follow where we would cover the geology in greater detail. Who could foresee that Fryx [Roald Fryxell] would be killed in a car crash in 1974; that our sample crates would take five years to make it up to the States (incomplete, as it proved); that Cynthia would refuse to share her data with us unless we recanted the old dates; and that after her death all the important Valsequillo materials would disappear from her files, both in the States and down in Mexico?[16]

The bone specimens from the excavations are at the heart of some of the confusions. Similar to the geology, the bones they were finding did not accommodate themselves to the archaeologists either. For one thing, being so far south of the northern glaciers, central Mexico could escape the radical climate changes that may have occasionally wiped out species. If you depend on a place such as Kansas for your grass and trees, and it snows and stays on the ground for a few years, things become bleak. Puebla on the other hand was a mile high, but if changes began to make things uncomfortable, critters could head down to the jungle and the beach.

The four-tusked gomphothere in the middle of the art piece was once thought to have died out a million years ago. And maybe it did, in the States. But Joaquin Arroyo, the onsite INAH paleontologist, told me that central Mexico was probably the only place where all three kinds of elephants—mastodons, mammoths, and gomphotheres—hung out in the same region at the same time.

Another big hole is that, after 40 years, the bones have not been thoroughly studied. In general, Joaquin also told me that there is still a great deal to do in order to reconstruct the faunal communities during various Pleistocene periods. Once Valsequillo research shifts into high gear, this research should assume the highest priority. Not only is it critical in itself, but when you find bone in that region, there is always the chance that spearheads, bone tools, or cobble tools might turn up.

This is why it is critical to recover every single bit of data that Juan Armenta Camacho collected—both notes and bone. INAH has its work cut out for itself, but Armenta's data will probably put them years ahead. And because Valsequillo is sheer Pleistocene gold wrapped in sands and silts, now that it's an open secret, INAH should be fighting off philanthropic gestures before too long.

"Rep"

With all this dancing in my already-dizzy brain, it was a relief to find a Hueyatlaco bone list written up by Mario Pichardo himself in 1969. It was considered the best list because it was based on the faunal remains from the excavated sites only. And it was written up before Pichardo and the others were aware of the U-Series dates.

As bone lists go in the Paleo world, they are often detested. They are despised for the same reason a shoebox of assorted artifacts is despised by archaeologists: no context. A list of specimens can come from anywhere, especially when it's just critter bones, and doubly especially when the stakes are high. Here's what Charles Repenning, a prominent paleontologist, told me about "lists."

> Lists don't mean a damn thing unless you know the guy and how good he is or can see the specimens and check for yourself. Typically a person writes a report describing each fossil and explaining why it isn't anything else and then summarizes with a list.[17]

Charles "Rep" Repenning, a USGS geologist and paleontologist for 50 years, was discussing Pichardo's 1969 animal list. I had sent it to him trying to get an idea of what it implied for the archaeology beds—such as, are there any index fossils in the bunch? Is this a late-Pleistocene group, or are they earlier? This was the first time I ever had to ask a paleontologist such things, but I understood his cautions.

I defended it based on the fact that we knew the sites and the general strata they came from, and that they were excavated by professionals who took notes and profiles. The bad news was the incomplete state of Irwin-Williams's archives.

In the end, the list was the best clue I had about the faunal remains. What did I have to lose? It was a start. Then there was all the crying and begging and whimpering until finally Rep felt sorry for the pathetic voice on the other end of the phone.

Tentative List of Fauna From the Valsequillo Formation

Tetela, Puebla, Mexico by Mario Pirchardo del Barrio, 1969. Virginia Polytechnic Institute

Asinus francisci.
Equus scotti.
Euceratherium collinum.
Tetrameryx suleri.
Capromeryx mexicana.
Camelops hesternus.
Tanupolama macrocephala.
Mylohyus fossilis.

Platygonus compressus.
Cuvieronius hyodon.
Mammut americanum.
Mammuthus columbi.
Canis dirus.
Dinobastis serus.
Cratogeomys sp.
Neochoerus sp.

Rep's Reply

```
Latest Rancholabrean is the same time as the
Wisconsinan glacial.
Equus (Asinus) tau (=francisci), earliest
Irvingtonian to Wisconsinan
Equus scotti, Blancan to Wisconsinan
Euceratherium collinum, Irvingtonian to
Wisconsinan
Tetermeryx suleri, mid-Irvingtonian to Wisconsinan
Capromeryx mexicana, mid-Rancholabrean to
Wisconsinan
Camelops hesternus, Rancholabrean to Wisconsinan
Hemiauchenia (=Tanupolama) macrocephala, late
Blancan to Wisconsinan
Mylohyus nasutus (= fossilis), Irvingtonian to
Rancholabrean
Platygonus compressus, latter Rancholabrean
Cuvieronius hynodon, C. sp. is Blancan to
Rancholabean
Mammut americanum, mid- Blancan to Wisconsinan
Mammuthus columbi, Irvingtonian to Wisconsinan
Canis dirus, Rancholabrean
Homotherium (= Dinobastus) serum, Irvingtonian to
Rancholabrean
```

Cratogeomys sp., Blancan to Recent
Neochoerus sp., Irvingtonian to Rancholabrean[18]
—ed. Same ref, Kurton Anderson

For Rep, the bones were not only older than the 25,000y scenario argued by Irwin-Williams and Denver Museum paleontologist Russ Graham, but he suggests they could be older than the 250,000y dates from the geochemists. For Rep, some of the animals go back so far that they may have been walking around when the last polar reversal occurred, c. 780,000y—the last time a directional compass would have pointed south instead of north. I fell down another elevator shaft.

Rep comforted me by saying he was only talking about the United States and that he did not know that much about central Mexico, Then he asked me if there had been any paleomagnetism studies in the region; apparently there had. Dr. J.C. Liddicoat checked the sediments along with Malde and Steen-McIntyre several decades earlier. The Hueyatlaco Ash and the artifact beds both showed modern polarity, so the site could not be older than 780,000y.[19]

Paleontologist George Jefferson from the Anza Borrego State Park, just east of San Diego, had a slightly different take on the critter list. In 2004, he e-mailed me some comments:

All of the taxa that appear on the list (some names have been changed), if correctly identified, co-occur during the Rancholabrean, and most are known from Wisconsinan localities (see Kurten and Anderson 1980). About half of the taxa first appear in the Irvingtonian or earlier in the Blancan, and about half during the Rancholabrean. Overlapping temporal ranges place the assemblage within the latter half of the Rancholabrean. Critical taxa here are Capromeryx mexicana, mid Rancholabrean to Wisconsinan, and Platygonus compressus, latter to terminal Rancholabrean.[20]

Both of these accounts differ from Irwin-Williams's conclusions near the time of her death. For her, the bestiary reflects a late Rancholabrean, which meant it fit with her arguments for a 20–30,000y antiquity for the sites. Problem was, there were no bison from the Tetela sites. The bisons came from Caulapan.

Also in 2004, Hal Malde wrote me something he observed from the critter list, that there were some glaring omissions from the record.

One peculiarity in the list is that it contains no aquatic forms, turtles, fish, water birds, etc. Also, there are no rodents, beaver, muskrats, etc. That is, it doesn't seem to be a living, indigenous assemblage of a riparian environment. Instead, the assemblage is of large animals of the kind that could have been hunted as game.[21]

When did the bison arrive in the Americas? Tony Barnosky e-mailed me saying that "around 230k for the New World is probably close." Similar to everything else about Valsequillo, a lot more work needs to be done on the bones. Again, everyone will benefit when Armenta's life's work is recovered and studied.[22]

Chapter 4.4

No Big Thing

It was the biggest rock we found that summer. Small, tabular, about 2.5"×1.5"×1/8 inch thick. An honest-to-goodness rock—our first after five weeks in the field. There were occasional gravels the size of rabbit pellets, but this rock was huge in comparison, and it came out of pure and very hard silty sand (in other words, no gravels). The flat piece of chalcedony was translucent when its retouched edge was placed in the sun. The other end looked to be a snap break. Mario was working his corner and pop, a small cube of silty sand came loose. And there it was on the bottom when he turned it over.

Small, plain, a dime a dozen in any other dirt site. In the regular world, no big deal; you can't give a utilized flake away. It has absolutely no monetary value, and you can make one in seconds. At Hueyatlaco, it was a huge deal. It was the "context" that made it priceless. Its context made it more than 200,000 years old.

Hueyatlaco: the greatest pre-Clovis site never known. We had been there for more than a month and no artifacts had been found. And then, in 2001, Mario flipped over the small square block of cemented sand and silt. Captured in matrix, was a micromini feature block all by itself. There would be no disputing where it came from.

The temptation to pull it free from the block was great. Mario was not about to do this. Once freed, it would rob the discovery of most of its power against any predisposed officials.

There were just enough hints to make the season a radical success, at least for me. Whether it was agate, chalcedony, or chert, terms that can vary between regions and geology departments, it was still the biggest rock uncovered at Valsequillo. In and of itself, it was an anomaly. The edge looked scalloped, as if it had been retouched.

It was *in situ* in a miniature feature block, similar to a piece of glass stuck in a brick. The block came out of the Valsequillo Formation left between two of Irwin-Williams's trenches. Mario turned it over and huzzah!

The others were not as certain. Some thought its rind looked akin to bone. If it was bone, it had been thoroughly petrified into a flint-like material. That meant that if it was a bone, it was a dinosaur's. Months later, word came down from INAH: It was not bone.

Several meters east, Joaquin came across the largest concentration of bone during the entire season. It started out as a bone that was going into a sidewall in Trench 2. He knocked out a 1×1 unit extension east of the trench, the bone pit. I haven't seen the report, but he found a horse jaw and several other bones including ribs. One of the ribs was flat. Ribs aren't flat. It had been modified.

In between the utilized flake and the rib, Valeria Cruz-Muñoz, Joaquin's assistant, found an isolated turtle shell in the middle of Trench 2—the first non-mammal remains identified that season. And what did they find just below it? Mammal vertebrae, back-bone parts of medium size. Was it an alter? Was it the remains of the Saturday night paleo special, Tortuga Mysteriosa? Coincidence? Alone, maybe. In between a utilized flake and a modified rib, maybe not. Because it was already a bona fide site, nothing prevented open speculation until the cows came home (which at Hueyatlaco was around 4 or 5 o'clock).

Meager evidence perhaps, but when the site is more than 200,000 years old, and it is a site that yielded plenty of artifacts decades earlier, it doesn't take a brain surgeon to take stock of the situation. One thing we knew for sure: 200,000-year-old archaeology in the New World was still as academically verboten in 2001 as it was in 1971. Nothing had changed. Step into a time machine and come out 30 years later, and it would be as if you never left, theoretically speaking.

Joaquin's "Pit of Bones"

A day or so after the removal of the turtle feature, a mid-sized long bone had been exposed extending east into the wall in Trench 2. It was about a meter below the tortuga, and a couple south. Instead of digging a "cave" into the trench's sidewall, they decided to sink a 0.5×1-meter unit over the bone.

When they got down to the bone level, they were faced with the highest concentration of bones encountered that summer. With patience and skill, Team Joaquin was able to extract an entire ancient horse jaw and more than a dozen smaller bones including some ribs. Once the report is out, we will know if the bones belonged to a single animal, a single species, or multiple critter types.

The big problem was the water table that constantly welled up the deeper they went. It was soggy and pretty miserable to work in, especially when it came to using plaster jackets to remove the bone. The Bone Pit was special for several other reasons, namely the stratigraphy and the general condition of the bones.

The sandy creek sediments seemed to give way to more clayish sediments (marsh?) further down in the unit. These were fairly thin, defined strata that seemed to shine when the eastern wall dried out. There was more talk about a facies change, where the sandy creek deposits graded laterally into clay lenses when the current ebbed. It was still under review when the project ended a couple weeks later.

Retouched flake kept in the matrix that contained it, a small feature block, so to speak.

A close-up of the flake's retouched edge.

A flattened rib that Joaquin Arroyo said was not natural because ribs are curved, suggesting it was modified by humans.

The top circle is the turtle shell, and below it, two mammal vertebrae. All photos by author.

More intriguing was the state of the bone. It seemed fresher, younger, in better shape. Translation: datable (??). During the collection of a bone, in a mix of pride and relief, Joaquin looked up and said, "We can date this!" Everyone knew exactly what he meant. *The bones were in good enough shape to date with Carbon 14.* Other bones followed. They looked younger and fresher than the usual manganese-stained, mineralized bones. In scientific terms, it meant wow. Simply wow.

If they *were* datable, then it would mean the bone pit was 40,000y or less. Was this offshoot of Trench 2 some entirely different geology? Was it a whole new series of beds? The fact that it was yielding younger-looking bones was exciting. An honest-to-goodness C14 date would be priceless. A Hueyatlaco first. Many had tried and all had failed to conquer Valsequillo's invulnerability to C14 dating. Finally, we had some promising contenders. The bone looked "ripe" enough for Joaquin to be excited, and it was contagious. However, if UNAM geologist Ana-Lillian Martin del Pozzo was right, and the geology of the bone pit was a facies change, C14 would probably fail.

It would take more than two years to learn the truth of the bones, and unfortunately it was bad news: The bones were undatable. Not enough apatite—not even enough for AMS, the radiocarbon technique that requires only a gram of organic material. Hueyatlaco had foiled us again. Marie Wormington was thwarted in 1962 when Humble Oil's radiocarbon lab couldn't date the bone. Vance Haynes and Irwin-Williams were similarly thwarted in 1969—again, not enough apatite. Joaquin's contenders now joined the group.

The overall drama of the events was subtle, akin to the temporal calm inside a hurricane's eye. Days were spent as any other day in the life of a two-month field project. The atmosphere was a mix of cool seriousness and boombox melodies. The crew excavated and took soil samples while others zeroed in on bone clusters. Sam had his diatoms. I took a lot of footage and pictures covering every inch of the exposures and whatever "specimens of interest" turned up. I used the "you-are-there," man-on-the-street approach. With footage, I could bring the geology home and show others how it looked. And now we might even have some artifacts. All was well with the world. It was a good beginning.

Because I didn't have to work—filming an event such as this is not work—it was easy to slip into those wider implications of what it was we were actually doing. I felt as if I were a Darwinian groupie exploring the Galapagos. Nothing could ever come close to the archaeological drama being played out at Hueyatlaco, especially if the huge dates panned out. The truth would be uncovered in the stratigraphy, and I'm not a geologist. All I knew was that a report would be forthcoming.

After I left, Pati found a flake in Trench 3, a couple meters below the Hueyatlaco Ash level. In 2003, Pati wrote a short article for Robson Bonnichsen's *Current Research in the Pleistocene* about the excavations and mentioned the flake, but there was no photo and no mention of the modified rib or the retouched flake. Unsolicited advice: check for traces of blood on the lithics.[23]

The INAH-UNAM crew was a great bunch of folks and we parted as friends. We all thought we would be back the following year. In the meantime, there were 10 hours of footage and more than 600 photographs to mess with. It was exciting. The academic tomb called Hueyatlaco was open to sunlight once again. What could be better than that? Then politics stepped in.

Chapter 4.5

Battleground for a Pleistocene America

Dear Clovis, Just Add Water

INAH's *First International Symposium for Early Man in America* took place in Mexico City in 2002, and Virginia was there to read a paper about Hueyatlaco's geology. Also present were Ruth Gruhn and Alan Bryan, two Canadian archaeologists at the vanguard of the pre-Clovis wave for decades, as well as Robson Bonnichsen and Michael R. Waters of Texas A&M University.[24]

The buzz on everyone's tongue: *Was Clovis First really dead?*

Many Clovis First myths had officially bit the dust a few years earlier at the 1999 *Clovis and Beyond Conference* in Santa Fe, New Mexico. It was a dream conference organized by Robson Bonnichsen and others. It brought together both insiders and outsiders to hash out alternative First American models; and there was plenty of room to look at dozens of Paleo-artifact assemblages, both known and strange, including Calico. Director Fred Budinger was on hand to talk about some new discoveries at the site. A number of archaeologists looking at the Calico display told him, "*They sure look like artifacts;*" but it was always when no one else was around.[25]

Originally from Idaho, Robson Bonnichsen was one of those Ph.D.s who was able to openly pursue pre-Clovis interests and still remain in the good graces of the SAA membership, or at least most of it. Even when he said nothing, Bonnichsen has been a visible nag (a negative symbol) to traditional Clovis Firsters for decades—his mere presence was a polite reminder of the opposition to their hegemony. Now they were forced to admit that trouble had come to Clovis City.

Clovis First was in bad shape. Emotionally, it was the great patriarchal glue that held everybody's world view together—pro and con. It was the grand tradition. Now Clovis was dying, and for many it was about time. The conference would serve as part wake and part wake-up call. Everyone was there. Some were solemn, some gloated, some were curious, some grieved, and others were incredulous.

The final nails in the coffin were:

❋ Thomas Dillehay's 14,000-year-old dates from his Mesa Verde site in Chile finally being accepted.

❋ Joseph McAvoy's 16,000-year-old Cactus Hill site in Virginia.

❋ James Adovasio's 19,000-year-old Meadowcroft Rockshelter in western Pennsylvania (an honorable mention because it has been known for decades but ignored for no good reason).

The coffin itself was provided by geologists who had declared that the great Ice-Free Corridor was still not ice free by the time the Clovis had settled in the Southeast. Adding insult to injury, the radiocarbon guys found another glitch in their C14 formulas, and had to add 2,000 years to all Clovis dates, which *really* closed down the corridor entry idea. Previous Clovis dates of 11,500y B.P. were now 13,500y B.P.[26]

Clovis First was dead. *What do we do now?* This is the question on every paleoarchaeologist's mind as I write. Deep down there's another question on every Clovis Firster's mind. *How wrong were we?*

And that's what was buzzing around the Mexico City conference. Nobody dared to bring up Calico, and only a few folks asked Virginia questions after her Valsequillo paper. Yet, Mexicans and other non-gringo archaeologists from Latin America and Canada were way ahead of the game. They knew Clovis was dead decades ago. Even Jose Lorenzo said so back in 1978: "It is surprising how such an inflexible position is able to obscure the scientific approach under a layer of pettifogging legal phraseology, proof, testimony, evidence and the like."[27]

Of course, there were some hangers-on in high positions who just could not let go. On the phone a couple years after the 1999 conference, Robson told me he had been assigned to visit various western state officials and inquire about the status of pre-Clovis discoveries and policies. When he arrived to query California's State Historic Preservation Officer (SHPO), he told me, "I was nearly laughed out of the room."

Texas A&M had become the new home of Bonnichsen's Early Man publishing empire, and he hooked up with another paleoarchaeologist, Mike Waters. Bonnichsen published the best and most up-to-date articles on both Clovis and pre-Clovis in a journal called *The Mammoth Trumpet* and the annual edition, *Current Research in the Pleistocene*.

Mike Waters accompanied Robson to the meetings in Mexico City. Waters is a geo-archaeologist—one of the first to be awarded a Ph.D. in geoarchaeology in the United States—and a rising star in Early Man research with strong ties to Tucsonans C. Vance Haynes (archbishop of the Clovis First Clan) and Julian Hayden (pre-Clovis sage).

From all accounts, Waters is a middle-of-the-roader who guards himself within defined limits, saying that the First Americans had to be modern humans. He debunks Carterfacts as geofacts. When the same kinds of things turned up in a Siberian site he dated to 400,000 years in 1997, they were labeled artifacts.[28] It was virtually the same middle-range position adopted by Marie Wormington, Irwin-Williams, and other non-Clovis Firsters 30 years ago when Valsequillo was still on the table. It is probably the most popular professional stance at this time. First Americans can only be modern humans. *Pre-Clovis yes; premoderns, no. Tall foreheads only.*

A Conference, a Dinner, and a Biface

Over dinner with Pati, Mario, and Ana Lillian, Virginia learned some of the best news in the last 30 years, something thought to be a pipedream, a fantasy, a hope against hope. Somebody found one of Hueyatlaco's real McCoys: a bifacial spearhead. It was in a dusty old Paleoindian exhibit in Mexico City's National Museum of Anthropology. Unlabelled, unidentified, forgotten, but unmistakable for the initiated, it was the same biface photographed in Figure 3B of the 1981 *Quaternary Research* article.

Are there more Valsequillo artifacts lying about in Mexico? More points, blades, flakes, along with Armenta's art pieces? His notes? His photo collections? How about the large 1 x 1-meter feature blocks?

From the beginning, it was Marshall's wish to rekindle the high level of professional interest that Valsequillo deserved. The Mexican Academy met him halfway. The gringo community? Probably not for several years. He thought they wouldn't budge without a televised documentary and maybe a book. In between, Sam would be working on several peer-reviewed microfossil papers, and Ted Timreck would be making a film on Valsequillo. Marshall was casting a wide net.

Then the surprise: Mike and Robson took the bait while it was still in the boat! It was 2002, and things were looking up.

Team Pre-Clovis

At the end of 2002, the *Mammoth Trumpet* made an announcement. Mainstream archaeologists were on the move, thanks to a retired philanthropic geologist. Joseph L. Cramer came out in a big way to provide funds for five different anthropology departments spread across the nation. Their unified mission: find the First Americans!

A Campaign to find the First Americans, by J David Meltzer, Ted Goebel, Vance T Holliday, Rolfe Mandel & Mike Waters

LIKE A MILITARY OFFENSIVE across a broad front, the Archaeological Research Funds endowed by Joe and Ruth Cramer are attacking the question, When did the first Americans appear here? Just as you would expect of a carefully planned military campaign, the strategy has been well thought out: divide the United States into five regions of archaeological interest; select five universities with the resources needed first to prospect for sites likely to bear evidence of early Americans, then to excavate identified sites; appoint as Executive Director at each university a scientist—a teaching professor, tenured or on a tenure track—with the training and experience it takes to plan and execute research; then endow a Fund at each university with enough money to fuel research in the region in perpetuity.[29]

Well...*almost* spread across the nation. The mission comes up a wee-bit short in the West in Las Vegas and Tucson, still quite a distance to the Pacific. The last time these towns saw the ocean there were dinosaurs. This seemed very odd, especially because the initial focus on first entry had shifted to the Pacific Coast and its islands. Great universities dot the coast. Another good reason for a Pacific outpost are the ancient interglacial terraces dotting the present Pacific coastline, north to south. They formed when Pleistocene sea levels were 6 meters higher than today. Carter was checking them out a half century ago.

One of Cramer's chosen sites was Texas A&M—coincidentally the realm of George Carter (*Emeritus geographicus*). He wasn't getting a penny, but Robson and Mike were. As leading paleoarchaeologists, they were obvious recipients of this award. They knew in a second what they were going to spend their money on: Hueyatlaco. After the conference in Mexico City, they went on a field trip to hunt it down.

Chapter 4.6

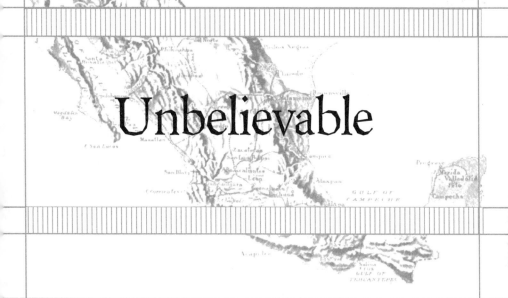

Unbelievable

May 2005: Hueyatlaco Strikes Again!

We had been waiting a full year for the new dates from Paul Renne and the Berkeley Geochronology Lab (BGL). In 2004, he had been hired by Mike Waters to take samples of the Hueyatlaco Ash and other related ash lenses on the Peninsula. He was dating them with the Argon/Argon method, a variant of Potassium/Argon (K/Ar).

Almost exactly a year had passed since Waters and Pati Ochoa returned to Hueyatlaco. Waters laid down a trench near INAH's never-dug Trench 4, parallel to and several meters west of Hal Malde's 1973 trench. Pati dug a parallel trench in the middle of the site starting at the Hueyatlaco Ash. Hal and Virginia were also on hand for the festivities. Waters says he found an inset composed of Beds C and E, the bifacial beds. Hal disagreed.

Diatom Duet

Meanwhile, Sam VanLandingham was working with the additional diatom samples and came up with something that amazed him. He discovered a unique diatom community nowhere before recorded in Diatomdom. He found it in the sediments that Waters believed to be insets. As Sam put it, it only turns up in only one other place in the world: in the sediments on the other side of Waters's alleged insets. Theoretically, the stream bed insets ought to be hundreds of thousands of years younger than the lake and stream beds outside his channel. The diatom communities should look completely different.

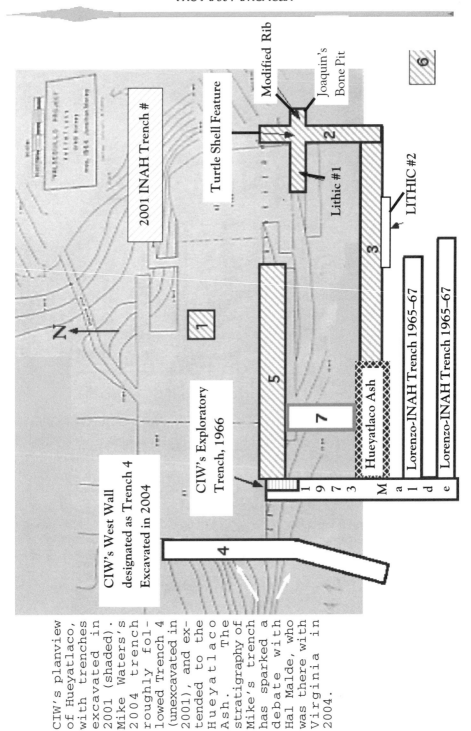

CIW's planview of Hueyatlaco, with trenches excavated in 2001 (shaded). Mike Waters's 2004 trench roughly followed Trench 4 (unexcavated in 2001), and extended to the Hueyatlaco Ash. The stratigraphy of Mike's trench has sparked a debate with Hal Malde, who was there with Virginia in 2004.

232

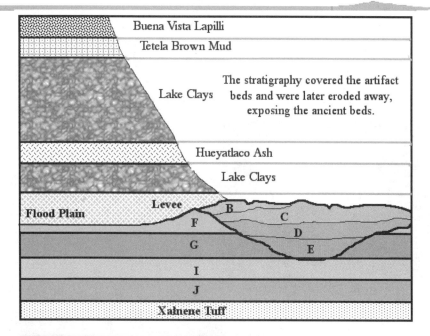

Buena Vista Lapilli

Tetela Brown Mud

Lake Clays — The stratigraphy covered the artifact beds and were later eroded away, exposing the ancient beds.

Hueyatlaco Ash

Lake Clays

Flood Plain — Levee — B — C — D — F — G — E — I — J

Xalnene Tuff

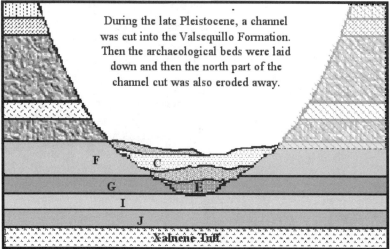

During the late Pleistocene, a channel was cut into the Valsequillo Formation. Then the archaeological beds were laid down and then the north part of the channel cut was also eroded away.

F — C — G — E — I — J

Xalnene Tuff

The current Hueyatlaco debate centers the west profile of a trench cut by Mile Waters in 2004. Top: Hal Malde's model for what he saw, which also accounts for Sam VanLandingham's diatom findings. Bottom: An approximation of Mike Waters's inset model, based on the theory that a late-Pleistocene channel cut down from the surface of the peninsula, and that the layers of sediments with artifacts are recent arrivals to the Valsequillo region, 20–40,000 years ago. Artifact Beds: C,E,I.

Robson Bonnichsen's digital photos of usewear evidence (gloss, striations) on Pedra Furada artifacts dated over 60,000 years old. Pedra Furada, a Brazillian rockshelter site, has been virtually ignored by the gringo archaeology community. It also has art. Photos: Robson Bonnichsen, courtesy of Niede Guidon.

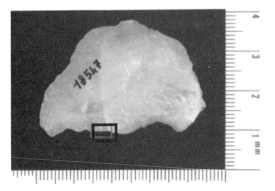

Figure 1. Dorsal side of flake exhibiting usewear characteristics. Box denotes the area seen in the subsequent micro-images.

Figure 2. Ventral side of flake. Box indicates the area seen in the following images and corresponds to the box on the dorsal side in Figure 1.

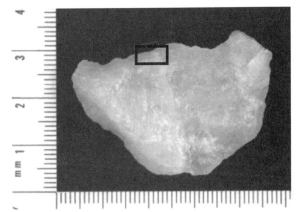

Figure 3. Flake tool with rounded and polished edge shown here at 40x.

Figure 4. Dorsal aspect of the edge shown here at 100x. Note that directional indicators, whch indicate tool movement direction, are generally oblique to the edge.

Figure 5. Close-up of the directional indicators in the upper left quadrant of Figure 4 shown here at 200x.

Figure 6. Close-up of tool edge in red box on ventral edge that has been smoothed and "lacquered" by silica gels deposited during tool use at 500x.

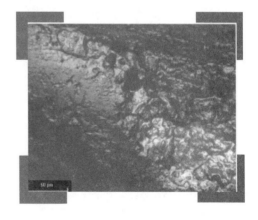

What are the odds of this one of a kind diatom match? I can't count that far. If Waters is right, how could there possibly be such a match? Diatoms are picky fellas, and for Sam it was a match of contemporaneity, a linkage that would stand up in a court case, similar to fingerprints or DNA.

An unconformity is a radical feature. It is not a blending of the old beds with the new in a soupy matrix. An inset implies a collection of sediments on top of an older and entirely different sedimentary feature. Alas, the microfossils and the grains were constant on both sides of the alleged unconformity. This bodes ill for Waters's inset hypothesis, and supports Fryxell's 1973 assessments that the sediments were part of the same deposition process. For the geologists, it was a big plus for their data pile.

Cowabunga!

When Paul Renne finally had something to say, people listened. The new Ar/Ar dates changed everything. The Ar/Ar dates were killer.

"1,900,000 years. That's the date Paul got for the Ash—1.9 million years. I think that's a minimum. It might be 2ma."

I didn't feel the recliner. I didn't feel much at all. I felt myself sinking into myself, trying to process something unprocessable, and yet this was the date from a top shelf lab by a pro who was selected by Waters himself. I told myself it was nonsense. It was ludicrous. It was just...just, uh, ah,—*say it!! say it!!*—impossible.

If the "250,000y (±100ky)" realm was not bad enough, now we have a date for an Upper Paleolithic assemblage that approaches the roots of the genus *Homo* itself. This was way beyond surprise. It was mental exhaustion. Now I knew how the earlier generation must have felt in 1968 when Barney Szabo reported his dates.

An e-mail arrived from Marshall a few months later and it was made clear that these were but preliminary dates. The dates were now younger. That was the good news. The bad news was that the dates were still 1,100,000 years old.

```
  Mike [Waters] had assured me over and over that
the first dates of 1.9 to 2 million years were pre-
liminary-only estimates. Later dating for the ash
was 1.1 million plus or minus 500,000 years. There
are two significant factors here. First, such a wide
allowance for error was the reason the archaeolo-
gists rejected the dates 30–40 years ago. They'd
never experienced such variations with radiocarbon
and tossed the dates. Second, subtract 500,000 from
1.1 million and you're just about at Farley's dates
[400,000 years]. I believe the Tetela Brown mud layer
came in at 800,000 and the Xalnene Ash at 1.3 mil-
lion, which you'll recall was a sample taken from the
```

alleged footprints site. Absolutely no conclusions
can be drawn in any way until the corroborating dating is complete.[30]

The bottom just drops, a stunned silence takes over. Which I guess is the goal of all great punchlines, or better yet, Zen koans. This was definitely a one-hand-clapping kind of date.

If true, this will become one of the most exalted punchlines in the archaeological record books, possibly even *The Guinness Book of World Records*. You wait and wait and wait. You chant the mantra that everything good is worth waiting for. And you wait some more. And when the waiting's over, your first reaction is spitting your coffee across the room. It ranks right up there with other greats, such as Zinj, finding out the world was actually round, and that God had a separate Creation on the other side of the world that He didn't tell anyone about.

At that time, however, theory had nothing to do with it. I was experiencing anxiety. It was time to kick back. This would require processing. It was time to call Jim Beam. He's not in? What about Mescalito? Yeah? Great.

Footprints and a Bony Brow Bone

If you use the word *blockbuster* too often, does it lessen the effect? Tough. Get used to it. We are living in an age of archaeological blockbusters. The Case of the Mexican Footprints is one of those, too.

During the 2004 fieldwork, an explosion went off a few miles away. While the Hueyatlaco Ash has received the lionshare of attention since the beginning, it was now showtime for the Xalnene Ash at the bottom of Adrian's Trench-Unit 1. It represents the bottom of the Valsequillo Formation and was not part of that formation. When you find yourself on top of it, you are no longer in the Formation. Now you need a jackhammer.

How old was the Xalnene Ash? Nobody knew. In 1981, J.C. Liddicoat et. al. estab-lished that the artifact beds and the Hueyatlaco Ash above them displayed normal polarity, so, younger than 780,000 years old. Previous dates put the Ash in the neighbor-hood of 200–400,000 years. He never looked at the Xalnene Ash; it would be older than that, but how much older?

Imagine Malde's surprise when Silvia Gonzalez announced in the press that she found human footprints smushed into the ash before it hardened, and that her dates suggested a 40,000-year-old antiquity. *Huh?*

Hal, Virginia, Mike, Pati, and Paul decided to take a field trip to see the "foot-prints." They were only a few miles away. For Paul it was the perfect site for an Ar/Ar sample of the Xalnene Ash—two birds with one ashball, so to speak. They all came away with big doubts and unimpressive pictures of the footprints.

On the other hand, Gonzalez's own photos of the footprints are much more im-pressive. It is an ongoing research project that is currently being explored. Gonzalez is

"Footprint" in the Xalnene Tuff, photographed during Silvia Gonzalez's investigation at the foot of Cerro Toluquilla, a few miles from Hueyatlaco. Photo: Liverpool John Moores University

presently involved in a large-scale project to date the local geologies, something we can all applaud because it will finally put Valsequillo back on the table.[31]

Hal was mucho troubled by the 40,000-year-old dates. He was not alone. For him, there was no way the Xalnene Ash dated to the Wisconsin ice age. Footprints or no footprints, it was not 40,000y. Period. If Gonzalez was right, then the entire hillside of Hueyatlaco's stratigraphy, lake beds and all, had to be less than her 40,000-year-old Xalnene dates. The whole world was watching the footprints. Malde was watching Gonzalez. If they are footprints, and they are 1,300,000 years old...wordless. It would mean that maybe our ancestors came across Beringia with the great mammoth migration.

An Eye for an Eye

He found it in a drawer or a box of bones in a museum in Jalisco, collected when Chapala Lake was low some decades ago. It was not an ordinary eye bone. It was way too bony. So Federico Solorzano went to France, and discovered that it resembled exactly an archaic human eye bone from the face of Tautavel Man, a fossil around 500,000y. He gave a paper in 2004 at the annual early man conference in Mexico City where Virginia spoke a couple years earlier.

> "Most people sort of just shook their heads and
> have been baffled by it," said Robson Bonnichsen,
> director of the Center for the Study of the First
> Americans at Texas A&M University.
>   "That doesn't mean it's not real. It just means
> there's not any comparative evidence."[32]

This had Valsequillo written all over it, but, similar to most of these kinds of "things," it too disappeared from the press. It had been reported in 1989 and then ignored. Now it came back for another "15 minutes" only to be ignored again. Maybe three times is the charm.

Robson Bonnichsen and Beyond

So much had happened during the past decade, and even more during the last couple years. Early in 2004, George Carter passed away at his computer working on his evil Asian chicken book. It was completed by his family from his notes. God bless.

Robson Bonnichsen was keeping busy. He was looking at the 16,000-year-old Topper Site artifacts in South Carolina, a site directed by ex-Clovis Firster Al Goodyear who taught at the university there. Under a Clovis quarry site, Goodyear found unimpressive flakes of stone in the pure sands of an old river bed. At first, the consensus was that it was just some detritus that leached down from the Clovis levels.

The 16,000-year-old dates coming out of there were similar to Cactus Hill, which had the closest thing we know of to a proto-Clovis tech, with blades and thin, but unfluted bifaces. Topper tech was more expedient and simple, and a good number of pros wrote them off as insignificant, even after Goodyear had shown them the results of local knappers who figured out how to make them with bend-break techniques.

Bonnichsen looked at the edges of the diminutive artifacts through his microscope and found usewear polish! No question. In this case it was aggregations of grass or wood residues that had thoroughly fused with the artifacts. It meant they were used, which meant they were artifacts. Pre-Clovis is not about pre-sleek arrowheads anymore. It will be determined by usewear whenever possible. Bonnichsen knew this for decades, and he now provided neo-rogue Goodyear the evidence he needed to fend off the geofactsters. It was a fantastic coup. A paper by Goodyear is in progress.

Bonnichsen's next prey were the artifacts from Punta Furada, Brazil, a rockshelter site run by Dr. Niede Guidon for decades and assiduously ignored by the gringo establishment. Their dates ranged from about 15,000y to 100,000y. Robson was finding usewear on those artifacts as well. Before he finished that study, Robson Bonnichsen died of a heart attack around Christmas of 2004. Niede Guidon told me he had sent him a very positive report with photos.[33]

The next generation would do well to use both Bonnichsen and Carter as shoulders to stand on as they pursue their craft.

Waiting Again

1,000,000 B.C. (or is it B.P.?)

It was not the punchline any of us expected. And it's not done yet. Protocols of science advise that Paul Renne defend his dates in light of all of the other dates from Hueyatlaco and El Horno. That is ongoing. The snag that I can understand is the polarity, and, if the artifact beds exhibit normal polarity, it means they are less than 780,000y. It is relatively easy to figure this out if you're really smart. And it is easy for someone else to check to see if you screwed up. So, I expect somewhere down the road someone will look at the polarity again as well.

Waters now asserts that the Bed I artifacts *must* belong to the very bottom layer of the inset feature. That Irwin-Williams was confused, and that everywhere she found a Bed I artifact, they were really from deep in Bed E. In other words, she screwed up the entire Bed I (unifaces) stratigraphy for the entire site. And then came the *Mammoth Trumpet* article on the Mexican footprints. It came out a year or so after Robson passed away. In a couple of background paragraphs on Irwin-Williams's discoveries and the geological research, the article totally trashed everything you have read up to this point. Essentially, everyone before Waters got it all wrong about the geology and the archaeology. The original team members were cast as either crazy fringers or as geological enablers for the fringers. It was all myth. *And after all we did for them.* It really made me wonder if the MT staff had a clue, whether they actually did any homework on the matter. But there's enough poetry for all, and in the end Waters had to make a huge concession.[34]

For Waters, there was no way Hueyatlaco had 1,100,000y-plus blades with unifacial retouch or anything else artifactual at that age. The very idea of million-year-old artifacts appalls him as it probably does most professionals. It was all nuts. There had to be a better way, some other way to date the "inset" artifact beds *directly*. Only this would clear the fog.

In the end it was unavoidable. The only datable material was the mineralized bone. The only thing that can date the bone is Uranium Series. Maybe it improved during the last 30 years. Several of us had mentioned using U-Series earlier in 2004, but Waters had his own agenda. He knew what he wanted to do, and Hueyatlaco wasn't going anywhere. He was no fan of U-Series—who is?—but now he was left with no other alternative.

Poetic in many ways. A full circle thing. Nostalgic, maybe. A return to the scene of the crime? Yes. The very technique that propelled the discoveries off the deep end a generation earlier is currently being pulled from the closet in order to resolve itself. In science, you call this "fun." Amongst mere mortals, it's gut-check time.

If he gets the hoo-ha dates directly from his "insets," it won't matter if he found insets or not. If he's right, it trashes the geosciences back to the stone age. It promises to be a great showdown. Time of truth and all that. And that is the tentative plan for 2006. But who knows what other tricks Valsequillo has up her sleeves? Rain? There's always rain.

Part V

The Puzzle Palace

The only way of discovering the limits of the possible is to venture a little way past them...into the impossible.

—Clarke's Second Law

Chapter 5.1

Negotiating the Impossible

New World

A lot has happened in the archaeology world since Cynthia Irwin-Williams passed away in 1990. Seems we underrated our ancestors yet again. Had she survived the decade, I would like to think that some of the findings discussed here would have renewed her faith and appreciation for the beings we call human. In light of these discoveries, I would like to think she would have thought again about the painful Valsequillo dates. And I would like to think that had she lived until December 2000, she would have read something that would have blown her mind: a possible solution to the Valsequillo riddle, a precedent for a blade and biface technology as far back as 330,000y. Yes, in Africa.

During the 1990s, Irwin-Williams would have experienced multiple shocks from multiple New and Old World discoveries that, little by little, and then by a lot, would strip away the impossibility of her impossible Mexican sites. One thing she would have learned was that there were more Clovis artifacts on a small Maryland peninsula than the combined take for Arizona, New Mexico, Colorado, and Utah. If she were alive now, she might have been torn in half, but somehow loving it. A western European ancestry for the Clovis paleoamericans, a branch of the European Upper Paleolithic in the New World. The Clovis homeland was not Siberia. It was Iberia. And it would have been suggested by an old friend.

Dennis Stanford and Dr. Bruce Bradley (flintknapping maestro) summarized their position in an abstract for the 2005 *Clovis in the Southeast* conference, hosted by

Al Goodyear, director of the Clovis and pre-Clovis Topper Site and the proud father of brand-new 50,000y-plus dates.

```
     Constructing the Solutrean Solution
     This paper summarizes the results of six years of
intensive research in which we assessed the avail-
able interdisciplinary evidence to see if the Solutrean
Solution Model is supported or should be rejected.
Our conclusion is that there is strong and compelling
supporting data and the model merits serious consid-
eration. In this regard, we address the issues and
opinions raised by other scholars who published nega-
tive "peer reviewed" papers seeking to "deconstruct
the Solutrean Solution" before we completed our stud-
ies. Our paper concludes with evidence to support the
view that Clovis developed out of an indented base
biface tradition that existed along the Mid-Atlantic
continental shelf.¹
```

I would like to know what Irwin-Williams is thinking now. No Bastille Day was quiet and no beret ignored when she was around. She had a deep fondness for France and French things, and here was another: Upper Paleolithic and Clovis, the two cultural periods she cut her teeth on. She must be smiling, shaking her head. A Solutrean-Clovis connection: Who would'a thunk it?

For a paleolithic francophile, what a world it would have just become. For old archaeology students, the French texts that became basic reading for acquainting ourselves with lithic technology have now become primetime reading for understanding the technological roots of Clovis. A direct technological ancestry, and not an independent invention as everyone wanted to believe. For flintknappers, you can only wonder what kind of discussions Francois Bordes would be having with Don Crabtree if they were still alive. The same goes for Thor Heyerdahl, who would be having discussions with just about everybody about 16,000-year-old Atlantic crossings and the economy of the Pacific's "kelp highway" that extends from Japan to Hollywood. Talk about a new world!²

And then there is the most recent addition to the Pleistocene extinctions theories. What caused the great mammal extinction at the end of the Ice Age during Clovis times? It was not the human blitzkrieg wrought by the Clovis hordes sweeping out of Canada. It was a supernova that took out North America—true catastrophism. This comes from the same Dr. Firestone from Berkeley with the ionic gizmo that can fingerprint objects to the sediments they came from. The blitzkrieg came by way of supersonic meteorites from the moon showering the earth, propelled by the force of an exploding star tens of thousands of years earlier. Some of the tiny moonrocks were found embedded in mammoth tusks. A New World cataclysm! If *that's* not romantic....³

Looking back, I don't know of another decade when so many separate archaeological fronts were so mercilessly pelted by discoveries so destructive to the status quo. Volumes will be needed to cover all the breakthroughs. Some were pleasing, but these others were. Let's just say they are still being worked out. The 21st century will inherit not only a new American prehistory, but an entirely new global prehistory as well. When archaeologists speak of "the New World" in the 21st century, it will be a reference to the entire planet, not just the Americas. Humans have just gotten older, and not just older but smarter, smarter beyond belief. And sexier.

When the waves of these disastrous/exciting turnabouts finally settle in, expect a business boom for therapists (or bars) specializing in academicians. Those who survive and/or relish in these events will party on. There's a whole new world out there, everywhere. Maybe even Antarctica. If you think that's an exaggeration, try this on. Popeye's ancestors go back to *Homo erectus*.

The idea of water travel in any Pleistocene migration theory was strictly taboo, except for Australia. In the Americas, it was land or nothing. Now everyone is a diffusionist by definition. That means Pandora's box has opened for good, and Isolationism is clearly dead. Now we must reconsider more recent immigrants, such as Carter's chickens, Japanese sailors, and Chinese Olmecs. *No! No! Clovis just got lucky, that's all.* Nice try.

The Pleistocene coastal approach to the New World had been discussed decades earlier by the enlightened Canadians. The gringos, however, claimed that the northwest Pacific coastline was blocked by glaciers, and that immigrants could not walk around them, so they didn't. Silly? You bet.

> Hypothetically there was nothing *wrong* with proposing a coastal entry, but it seems the Clovis school argued: "the west coast might have been the route by which people entered the Americas, but the evidence will never be found to prove it was the route, therefore it wasn't the route."[4]

Kind of leaves you breathless. There were no boats allowed in migration theories if you wanted a Ph.D., grant, scholarship, or anything else official. The 60,000y Aussie precedent never fazed the Brahmins in archaeology and anthropology. It was easy to argue that island hopping to Australia was one thing, but navigating the thousands of miles across the Pacific to the Americas was quite another. Maybe it was easy to forget that there was a great string of island-hoppable islands leading straight to Alaska, not to mention the coast of Beringia itself.

Folks are singing a different tune these days. The new navigationalism will have a great impact on the Academy. In a fine *Atlantic Monthly* article called "The Diffusionists Have Landed," Marc Stengel explores new sets of questions about who the new First Americans might have been.

> How might the pre-Clovis settlers have arrived? One explanation is that early immigrants floated down the western coast of North and South America in small

boats. This theory, considered heretical when, nearly three decades ago, it was proposed by the archaeologist Knut Fladmark, of Simon Fraser University, has been gaining adherents of late. Researchers such as Dennis Stanford, the chairman of the anthropology department at the Smithsonian Institution; Carole Mandryk, an associate professor of anthropology at Harvard University; and Daryl Fedje, an archaeologist with Parks Canada, are urging their colleagues to consider that canoe-like or skin-covered boats—prototypes of Inuit kayaks, perhaps—might have aided migration toward the end of the last Ice Age, around 14,000 years ago.

Jon Erlandson, an anthropologist at the University of Oregon, has pointed out that boats were used in Japan 20,000 years ago. By Fladmark's estimate, travelers paddling six hours a day could have made the trip from the eastern Aleutians to Chile in just four and a half years. This route might also help to explain [an 11,500y female skull] Luzia's presence in Brazil: the anthropologist who first noted her unusual features believes that her forebears originated in Southeast Asia and migrated "northward along the coast and across the Bering Straits until they reached the Americas."

[Mike] Xu, for one, is amused by this archaeological approximation of a drag race backward in time. Although he welcomes any willingness among traditional academics to question the established settlement dates, he is puzzled by their apparently exclusive fascination with older contact. "It amazes me...that while there are authorities who propose visits to North America by boat some twenty-five thousand years ago," most orthodox academics insist that contact across the sea in the past 3,000 years is "simply unthinkable."[5]

Michael Xu has a point and Betty Meggars probably agrees. If archaeologists are now talking about 20,000y boat trips down the West as if it were yesterday's news, why do the same folks get so hot and bothered about possible contacts a few thousand years ago? Could it be that old habits die hard? *Post academic shock syndrome* is a delicate condition. Ask the geologists who, in 1970, had to endure the onslaught of plate tectonics after decades of ridiculing it. *No. Simply no. No way. Aw, shit.*

There is another aspect to boats with respect to demographics. It was estimated that it would take four-and-a-half years to make the trip from Beringia to Chile, or maybe five because they stopped and partied in Frisco. Think of that duration. It is perceivable, even if it takes 10 years because the entire coastline is heaven and there's no hurry.

Maybe it takes a generation. Every group probably had its explorers and scouts who could make the trip a bit quicker. All in all, with boats, you could travel the length in five years. This is all very well and good, now. But it wasn't too long ago we were still thinking in terms of thousands of years, on foot. As recent as 1998, a linguist from Berkeley estimated that "it would have taken about 2,000 years to travel on a beeline at a good clip."[6]

If you are walking, it takes 2,000 years "at a good clip," versus five years to cover the same distance in a boat. If you have spent the last 30 years thinking in terms of millennia for moving north to south, and then you wake up one day and find they had boats and it was only a matter of years? And that they were doing it since the Pleistocene? That's quite a jolt. Figuring out who was where, and when, and with what, will take a radical change in thinking.

What inspired this theoretical hardness that permitted nothing outside the boatless Isolationist box? Was there a mass conspiracy to defraud the public by a cabal from the original skull and bones society? Are the secrets buried next to The Ark in some Pentagon-subsidized Smithsonian warehouse and kept out of public hands because we cannot handle the truth?

Dream on. It was the Paleo experts *themselves* who could not handle the truth. Clovis First/Isolationism was guided by a consensus mentality, a groupthink that reason could not penetrate. *What's the use of wasting time and money trying to prove yourself wrong when you know you are right?* In the end it was nothing but wishful thinking, an obsession that stunted the development and maturation of First American research.

In spite of the tonnage of "science" being thrown at the problem of American origins for a half-century, nobody seemed to want to concede the negative evidence building up against the Clovis First model. They still couldn't answer a simple question. Where the hell is the Clovis Trail? Maybe it had to do with the shear absence of Clovis or proto-Clovis sites in Canada, Alaska, or Siberia?

Didn't phase them a bit. When the need for a Plan B arose, everyone was left floundering.

The loss of [the Clovis] paradigm has thus plunged American archaeology into a new period of tumult and uncertainty over its oldest mystery, one critical to understanding how modern humans spread out through the world. [7]

Maintaining Sobriety During a Paradigm Collapse

As I read once, *a paradigm is what you think about something before you think about it.* This might work during a time of paradigm stability, but what happens to this sublimity when the wheels come off? On one hand, there is always the fear that some will begin to lose their conservative moorings and uncontrollably begin thinking all kinds of wild and crazy things. The fringe is still the fringe, and we must guard ourselves against getting drunk on all of the forbidden possibilities. On the other hand, open minds are needed and, as Carl Sagan preferred to say, "an open mind doesn't mean that your brains fall out of your head." How do we achieve a balance?

"Through the idea of 100,000-year-old ocean-going boats is only slightly more believable than the brought-here-by-space-aliens theory, a later migration involving small skin boats moving in short jumps down the West Coast is more plausible."

—Blake Learmonth

Adam and Eve were Aliens

Homo alienensis

100,000y seafaring

OUTER FRINGES
Wackydoodleland
"...for madmen only"

40,000y

Moderns-First Model
Neo-Orthodox
Cutting Edge

12,000y

The Great Wall of Clovis
Clovis-Isolationist Model

The Learmonthian Model

A view of the new fringe based on Blake Learmonth's pronouncement. In the New World, 40,000y archaeology is okay, but only just okay. Any claims for anything older will probably still engender scorn for their ludicrous erroneousness, especially if it includes seafaring 100,000 years ago.

Out of the political chaos of First American research a voice rang out defining the new limits for the new and improved watery frontiers of the New Orthodox. For those of us still lost at sea in the dark, Blake Learmonth has thrown us a quantitative liferaft.

> Though the idea of 100,000 year old ocean going boats is only slightly more believable than the brought-here-by-space-aliens theory, a later migration involving small skin boats moving in short jumps down the West Coast is more plausible.[8]

This is a common device where we compare one dumb idea to an even dumber idea, and it serves to warn the confused readership about what should and should not be taken seriously. If by chance down the road we *do* happen to turn up 100,000y seafaring by implication (say, by finding 100,000y sites in Australia), then it does not mean that Learmonth is going to move to Roswell and begin spending his nights scouring the sky through his new telescope.

If 100,000y navigation becomes a scientific fact somewhere down the road, it will not add one whit of credibility for the brought-here-by-space-aliens theory. And even if our ancestors did reach Australia at 100,000y, that's still a far cry from following the Ring of Fire up and around to Malibu. As metaphors go, the message is clear. If you begin to argue for 100,000-year-old navigators, then you, similar to all those in the E.T. ancestors camp, will inherit a professional stigmata that will follow you to the grave. So you better not.

So is it okay now to clean the slate of all the ridiculing and seriously reconsider Valsequillo, Calico, and Pedra Furada? It's okay, right? It's a new age, right?

Fugeddaboudit! No way, no how! Talk about brains on the floor!

A 40,000-year-old cellar for the American paleolithic is about as far back as anyone is willing to go, publicly at any rate. In this sense, Learmonth's model still holds.

Valsequillo is still impossible. It has an extra zero. It was clear that no further answers were to be found in the Americas, so I had to go overseas (online) to scour the human record for other impossible things—all peer-reviewed of course—but nevertheless, just can't be. In the end, I found out that *mind-boggling* was a better word than *impossible*. Impossible just adds subscribers to skeptic societies. Mind-boggling concedes that sense of wonder and curiosity in the face of a reality capable of utter transformation with the next shovel of dirt: part romance, part humility, part caution, and part scotch.

How smart were we and when? What exactly *is* meant by "modern" and "intelligence," and how are they represented in artifact form? The answers would be in the Old World's archaeology of human intelligence. They weren't hard to find. Archaeological headline Websites made gratification instant, and often because extra zeros were exploding all over the place. There's an archaeological renaissance going on, about 2 million years worth. The evolution of intelligence is getting a makeover.

Chapter 5.2

I, Species:
The Mods

For the neo-traditional archaeologist, common sense says that the First Americans have to be modern, and "modern" begins at 40,000y. Neanderthals never got to East Asia, as far as we know. This left only *Homo erectus* as the culprits of Valsequillo and Calico. The only way this could ever be accepted would be to find a near complete *erectus* skeleton or a complete skull somewhere in the New World, and then have a field trip to make sure.

Everything tells us that anybody we find here came from the Old World. There is no credible evidence for a separate in-house version of human evolution in the Americas. The monkeys were different. They had prehensile tails, which, evolutionarily, inspires wild speculation. What if? What would we look and be like with tails that worked?

Traditionally, any and all signatures of early human intellectual development were strictly Old World concerns. Valsequillo makes it a New World concern. If humans were in Valsequillo by 200,000y, then they had to come from the Old World. That means they had to have the tools, the intelligence, the social integrity, and the food-on-the-hoof-know-how to make the trip across Beringia. That's huge in itself. Then the stinger. The technology they were using in Valsequillo did not show up in the Old World for another 160,000 years or so. When it did, it signaled the dawn of the Upper Paleolithic, the first modern humans. But this was central Mexico before we were modern…and there were modern tools, and round and round we go.

There's a vast middle ground that separates Us from *H. Erectus*. Archaic *Homo sapiens* are akin to half and half. According to academic culture, we are *Homo sapiens* (man who thinks). Sometimes archaic humans are given separate species names; sometimes they are regarded as a subspecies, or race. These archaic types may have been around for half a million years, and if we could have babies together, then they were us. So maybe the question is not so much whether the First Americans were modern, but whether or not they were modern enough.

Would it be enough if the First Americans were a variety of archaic *Homo sapiens*, such as Germany's *H. heidelburgensis* or Africa's Rhodesia Man? Or was the crossing limited to us thoroughly modern humans, the Mods, *Homo sapiens sapiens*, "man who thinks he thinks." Because the Mods didn't show up until 40–50,000y, that pretty much establishes the temporal cellar for the First American. If the first Mods turn out to be 60,000y or 75,000y, then the gringo Orthodox might be compelled to adjust its assumed time depth for American archaeology accordingly. Afte rall, Australia has 60,000-year-old sites. But 200,000y? 300,000y? 500,000y? *No chance.*

But that was then. This is now. For the past decade there have been some remarkable paradigm busters going on around the world. When challenged with negotiating an alien idea such as a 200,000y Upper Paleolithic horizon in the Valley of Puebla, it was useful to examine it in light of these new impossible discoveries, and then connect the new dots and see where we come out. Some of these discoveries are right on the cutting-edge of what could be accepted. They were low on the totem pole of the impossible, and are given a rating of simply *amazing*. It was the *oh, my God!* ones further up the pole that really caught the experts by surprise—that is, once they decided not to rebury the stuff or pretend as though it never happened. (That's a joke.)

To set the stage, summaries defining what is meant by "modern" are given here. Currently there are two distinctions for the term *modern*, depending on if you are talking about *modern physical structure and anatomy* (skull, skeleton, body, c. 180–200,000y) or talking about *modern behavior* (40,000y). The summaries here relate to modern behavior. Sally McBrearty and Allison Brooks list significant benchmarks that can serve as an intellectual gauge for the wonders discovered during the wild 1990s and beyond.

Archaeological Signals for Modern Behavior

The European Upper Paleolithic, because it is known to be the product of *H. sapiens,* is often used as a standard for modern human behavior, which is contrasted with the European Middle Paleolithic produced by the Neanderthals. The literature converges upon a number of common ingredients thought to characterize modern human behavior:

✳️ Increasing artifact diversity.

✳️ Standardization of artifact types.

✳️ Blade technology.

✳️ Worked bone and other organic materials.

✳ Personal ornaments and "art" or images.

✳ Structured living spaces.

✳ Ritual.

✳ Economic intensification, reflected in the exploitation of aquatic or other resources that require specialized technology.

✳ Enlarged geographic range.

✳ Expanded exchange networks.

[T]his inventory...reveal[s] assumptions about underlying hominid capabilities. We would argue that modern human behavior is characterized by:

✳ Abstract thinking, the ability to act with reference to abstract concepts not limited in time or space.

✳ Planning depth, the ability to formulate strategies based on past experience, and to act upon them in a group context.

✳ Behavioral, economic, and technological innovativeness.

✳ Symbolic behavior, the ability to represent objects, people, and abstract concepts with arbitrary symbols, vocal or visual, and to reify such symbols in cultural practice.[9]

For those who like to see things in pictures, a graph by Dr. Brian Fagan says it all.[10]

In short, premodern humans—pre-*Homo sapiens sapiens*—were still a few cards short of a full deck, a few fries short of a Happy Meal, not the brightest bulb in the box, and, if you are Down Under, one stubbie short of a six-pack. Maybe they attained the intelligence of a small child with their short attention span. They were incapable of abstract thought and probably couldn't talk beyond a grunt. You know, cavemen.

The secret? Our raised foreheads. The front part of the brain developed, and made us into the kind of big-brained beings we turned out to be. Abstract thinking, planning, community management, economies, hunting strategies, perhaps language itself, were all thought to be modern qualities care of our new foreheads. Neanderthals had brains as big as or bigger than ours, but no foreheads to speak of.

At least this was the shape of things around the time Irwin-Williams died. It was why Valsequillo was still impossible, not just from an Asian Connection perspective, but from a fundamental, evolutionary perspective. To say the artifacts were 200,000y was an affront to the entire world of human evolution where it was most vulnerable: that final phase of transformation from bony-faced hunks into the gods and goddesses we ultimately became.

But then, seemingly all at once, in what can be described as a cascade of discoveries from around the world, the standard premises for "modern human behavior" were stood on their heads. Several of these discoveries involved archaic humans, others involved much more distant relatives. They are important to pursue because together they begin to refute what American archaeologists have condemned as the "impossibilities" of Valsequillo in particular, and pre-modern invasions of the New World in general.

It turns out that a tall forehead and a big brain weren't such a big deal after all. As for the incapacity for abstract thought prior to 40–50,000y, that turns out to be a bunch of hooey, too.

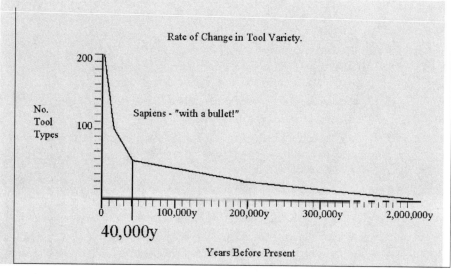

Brian Fagan's model for the rise of the Mods. Based on the number of "official" tool types before and after the great transformation, the same meteoric rise implicitly applies to modern intelligence. All of our pre-sapiens ancestors are left behind in the dust.

The Nookie Factor, or Sex and the Single Species

Archaic *H. sapiens* are shelved somewhere between 600,000y and 50,000y, somewhere between *H. erectus* and the Mods, and may or may not include Neanderthals. It could be a region-by-region thing because Neanderthals were limited to Europe, western Asia, and north Africa.[11]

The idea is that Neanderthal evolved directly from *H. erectus* around 200–300,000y-plus, and were stuck in Europe during a glacial period, separated from contact with others until the Upper Paleolithic. This separation resulted in the unique characteristics of Neanderthal when compared to all other human family members; or Neanderthal came from *H. heidelburgensis*, an archaic *Homo* species from Germany that dated as old as 400–500,000y, who in turn had evolved out of *H. erectus*. Or *H. heidelburgensis* may actually belong to the *Homo Sapiens* camp (that is, *Homo sapiens heidelburgensis*). Nobody knows for sure. Confused? Who isn't?

Under the covers of ancient life remains hidden one of the most significant dimensions of premodern life—namely, the *Nookie Factor*. By definition, a species cannot successfully mate and have viable offspring with another species. When applied to the human dimension, the designations *H. heidelburgensis* and *H. neanderthalensis* mean that there might be nookie, but no babies. The same applies to trysts with *H. erectus* and *H. sapiens* as well.

If the designations are those of subspecies ("races"), such as *H. sapiens heidelburgensis* or *H. sapiens neanderthalensis*, then physical anthropologists should expect several hundred thousand years of variation arising from a nookie heaven that potentially gave rise to all sorts—and much more so if *H. erectus* was also part of it. How does *H. erectus sapiens* sound? If everyone from *H. erectus* forward could have kids with everyone else, it would certainly give an added dimension to the name *erectus*. In the end, DNA comparisons might be the only way to reach solid conclusions about who was the same species and who was not.

To nookie or not to nookie: That is the question. It is for this reason that you are warned on the first day of Physical Anthropology 101 that the world of human evolution is divided into splitters and lumpers. For some, each discovery means a new *Homo* species. For others, *H. erectus* and *H. sapiens* are actually the same species, separated only by race. And then there are combos in between the extremes. It is a room of mirrors, and new discoveries expand the debate. One thing to keep in mind: *Homos*—both guys and gals—were sexually "on" all the time, 24/7/1,000,000s. Could it possibly be that at least some of our early hunting and warfare strategies grew out of "guys night out"?

The nature of genus *Homo* is still to be determined. Babies or no babies is a cut and dried division, and serves as the definition of species. Practically, however, we should never ignore the nookie factor, and those trillions and trillions of sperm that were floating around for the last million years. God might not play dice with the universe, but this is pretty close.[12]

Chapter 5.3

What a Piece of Work Is (Pre-Modern) Man

For millions of years, mankind lived just like the animals.
Then something happened which unleashed the power of our imagination.
We learned to talk.

—Stephen Hawkings[13]

Living the Great White North

What were we up to 400,000 years ago? We were learning about living in the cold, an education that was not supposed to happen until the Upper Paleolithic, ca. 30–40,000y. Two sites were announced almost simultaneously in the mid-1990s that served as a double-barreled wake-up call. Diring Yurick, Siberia and Schöningen, Germany, at around 60-degrees north latitude, were at least 400,000 years old.

> The Center brought Yuri Mochanov and wife Svetlanna Fedoseva to the US to report their very important Diring Yurick site, located on the Lena River about 140 km upstream from Yakutsk, Yakutia, Siberia. The

Mochanov site is located at 61 degrees north latitude and is very important to our understanding of when humans were able to penetrate the far north. The Center assisted Mochanov with presentations at 12 locations in the west, central, and eastern United States, including the Yacht Club in Greenwich, Connecticut. This adventure received lots of press with articles in numerous newspapers and *Science*. After Mochanov's departure, Mike Waters at Texas A&M University ran a series of thermoluminescence (TL) dates on the deposits above the artifact layer. The date suggested the site is minimally 400,000 years old, while the cultural deposit could be considerably older. These dates would suggest that *Homo erectus* penetrated the far north—perhaps during an interglacial. If early humans could have lived at Diring in the far North, they could have also come to America. Thus, the search must go on.[14]

During the mid-1990s, Mike Waters was involved with one of the most significant Siberian sites ever dated, Diring Yurick. Above and beyond the usual catcalls by the usual gringo geofactsters, Waters realized that the broken pebbles and cobbles were real McCoys. Broken quartzites and other rocks were featured around much larger rocks called anvils. The deposit itself was largely airborne sands and silts. There was no way these agencies broke the rock in place and positioned them around boulder-sized rocks. No way. No how. Those who claimed such were prisoners of Clovis-think.

The technologies used were bipolar flaking and direct percussion flaking, *primary reduction techniques* that have been around since Day 1, which currently dates back to about 2.6ma. When I saw the anvil features, it reminded me of my backyard in San Diego during the 1970s, where I experimented with bipolar flaking; isolated anvils surrounded by broken quartzites and other pebble types. Nostalgia happens in the strangest places.

"They're definitely human-made artifacts." Waters believes their existence at 61 degrees north, about the same latitude as Anchorage, Alaska, demands much more research in the Lena Basin. And he would like to do more TL dating of samples from immediately above and below the cultural surface.[15]

Diring Yurick was one of many sites unearthed by Yuri Mochanov since the 1980s. Previous TL dates gave results in the neighborhood 1.5ma and older. Diring became notable because Water's work is respected in gringodom, as is Steve Forman's, a sharp thermoluminescence (TL) expert from the University of Illiinois at Chicago.

Not too long ago, the earliest Siberian sites hovered around 13,000y, fairly contemporary with the Clovis, and a good chunk of the evidence used to argue that folks could not adapt to arctic environments until that time. Sites such as Sheguiandah in Canada and Calico were disputed because (everyone knew) no one could adapt to Siberia so early. Now that we know they could handle Siberian cold more than 400,000 years ago, it indicates they were intelligent enough to cross Beringia.

The tools themselves were no big deal. Same ol for eons. Only stone survived; no bone or wood. We don't know exactly what they were doing or making with the tools. Bone and wood artifacts older than 40,000 years might as well be pipe dreams. And the Siberian sites had none. Epistemology is a bitch, and archaeologists are inclined to underestimate signatures of intelligence before they overestimate. Better cautious than a loony. In the end, little or no evidence is little or no evidence, and, when you have no idea what these guys were doing with wood and bone, what can you do? It is just one of those frustrating limitations you learn to live with when you're interested in early man.

And then came the Schöningen javelins in northern Germany, a paradigm buster deluxe.

> Working in a coal mine: the Schöningen spears
> "Just occasionally, an archaeological discovery leaves one speechless. Reasons usually concern the degree of preservation, the unexpectedness of the find, and its wider implications. The discovery of complete, unambiguous throwing-spears 380,000 to 400,000 years old at Schöningen in Germany...meets all these criteria."[16]

In flint-rich Europe, the stone artifacts are a bit easier to discern from naturally broken stones. Flint leaves highly defined flake scars, the flaking is easier to control, and, in general, patterns of intentionality are easier to see. That's why Leakey liked Calico. But everyone was still left with a big gap in the technological picture of things, namely the absence of tools made of wood, bone, and other organic materials subject to decay.

Sometimes you can guess but you don't know. Microscopes can sometimes show what kind of material, such as wood or flesh, was being worked on. We had no real evidence for what they might have been making with those simple tools and had little other alternative but to think that simple tools meant simple minds. Don't believe me; check Dr. Fagan's chart again.

And then in the harsh subarctic environment of northern Germany, where no premodern presence was thought possible, Hartmut Thieme found a mother loade of wooden artifacts, including spears, javelin-shaped spears! Weighted nearer the tip, *exploiting the same principles of aerodynamics built into modern Olympic javelins*. Without a doubt, the spears were made with throwing in mind. It was an eye-opener. Javelin spears meant group hunting, planning strategies, teamwork...and language?

Along with the spears, Thieme's team also recovered:

✳ 14 complete horse skulls and 10,000 bones from horses.

✳ Several dozen stone tools used for butchering carcasses and scraping hides.

✳ A large bison bone with multiple indentations, probably marks from cutting hides into clothing or leather straps.

Translation: Amazing.

No human or humanlike fossils have been found at Schöningen, leaving unclear the identity of the spear makers. Thieme regards them as *Homo erectus*, Roberts tentatively assigns them to an early version of *H. sapiens*, and Christopher B. Stringer of the British Museum in London thinks they may have been predecessors of Neanderthals.[17]

In the Land of Nookie, they could all be talking about the exact same "thing."

The subarctic wooden javelins from northern Germany are amazing discoveries because it moves back the "modern behavior" clock several hundred thousand years. Stone-wise, it was the same tool kit that had taken them to Asia and the South Paciifc. The Schoningen javelins put us on notice. Simple tools no longer implied simple minds.

Now, this is great and all that, but it might turn out that the spear makers were actually an early form of us, an archaic *H. sapiens*. If so, then it will not destroy the evolution model we have now, only extend the period where modern humans were modernizing. Upsetting, for sure, but not devastating.

The Traveling Ergasters

A politically incorrect description of *H. habilis*, our 2.6–1.7ma pre-*erectus* chimp-sized ancestor with its even simpler *Oldowan* tool kit (Mode 1), could go something similar to this. These 4-foot-tall neophyte bipeds with pea-brains less than half the size of ours never ventured from their sub-Saharan East African homeland, the only region their remains have been found. These half-wits were probably lucky if they made it through the day without becoming some carnivore's tasty morsel. Talk about mentally challenged! How they *ever* survived long enough to evolve into the bigger, taller, bolder, brainier, hand-ax-wielding *H. Erectus* a million years later is anyone's guess. Even so, "Handy man" was probably the first ancestor to use stone tools on a semi-routine basis.

And then it happened, near the Silk Route in Georgia, southern Russia. It happened before the announcement of the javelins, but the experts gave it a no-never-mind for almost a decade until it happened some more and it came back to haunt the experts again, bigger and badder than before. It even had fangs! Fangs! *Homo lonchenyensis*.

The discovery was of such magnitude that to call it "amazing" is an insult. This thing that happened zooms up near the top of the impossible totem pole, the height of absurdity. It prompted something you never hear anymore, not publicly, not since the Inquisition on the Planet of the Apes. This is the *"Let's just rebury it and forget it"* level. It approaches the emotional apogee reached by the Valsequillo discoveries though with one saving grace: The Georgian scientists, unlike the gringos, didn't ignore it. Nope. They kept digging.

The 2001 *National Geographic* article exploded off the shelves. "The 1.75-million-year-old pioneer," found beneath the ruins of Dmanisi, a medieval town in the republic of Georgia, had a teeny brain, "huge canine teeth and thin brow too apelike for an advanced hominid." This skull, the other bones and artifacts punched an immediate and inescapable wormhole in the evolutionary playbook. What the hell was *this* doing *here?*

"This skull reopens so many questions about our ancestry that one scientist muttered: "They ought to put it back in the ground."[18]

Welcome to the realm of the absurd. This is where the "Put it back in the ground" syndrome is considered the humane thing to do. Here it is exposed as an exasperated jest, a frustrated joke looking for a bar. Somebody or something new just turned up in the neighborhood, upsetting the applecart and forcing everyone back to the drawing board, and any other metaphor you wish to add while they're rewriting the textbooks. If there was ever an equal to Olduvai's Zinj, the Dmanisi discovery was it. In 1960, Zinj forced everyone to look south. In 2001, Dmanisi forced everyone to look north again.

There is something/someone similar to a *Homo habilis* who could be an early type of *Homo erectus* called *Homo ergaster*. Quite short with longish arms and a small brain. With fangs. Nobody saw fangs such as this before. And talk about romance! One of these folks ended up as cat food 1.8 million years ago. The archaeologists knew this because the two holes in one of the skulls were made by a saber-toothed lion.

Anthropology is now forced to reconsider the entire complex of faculties that were squeezed into the nutshell that is the Dmanisi brain. A brain with intelligence, consciousness, self-awareness, abstract thought, planning, internal dialogues, dreaming? Whatever the speculation, the pea-brain was able to figure out a whole lot of stuff to take off from Olduvai almost 2 million years ago. They traveled thousands of miles over new ground into new environs with new animals, plants, diseases, and poisonous beasties. How could they have done it without at least some of the Upper Paleolithic qualities and faculties already in place? One thing is certain: Lower Paleolithic demographics just got a lot more complicated.

Discoveries of this magnitude sometimes lead to heavy drinking, or the earthquake feeling when terra firma turns to jelly. For the enlightened scientist, this kind of turnabout is greeted like a sudden thunderstorm, a sobering plunge into a mountain stream.

> Science is a process of discovery, not confirmation. Let us allow for the occasional, delicious surprise that makes us rethink all we thought we knew.[19]

Translated: Last one to the bar is an idiot.

History of the Fanged One

The story began at a medieval villa overlooking the Silk Road. Granaries in the medieval compound exposed bone beds, Pleistocene bone beds that contained simple stone tools. Excavations resumed during the 1980s. Then, on the last field day of the 1991 season, a human-like jaw with all its teeth turned up in beds dated between 1.2ma and 1.8ma. It was the oldest hominid bone ever found in Eurasia. Several years later the archaeologists found the skulls, and the world of human evolution stopped on a dime.[20]

For University of Binghamton's Philip Rightmire: "There's no reason to downgrade these early Georgians on the IQ scale. They took a long hike and they made it."[21] They made it to a beautiful spot between the Black and Caspian Seas, a place with plenty of water and critters. They made it to a place close to 3,000 miles away from Olduvai Gorge. Maybe they followed a migration of critters out of Africa. And did they stop when they reached Dmanisi? Did the animals they were following stop? When they arrived, did the critters keep on moving east along the Silk Road? Was it already an age-old animal route?

During 2001, while we were working Hueyatlaco, some surprising dates came out of the Nihewan Basin southwest of Beijing, at a latitude of 40 degrees north. They dated deposits of simple pebble tools and came up with 1.3ma, becoming the oldest sites in northern China. About a year later, new dates would clock in at 1.66ma.[22]

They were probably not part of the Dmanisi clan, but it does increase the antiquity of northern living back another million years. To date, no remains of *Habilis/Ergaster* have turned up in China, only *Erectus*. They probably came from the south because there are 1.8ma dates from Indonesia. But a Silk Road connection is still a possibility...maybe?

Chapter 5.4

Homo erectus popeyensis

Popeye the Java Man

This is the "all bets are off" level. Here, absurdity takes the backseat and chaos takes the wheel. The face is wild-eyed, a mix of Vonnegut and Dangerfield. This is a zone so wild it's beyond fiction. Fiction doesn't have a chance here. It is a level where the unspoken, unheard of, and unimagined becomes fact. Day becomes moonlight and nothing can ever be the same again.

It happened on Flores Island, the Hobbit island, but decades earlier before the Hobbit was found. In fact, the Hobbit was found because they were looking for more of this other thing that was discovered, a thing that was forgotten then rediscovered a couple generations later. What happened is best called a realization, a realization that put the entire Academy smack dab in the middle of the Twilight Zone, like it or not.

It started almost 40 years ago when stone tools were reported on Flores Island in the late 1960s. Then it was tossed from the corporate memory, Valsequillo-style. Too old. Then a new interest began in the mid-1990s by someone who had a keen curiosity. *That's odd. They're not supposed to be here.*

This work appears to confirm an older idea, first floated in the 1960s, that stone artefacts from Mata Menge (central Flores) were found in association with an extinct fauna (fossil elephants and others) thought to be about 750,000 years old. The idea was rejected at the time because few archaeologists accepted that the stones were definitely of human origin, or were the same age as the fauna. However, Mike Morwood (University of New England) and colleagues revisited the area and have now published details of at least 20 stone artefacts found *in situ* (14 from Mata Menge, six from nearby Boa Lesa). The researchers are convinced that these are in fact stone tools. And age estimates (based on fission track dating of sediments below and above the artefacts) demonstrate they must be between about 880,000 and 800,000 years at Mata Menge and older than 840,000 at Boa Lesa.[23]

And so another monumental discovery was slapped away from an entire generation because it didn't make sense and it just couldn't be and we know best. *Homo erectus* artifacts were found on islands located between Indonesia and Australia. Flores Island was separated from everything by a deep trench. It was a lost isle where lizards grew into Komodos and rats were the size of pigs, and elephants shrunk. The artifacts together with the elephant bones were more than 840,000 years old. The only way to reach the islands was by boat. Navigation almost a million years ago. Navigation against stiff currents, too. It is not a lake down there, but that shouldn't matter either, because 840,000 years ago there was not even supposed to be a concept for boat, raft, or any of that.

They cruised the Flores Straits!

Even with the lowest sea levels imaginable, Bali appears never to have been connected to Lombok, nor was Sumbawa connected to Flores. Therefore the new findings from Flores, although still not accepted unequivocally, suggest that whoever made the artefacts (probably *Homo erectus*) would have had to have made two sea crossings: 25 kilometres from Bali to Lombok (which was probably joined with Sumbawa at low sea levels), and 19 kilometres from Sumbawa to Flores.[24]

Popeye Erectus. Contemplate on that, Grasshopper, and you will know true humility. Or complete madness! Is there a difference? I don't know anymore.

Similar to Valsequillo, the actual Lower Paleolithic sites on Flores are almost as interesting as their impossibility. The mind of the archaeologist confronted by the chance of becoming the world's most celebrated buffoon acts carefully, cautiously, and suspiciously. To find something as ridiculous as *Erectus* sailors carries with it an enormous risk. You had better be sure, because even if you are correct you run the risk of sheer rebuke if you don't play your cards right. Louis Leakey found this out the hard way at Calico. When fate and curiosity carry you to a previously unaddressed dimension of the Fringe, when the whole world is watching to see whether a century's worth of intellectual profiles for preMod behaviors will be utterly trashed, you had better be your own best devil's advocate.

The honor fell to Mike Morwood who proved to the world he was up to the challenge. To the world's good fortune, the geological focus posed by the Flores Island team was top-rate. Geological concerns and the standards applied are fairly universal. In an Aussie TV interview, Morwood admitted:

> I think they would cause people to rethink about the capability of early humans. If by eight hundred and forty thousand years ago ancestral humans could make a series of water crossings to get right out into eastern Indonesia, then clearly we're dealing with a highly intelligent animal.[25]

When asked in the same 1999 interview what he had in mind to do next, Morwood wanted to look for younger sites on the island, in the 50–300,000 range. If they existed, maybe it would shine more light on what he was really interested in: the initial colonization of Australia.

What he found next really shook up the world. He found skeletal remains dubbed The Hobbit, about 18,000 years old. Team Morwood called it a new species, *Homo floresiensis*. The debate continues on cable science shows. Some say microencephaly, a disease that distorts the skeleton. Some say they were just short island people. When challenged, he found additional remains of more than half a dozen individuals that matched the first. In the meantime, it seems Popeye *erectus* became a nontopic.

Personally, if forced to choose, you can have the Hobbit. In terms of significance regarding our intellectual legacy, *erectus* navigators are indescribably more important.

During this period of Hobbit madness, something else equally mad happened. The chief physical anthropologist of Indonesia, who was not in on the discovery, snuck into the Flores lab where the Hobbit bones were stored and carried them away, possibly damaging them in the process. Hostage negotiations are continuing.[26]

Practicing Pleistocene Seafaring

If you have been a member of the Anthropology club, you should be hearing screams from all those paradigms about ocean travel and premodern intelligence. They are drowning under the *Erectus* boat. And though this is all taking place down in Indonesia, we shouldn't take our eyes off Morocco—Gibraltar and probably the Mediterranean in general. If *Erectus* was rowing in the heavy currents of the Flores Straits, Gibraltar would have been a Sunday picnic.

Erectus sailors means a lot more than merely going back to square one. At the very least it means going back to the square root of one, which is the same as "one" but you have to know a lot more to know why. It will require a whole new understanding of the pre-*Sapiens* brain. *Tall foreheads need not apply.*

If *Erectus* was making seaworthy boats at 840,000y:

❋ What technologies and knowledge and training are necessary to conquer short-range sea navigation?

❋ When did they learn to swim?

❋ When was the first bodysurfer?

❋ Did they dive for clams and oysters?

❋ Did they have fishing gear (spears, nets)?

❋ What else were they making?

❋ What is the learning curve for an 800,000-year legacy of navigation?

❋ What effect is early navigation going to have on Lower and Middle Paleolithic demographic modeling?

❋ Does it support the Sea Food is Brain Food hypothesis? The Aquatic Ape hypothesis?

❋ What does it take to build a seaworthy boat? The technological knowledge? The materials, cordage, and knots? Fording the rough currents? Knowing weather? Language?

Many professional minds, once chained to the land by the professional threat of ideological heresy, are now unleashed, free to openly pursue the sea as an archaeological medium of travel and communication, if not for the sheer challenge.

In this regard, Robert Bednarik is light-years ahead of most. A nondegreed Aussie expert of primitive technology and art, he had already shown how Aborigines may have first arrived in Australia. When news of the *Erectus* tools on Flores Island hit the fan, Bednarik was at it again. Initially, when faced with this impossible discovery, some thought of accidental drift, with Early Man hugging to thick mats of vegetation that form near the local south Asian coasts.

That speculation doesn't float, contends Bednarik. Only a craft propelled by its occupants could negotiate the treacherous straits separating one Indonesian island from the next. To back up that claim, he launched a project in 1996 to determine what Stone Age groups would have had to do, at a minimum, to reach Flores and its neighboring islands.

Nearly 12 hours later, after covering a distance of 30 miles, they completed their journey–just barely.

...Bednarik and a team of Indonesian boat makers and craftsmen built the raft out of natural materials, using sharpened stone tools comparable to those wielded by *H. erectus*. Despite the simplicity of such implements, prehistoric island colonizers must have possessed a broad range of knowledge and skills to assemble rafts on a par with Nale Tasih 4, Bednarik holds.[27]

Learmonth Model Revisited

Blake Learmonth told us that "seafaring 100,000 years ago" was just a bit shy of UFO ancestry. If this is correct with respect to the Fringe, then we are faced with a universe that did not exist until now. UFOs are the standard bearer of the outermost fringes of the Fringe. If an academic believes in UFOs or "seafaring 100,000 years ago," s/he will believe in anything, uncritically. Nothing s/he ever says will have any credibility and s/he might as well commit her/himself to rehab before someone else does.

So how do things measure up now that there are 840,000 year old *Erectus* sailors? The question can take the shape of a common formula.

If A is likened to B, then C is likened to D.

If a belief in "seafaring 100,000 years ago" is likened to a belief in UFOs,

then the knowledge of 840,000y seafaring is likened to _____ (fill in the blank).

See what I mean? It's clean off the charts. An entirely new dimension. Perhaps it is something only Rod Serling could fathom, or a Zen master clapping with a hand behind his back holding a one-ended stick. For chess players, "*Erectus* navigators" is finding out that a pawn has all the powers of a Queen at the beginning of the game. For brain scientists, these guys were supposed to be playing with a few shy of a six-pack. The fanged *Ergasters* even less so. Words cannot do justice. Perhaps poetry. Shebang doodly-wop.

Hungry Brains

Into this period of productive chaos came another stab at the good old days. This one dealt with how we got our big brains in the first place. First, there was a headline in 2001: "Beach Tools: The First Things That Humans Did After They Evolved Was to Head for the Beach." The 125,000-year-old tools were found mixed in with fossil corals

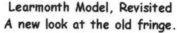

Learmonth Model, Revisited
A new look at the old fringe.

840,000y

**Indonesia
Earliest Navigation**

"While the technology and production of the stone artefacts do not attest to any extraordinary skills for Homo erectus, affirmed sea crossings 840,000 years ago would have several interesting implications. Some archaeologists have argued that substantial sea crossings demand language and intellectual abilities not normally associated with Homo erectus."
Malcolm Ritter, Ancient Mariners?

**UFO
Ancestors**

**100,000y
Navigators**

"Though the idea of 100,000 year old ocean going boats is only slightly more believable than the brought-here-by-space-aliens theory, a later migration involving small skin boats moving in short jumps down the West Coast is more plausible."
Blake Learmonth

To Scale

The Homo erectus sailors of Flores Island have now trumped all previous assumptions about our species's inclination to cross heavy seas. It dwarfs Learmonth's limits of the fringe by hundreds of thousands of years. If claims of 100,000-year-old seafaring were tantamount to claims of alien ancestry, then what would compare with 840,000-year-old seafaring? The Flores Island sailors have totally trashed all previous models of what we thought the evolution of intelligence was all about, and they trashed it with the same simple stone tools they had been using for a million years.

and oyster shells, "a sign that the human romance with the seaside is as old as the species itself." Species meaning the Mods. It was an announcement greeted with excitement because the discovery could indicate the "beginning of the human love affair with seafood, boats, and all matters maritime."[28]

It does not seem to matter that the Flores *Erectus* discoveries were published more than three years earlier and dated more than 700,000 years older. Everyone wants to be first. But you can sense the excitement in the writing. This was huge. Seashore adaptations tied to early modern humans "signals a sea change in human behaviour." Apart from the pun, it opens up the minds of many that, wow, maybe these guys were smart enough to realize the richness of shoreline environs at 125,000 years ago. It is obvious from Morwood's discoveries that *Erectus* had been hip to these advantages for eons.

Was there something about seashore living that started things off, intellectually speaking? We have been looking for the missing link for 150 years. What if it was a shazam diet, and not a shazam moment, that inspired the change? For Dr. Stephen Cunnane, a metabolic physiologist at the University of Sherbrooke in Quebec, it makes sense. "When early humans started to fish, they also began feeding their hungry brains."[29]

Anthropologists and evolutionary biologists usually point to things like the rise of language and tool making to explain the massive expansion of early hominid brains. But this is a Catch-22. Something had to start the process of brain expansion and I think it was early humans eating clams, frogs, bird eggs, and fish from shoreline environments. This is what created the necessary physiological conditions for explosive brain growth," says Dr. Cunnane.

The big quesiton is which came first—the bigger brain or the social, linguistic, and tool-making skills we associate it with?

But Dr. Cunnane argues that most anthropologists are ignorant or dismissive of the key missing link to help answer this question: the metabolic constraints that are critical for healthy human brain development today, and for its evolution.

Human brains aren't just comparatively big, they're hungry. The average newborn's brain consumes an amazing 75-per cent of an infant's daily energy needs. According to Dr. Cunnane, to fuel this neural demand, human babies are born with a built-in energy reservoir—that cute baby fat. Human infants are the only primate babies born with excess fat. It accounts for about 14 per cent of their birth weight, similar to that of their brains.

It's this baby fat, says Dr. Cunnane, that provided the physiological winning conditions for hominids' evolutionary brain expansion. And how were hominid babies able to pack on the extra pounds? According to Cunnane, their moms were dining on shoreline delicacies like clams and catfish.

"The shores gave us food security and higher nutrient density. My hypothesis is that to permit the brain to start to increase in size, the fittest early humans were those with the fattest infants," says Dr. Cunnane, author of the book *Survival of the Fattest*, published in 2005.

Controversially, according to Dr. Cunnane, our initial brain boost didn't happen by adaptation, but by exaptation, or chance.[30]

From the Evolution page from U.C. Berkeley, we learn that:

Exaptation [is] a feature that performs a function, but that was not produced by natural selection for its current use. For example, feathers might have originally arisen in the context of selection for insulation, and only later were they co-opted for flight. In this case, the general form of feathers is an adaptation for insulation and an exaptation for flight.[31]

So there you go. The idea here is that we got smart by chance, serendipity, accident, dumb luck, and/or providence. The debate continues to howl, but it does offer a positive light on how Popeye Erectus figured out seafaring.

It seems as though the idea that *Homo* has had a long, intimate affair with the seashore is gaining steam. In the future, there's a chance that the new generation of explorers will find out whether the Aquatic Ape Theory is really where it's AAT.[32]

The realm of questions that are opening up has broadened beyond everyone's dreams of just a decade ago. Metaphorically, if 20th-century understanding is represented by our solar system, the Wild 1990s ushered in some archaeological worm holes that are moving us toward the galactic.

Halfway There

At Valsequillo, the discoveries were impossible on the grounds of being too early and too sophisticated.

Presence

Were pre-Mods smart enough to make it over to the Americas 200–400,000 years ago? The impossible discoveries at Diring, Schöningen, Dmanisi, and Flores Island all

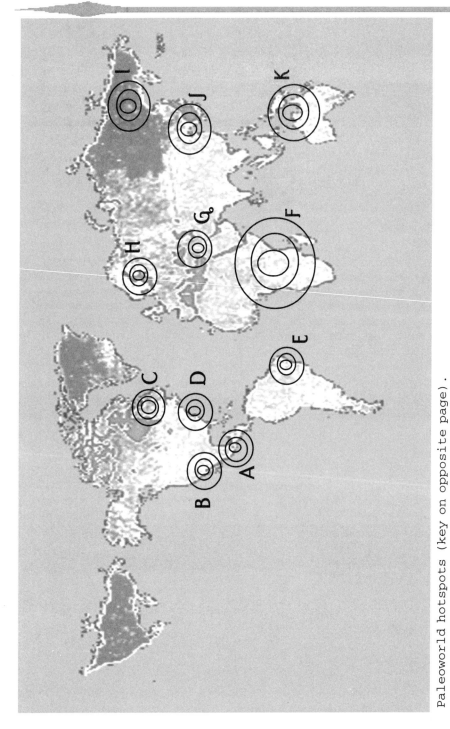

Paleoworld hotspots (key on opposite page).

had simple stone technology. With these "simple" stone tools, they conquered their world, a world that is now vastly larger than it was a mere decade ago. Diring showed we had the wherewithal to handle Siberia more than 400,000 years ago, and Schoningen, at the same antiquity and latitude, gave us modern javelins. And now the adaptive genius of the 1,800,000-year-old *ergasters*, with and without fangs. All of these folks survived using the simplest of stone tools.

A million years later, Popeye *Erectus* is island-hopping. It still takes my breath away. Similar to the way Zinj added a quick million years to the human past, *Erectus* popeyensis has added nearly a million years to our mental, linguistic, and apparently ocean-loving past. Personally, it was about the most impossible thing that I never imagined. UFOs may be total fantasy, but we sure have tons more information about them.

What's in the folder for *Erectus* navigation?

What folder?

Actions speak louder than theory. Everyone from brain scientists to theologians will have a lot to mull over in the next century. Which one of these pre-Mods would *you* put in a zoo?

The temporal impossibility for pre-Mods in the Americas has been negated and the odds have lessened. Valsequillo contemporaries in the Old World had indeed surpassed all expectations for widespread northern living on par with the needs for crossing Beringia when the conditions were right, probably decided by the migrating herds themselves. Taking these revolutionary finds together, there is no valid reason to automatically condemn research grants testing America's potential for Middle Paleolithic period sites, especially if they are tied to paleontology.

Sophistication

Hypothetically, let's say this reasoning passes the smell test. Then we are left with the riddle inside the enigma: Valsequillo's advanced technology, the true festering thorn of the mystery.

Location of the major discoveries mentioned in the text	
A: Valsequillo 250,000y	**F: Africa, Middle Stone Age** 330,000-40,000y
B: Calico/Mojave/SoCal 250,000y-plus?	**G: Dmanisi, Georgia** Habilis Ergaster 1.8Ma
C: Sheguiandah, Canada 130,000y	**H: Hanover, Germany** Javelins: 400,000y
D: Topper Site, S.C. 50,000y	**I: Diring Yurick, Siberia** 400,000y
E: Brazil Pedra Furada 50-100,000y Toca De Esperanca 250,000y	**J: Nihewan Basin, China** 1.6Ma
	K: Flores Island Popeye Erectus: 840,000y The Hobbit: 18,000-90,000y

Chapter 5.5

The Revolution That Wasn't

The Riddle Wrapped in an Enigma

Returning to Arizona, all through the trip back on the bus, the plane, in the airports, while I was sidelined in Waco, and for months afterward in Tucson, the war of ideas and impossibilities raged in an already dizzy brain.

Valsequillo was a geological problem. The fact that it was an archaeological no-brainer took a lot of pressure off the team. It had already been established as a site decades ago. Who gives a damn what kind of artifacts they are? The point is, they were artifacts. Period. End of argument. In the science world, it does not matter if it's spear-heads, a flake scatter, a jaw, a hearth, a footprint, or a house ring. It all means human presence to the scientist. Even vanished artifacts do not matter when you have photographic evidence, artifact casts, and surviving notes and witnesses. Presence was established. But the artifacts were Upper Paleolithic and the presence was *screaming* a quarter- million years. And the mental civil war started its cycle again without resolve. Scientifically there was no problem. Archaeologically, it was crazy.

Valsequillo, the sleeping dragon, has once more become the 900-pound gorilla in the middle of America's Pleistocene—200–400,000-year-old geology containing 20–40,000-year-old artifact types. What's going on?

If there is any hope for penetrating the mystery of the Valsequillo discoveries, it is fairly clear that all American archaeologists, North and South, have to begin on the same page. A hypothesis is needed that is both agreeable and testable. It comes from a prominent

Clovis Firster's response to a question about what he thought of the Valsequillo discoveries. The response: There was no way they were making bifaces 200,000 years ago.

After all this time, there has been no proof whatsoever that the U-Series dates and other geological indicators were way off base. That is where we find ourselves today. At the time of this writing, Renne's million-year-plus dates for the Hueyatlaco Ash are still unresolved by his own admission, and so will be left out of consideration for the time being. If they turn out to be true—and thus negate all previous geochronological techniques thrown at the site—then another book is in order; not by me, though. I'll be in rehab.

Hypothesis

There were no blade and bifacial thinning technologies being practiced 200,000 years ago.

If the statement is true, then we reach a dead end, which is where the situation was before 2001. It would affirm that no blade or bifacial thinning techs are located in 200,000-year-old sediments anywhere in the world.

If a material precedent for bifaces and blades dating 200,000 years ago can be established, then we have negated the hypothesis and we continue. A technological precedent would negate the contention that Upper Paleolithic artifacts at Valsequillo are an impossibility. If these types of artifacts exist elsewhere in the world, contemporary with the 200,000-plus Valsequillo dates, then the onus of impossibility is removed. And if it is removed, then the world model for Upper Paleolithic itself would appear to be in need of a makeover in order to fit the new evidence.

To accomplish this, to negate the hypothesis, a single precedent is required from somewhere in the Old World where sophisticated blades and spearheads were being made 200,000 years ago. That's all! Finding these kinds of artifacts in the Old World sites of a similar antiquity would remove the burden of archaeological disbelief. It would also provide a measure of support for previous USGS dating.

The African Middle Stone Age

There had to be a rational explanation. There was. Most archaeologists just didn't know about it yet. This is what would have blown Cynthia Irwin-Williams's mind. Around the time Bob, Chuck, and I met up with Mario, Pati, Adrian, and Joaquin in Mexico City in late 2000, an article was published in the *Journal of Human Evolution*, an article that took up the entire issue. There was indeed a precedent. The artifacts had been known for a long time, but they couldn't date the things with C14, so the archaeologists just figured they were around 40,000y at most. New dating techniques were beginning to sort things out. Blade technology was being clocked in at 330,000y. Bifaces were closer to 230,000y.

When the Leakeys found Zinj, it turned everyone's search for the human heartland from Asia and Europe to Africa. Prior to that, Africa was considered a backwater to our evolution. Similarly, the search for the origins of modern "behavior" and the Upper Paleolithic Revolution has also been focused in Europe and Asia, largely because sub-Saharan Africa was considered a cultural backwater where modern behavior arrived much later.[33]

The Wild '90s, with new and improved dating techniques, changed this too. The Middle Stone Age (MSA) was beginning to look a lot more sophisticated.

"The Revolution That Wasn't"

If a revolution takes a hundred thousand years, is it a revolution? I think this is the question behind the title of an explosive peer-reviewed article in the *Journal of Human Evolution*, published on the eve of the new millennium by Sally McBrearty and Allison Brooks: "The Revolution That Wasn't: A New Interpretation of the Origin of Modern Human Behaviour."

Reading the summary seemed similar to a "Zinj" replay. Everyone's looking for the first evidence of modern humans, which everyone knows is somewhere in Europe or Asia or northern Africa. They've known it for a century. All of a sudden some headlines make the Eurasian School of Modernity balk. The biologists looking at DNA figured out that we all descended from the same mother. Mitochondrial DNA is something only passed along the female lineage and, based on the voodoo they do, the biologists figured out *Eve*—the name they gave our first mother—must have been living around 150–200,000y. Supporting this scenario were the discoveries of several thoroughly modern skeletons turning up much earlier in Africa than in the two northern continents. When my cyberjourney began, the most recent discovery was in east Africa; it was also the oldest, clocking in at 160,000y. A couple years later, another modern specimen jumped from about 140,000y to about 190,000y.[34]

Yep, those crazy Leakeys were at it again. In fact, they were at it again almost 40 years ago and didn't even know it. It was 1967. There they were, Richard, son of Leakey, and his crew, hunting as only they can for evidence of early man—younger than a million years need not apply. And then they found some bones, but pshaw, they're modern. No more than about 130,000 years old, if the Uranium/thorium dates were right. "Shucks, false alarm." They shrugged their shoulders. *Better luck next time.* They were modern, and Richard Leakey was looking for australopithecines such as Zinj, or his more gracile relatives. For Team Richard, it probably wasn't worth an imported beer. So there they sat for decades in a museum box, Leakey throw-aways, lonely and forgotten. Then in 2005, Ian McDougall from the Australian National University in Canberra and others, decided to redate the bones and came up with a date of 190,000 years old, making these skulls the earliest "modern" specimens in the world.[35]

These new finds, along with the DNA data, have stretched our modern structural antiquity back to about 200,000 years. The UP gang argues that our behavioral modernization began 150,000 years later, around 50,000 years ago, the same time they left

Africa. Then, bang! We rocket ahead in smarts, as in Fagan's chart. Modern structure did not mean modern behavior, and it did not mean blades and bifaces. In Europe and western Asia, this shift in technology was abundantly recorded in the sites. Discerning UP from MP was easy. UP deposits were immediately recognized by the blades that turned up everywhere. In Africa, not so much. The MSA grades into the Later Stone Age so that maybe the best you can discern is a rough proximity of the transition.

The opposite was true of the African Early Stone Age transition into the MSA. It was defined, and it was amazing.

Finding a single or occasional blade in any industry may be due to accidental production. A flake with a length that is two times its width can be made any number of ways without trying, even sideways. When a degree of density and formal regularity of blades begin turning up, invariably some of the blade cores also turn up, and both show purposeful, intentional behaviors. For McBrearty and Brooks:

> Blade production...requires the cognitive skills to perceive artifact forms not preordained by the raw material and to visualize the manufacturing process in three dimensions, in addition to the dexterity to carry out a complex series of operations and corrections as the process advances.[36]

One of the earliest "possible" blade industries occurs in the Levant, northeast of Egypt, and is poorly dated to between 250–350,000y. The best of the earliest dated sites containing blades are in eastern Africa beginning around 300,000y. Retouched projectile points begin to turn up around 235,000y.

> The Kapthurin Formation, Kenya, provides unequivocal evidence for early African blades in a late Acheulean [late ESA] industry....Trachyte blades were recovered from both surface and excavated contexts at the site of GnJh-03. The [blades] occurs *in situ* at a depth of ca. 3 m below the base of K4, a volcanic unit. Conventional K/Ar dates for K4 indicated an age on the order of 240–250,000y; a current program of redating by Ar/Ar indicates the true age lies closer to 280,000y....Both unidirectional and bidirectional blade removals are represented; blades show both plain and faceted platforms. Distinct levels of skill are reflected in the different refitted sets, and the most skilled knapper was able to proceed through a long series of blade removals to core exhaustion. The resulting blades are remarkable for their length, thinness and flatness. The Kapthurin Formation blades demonstrate the presence of a fully conceptualized,

well-executed method of blade production, and high
level of technical competence in east Africa before
280,000y.[37]

Then they discuss how the African MSA differs from the Eurasian Middle Paleolithic and its Neanderthals.

Pointed flakes and blades seem to be target forms
for many MSA toolmakers, and retouched points are
among some of the earliest MSA artifacts at 235,000y.
The large numbers and careful design of points in the
retouched component of many MSA assemblages and the
relative lack of emphasis on scrapers, are major
differences between the African MSA and the classic
[Neanderthal] Mousterian of southwestern France.[38]

Another flip-flop was knocking at the gates of orthodoxy.

The new MSA dates demonstrated that the new fangled artifacts such as blades and
bifaces first start appearing about 200,000 years earlier than their European counterparts. First the blades turned up, and points made out of unifacially retouched blades.
Around 180,000y there are actual bifaces, and not just one kind but a variety.

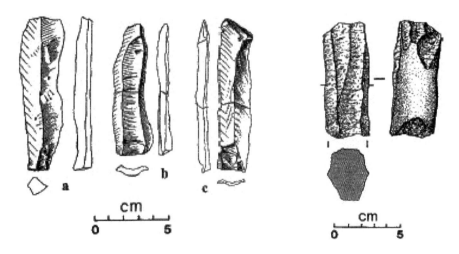

Blades and a blade core from the African Middle Stone
Age, beginning around 330,000 years ago. Blade technology appears at the start of the MSA. What happened
330,000 years ago when we invented prepared platforms?
What does it say for the mind that figured it out?

The rise of prepared platform techniques in flintknapping as far back as 300,000y-plus is jaw-dropping. Preparing a platform consists of sculpting a striking platform that will facilitate the removal of the type of flake or blade you want to produce. It makes the fracture more predictable. Skill, foresight, prediction, and a whole host of perceptual and physical memories come into play, an interplay of force, mass, gravity, and a subtle coordination that can be improved upon with practice and innovations.

Smaller points also suggests an evolution in the types of shafts that the points will be attached to. Because the wood doesn't survive you can only surmise, but McBrearty and Brooks discuss possibilities about the early MSA invention of the throwing stick (atlatl) and they even suggest the invention of the bow and arrow—based on the small size of some of the points.

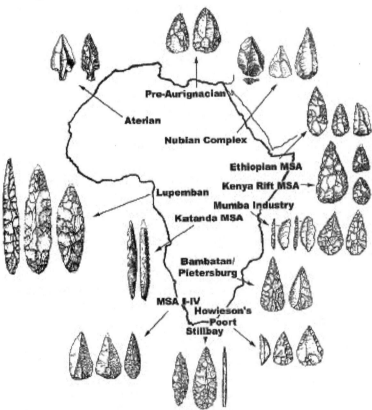

Bifacially flaked spearheads from Africa's Middle Stone Age, 330,000 - 40,000 years ago. Was this the origin of the Eurasian Upper Paleolithic? Of modern intelligence? Is there a better candidate? In the meantime, the Middle Stone Age technology satisfies the role as a precedent for the impossible Valsequillo artifacts.

The African Middle Stone Age serves as a temporal and technological precedent for Valsequillo's impossible stone tools and art. Valsequillo is no longer alone in the world for having such modern tools in such an old geology. The African MSA disproves the hypothesis that *"There were no blade and bifacial industries operating 200,000 years ago."* The past decade of work shows that the MSA has Upper Paleolithic artifacts as early as Valsequillo. Valsequillo *has* a technological precedent.

On and On and On...

They say that every discovery or answer begets dozens more questions. They are right. If these uppity techs were developed in Africa, and they somehow reached Central Mexico by 200,000y, how on earth do we explain their absence in Europe and Asia until 40,000y? How could MSA folks reach North America and not spread the "news"— the new technologies—in the east Asian regions they passed through to get here?

Nag, nag, nag...

Had archaeologists engaged their curiosity 30 years ago, both at Flores Island and Valsequillo, we may have had some answers by now.

Is it possible that our ancestors made some headway in boatcraft and navigation during the subsequent hundreds of thousands of years since Flores Island? For example, did pre-Mods venture out to the Canary Islands during low sea level periods? Could it be that there were actually some pre-Mods who explored the Atlantic, getting caught up in the currents and tradewinds that typify Hurricane Alley between west Africa and the Caribbean, maybe as early as 300,000 years ago, and so account for the 200–300,000y pebble tools found in Toca de Esperanca in Brazil? Though it may be close to unthinkable for land-lovers, there are modern precedents for making the trans-Atlantic trip in rowing craft. In fact, it has become a tournament.

British Pair Becomes First Mother and Daughter Team to Cross Atlantic in Rowboat
Wednesday, May 5, 2004
(05-05) 09:03 PDT BRIDGETOWN, Barbados (AP) —
Sarah and Sally Kettle have become the first mother-daughter team to cross the Atlantic in a rowboat.
The British pair set off in a 23-foot plywood boat, the Calderdale, from the Canary Islands on Jan. 20, along with 13 other boats racing in the Ocean Rowing Society's Atlantic Rowing Regatta.
Sarah, 45, and Sally, 27, arrived late Tuesday night in Barbados after the 2,907-mile journey.
"Fantastic, absolutely fantastic," Sarah Kettle said.
She said the trip was fueled by chocolate.
"We ate so much chocolate. I never ate so much chocolate until now," she said.[39]

Chapter 5.6

Dancing With Bison

When I was a boy of 14, my father was so ignorant I could hardly stand to have the old man around. But when I got to be 21, I was astonished at how much the old man had learned in seven years.

—trad. Mark Twain

Translation:

14 year old=anthropologists, archaeologists, you, me, brain scientists, kids, and other intelligence experts.

Father=pre-modern humans.

The Puzzle Palace

Prehistory as a puzzle palace is an apt metaphor. The puzzle field is the earth, and its onion-like layers are time periods. It's a done deal. It is preexistent because it already happened, so the pieces that have survived *must* interlock, across and down. It just needs to be figured out, and that requires knowledge of the material evidence in its myriad forms. Intelligence clearly has a longer history than we are used to dealing with. This is not the rudimentary intelligence of social animals, but the intelligence of ocean navigation and epic overland journeys to Indonesia, Russia, and Eastern China by 1.6ma. This is not theory. They pulled it off. It would seem we are faced with an extra million years of modern-like intelligence to deal with in the Old World; in the New World, maybe a bit less than half that long. It will probably depend on whatever they figure for Calico's age.

What is not a done deal is our future. Will our species be around long enough to actually figure out the whole 3-million-year package? Consciousness, the mind, intelligence? Groundbreaking discoveries continue to pop up all over the place, all peer-reviewed, and it seems we are on the edge of filling in some huge gaps in the psychological evolution that is our species. Parallel to these discoveries, post-Genome Project biologists are beginning to peer into consciousness, considered by some to be the next true step toward human understanding in science.[40]

Ours is a legacy of consciousness and how it reacts to Nature, its own self, and the unknown. When did we begin to talk to ourselves? When did we realize we were talking to ourselves? When did we first experience deception? Self-deceit? Lucid dreaming? Figuring out the when's and where's of these capacities are all premised on whether we ourselves last long enough to figure it out.

In a few short years, the world of *Homo sapiens* is again turning the planet into a slaughterhouse on the verge of a global meltdown (on many levels). Just like that! In a heartbeat. A moment ago, the child and elder were paddling west, carrying a torch to guide the sun when it wakes up on the first day of a new millennium, and so ushered in the biggest New Years party the world has ever known. More people partied about the same thing on that night than at any time before. The whole world was watching. And there was a good, very renewing thing about it. We were in touch on a global scale.

Before you know it, we are blowing each other up, and everyone is told to be very afraid and suspicious of each other, as in the bad ol' days. Madness in a heartbeat. Care or carnage: that's the choice of our species now and forever.

Wouldn't it be nice to know where we came from and how we developed before we scare ourselves into oblivion? While we still have a cultural infrastructure that supports the research? We are close to scoring some real answers, and not just here in the Americas; time is needed to process all the new data. These new discoveries have added dimensions to our legacy scarcely imagined a decade ago. Our true nature as a species is still a question. Are we, by nature, killer apes or killer lovers?

The "New" New World

The sooner we know where pre-Clovis horizons are, the sooner we'll know what to look for and what to keep from being destroyed before we get a good chance to look at it. Bone beds and stone quarries would be good first bets. Sheguindah's quartzites and Calico's semi-precious cherts will make excellent study collections because there are so many specimens. Bone beds from the Middle Pleistocene forward are now potential goldmines. Elsewhere, folks might want to start taking deeper peeks under their Clovis sites.

How do kill sites look without bifaces, without stone spearheads of any kind? Without stone? A kill site without arrowheads might look very different from the Clovis kill sites we know and love. So might the tools, like the bone tools?

The puzzle pieces of human evolution are materially finite. The pre-Clovis record is fragile and easily destroyed. That record will be largely composed of faint vestiges of human presence captured in the ancestral dust, mere fingerprints in a Clovis world that demands skulls, if not skeletons.

Valsequillo could easily be one of a kind. It would be hard to imagine another region so generous in Middle Paleolithic bones and artifacts buried in sand and silts. The Lake Manix region surrounding Calico would be a good second. But what of all those other sites that didn't quite measure up? (For Euros such as Francois Bordes and Mary Leakey, Calico measured up.) These "lesser" sites might not have been strong enough to bust the Clovis bubble, but things have changed, and that bubble has long been popped. Now these lower-tier sites don't have to prove immaculate presence. Now the pressure is on us to *expect* earlier, non-bifacial thinning, agnostic artifact types. Now it will be up to us to explain "why" a certain broken stone cannot be an artifact instead of blindly assuming geofacts. To this end, presence/absence recognition needs to be upgraded.

Experimenting with bipolar flaking is definitely a start. A few centuries ago in Europe, flake scatters were regarded as places were witches blew up. While most all archaeologists are (or should be) hip to direct percussion and pressure methodologies, bipolar assemblages might as well be places where witches blew up.

Bone fractures and taphonomy could become the meat and potatoes of the new American archaeology. In the end, exposing our deep New World heritage may depend on bone beds. Where bones survive, maybe there is some of *us* in the mix.

Translated: Track down your friendly neighborhood Pleistocene paleontologist. Bow. Present the customary imported six-pack. And this is what you ask: "Seen any anomalies lately?"

Anomaly Heaven

```
    I met Roald Fryxell. He gave a talk at the Udden
Club. I remember sitting in the laboratory afterward
and he told me about a site that he was working on in
Mexico. I don't remember exactly the name of the
site. He found some really early kinds of tools. He
dated the site five or six different ways. It was too
old for Carbon-14. It was a very old site. He had
primitive tools. He had volcanic ash that he dated.
There was a basalt flow that blocked a lake. They
were able to date that using a uranium dating technique.
The fossils were much older than recent material. They
```

did hydration studies on flints [volcanic glass-ch] to get an age. All the dated material was more than 100,000 years old. Of course early humans in the new world at that time had only been dated to seven or eight thousand years. He worked on an early man site in Washington State. Nobody would believe that work in Mexico because it was way too old. I never forget him telling me that. It was just a few months after that he was killed. He was out in the field and was going to town to give a talk. They think he fell asleep and got into an automobile accident.

"The reason I remember that, as a paleontologist, I always thought that if humans were chasing mammoth and mastodons and bison and large mammals up in the arctic, when those things migrated into the new world, I always thought that man would be right behind them. Just about four or five years ago we discovered a site here. It was the same kind of thing. We dated it every way possible. It was close to 200,000 years old. Nobody believes that one either. People will argue about it whether it was fossil that was deposited and then reworked into a younger deposit. So there are many academic arguments. But I have never forgotten that and tend to think that he was probably right. It was probably that old. I think our site is as old as that. I think someday you will find somebody publishing on a paleolithic discovery in North America.[41]

If monitoring behind bulldozers and bellyloaders is one's idea of a romantic profession, it ceases to be after the first day, unless you have a thing for diesel fumes. It is a marginal type of work because you usually get to do it when there is a good chance there is only a slight chance of finding anything. For example, if there are sites in an area and they have been avoided or excavated, the contract archaeology company often leaves one or two fieldworkers behind to follow the mechanical dinosaurs in case anything else turns up. This also applies to paleontologists.

More than a decade ago, in National City, California, south of San Diego, a SDNHM paleontologist was monitoring an area where there was a slight chance that California Department of Transportation (CDoT) roadwork would turn up old bones. Fossilized bone sounds different from hardened mud and sand when scraped by a bulldozer's blade, and this sounded like bone. He called the bulldozer off the spot and brushed the ground looking for the source of the "noise."[42]

Anomaly 1

It was a circular outline, but it was not bone. It was a tusk, probably mastodon. Because it was circular, that meant it was a cross-section of a tusk. It was a cross-section of a tusk, a tusk that had been buried vertically in the ground...similar to a post.

What could have naturally buried a tusk that stood it up in a vertical position?

Once excavated, the paleontologists had to append that question.

What could have naturally buried a tusk in a vertical position that penetrated at least three strata of a buried flood plain?

The deposits were made up of hardened sands, silts, and clays. Similar to Valsequillo, this meant a low energy, gentle burial, only slower. There were no gravels. This was later supported by the articulated nature of the buried remains of many other critters. From reconstructions, the burial context seems to have been caused by a rising ocean level and the resulting back up of the local drainages creating a marsh-like zone. The gentle deposition of sediments kept the bones in place for the most part. A horse was uncovered, a near-perfect burial except the head was missing, which is not rare in paleontology.

Anomaly 2

What is rare is to find the remains of animals in fairly good shape while another one next to them is smashed to smithereens, as if it got run over with a steamroller. This was the mastodon. The bones were broken when they were still fresh (green).

Anomaly 3

What was also strange was finding several small boulders (roughly about 20 pounds) and a couple of broken cobbles in a fossilized marsh. The larger stones were typified as "anvil-sized," but could also be viewed as large hammerstones, possibly using two hands. A couple of the larger stones were found amidst bone clusters. Referred to as "erratics," it means that the presence of these stones is unexplainable, out of place. There is no natural riverine agency that can select certain heavy stones for transport, while only carrying silts and clays over flat ground. It drove a local geology professor batty. Several of the smaller cobbles were found broken, with sharp refittable bits and pieces scattered about the site. This meant they were broken up onsite in a muddy matrix. How did the boulders get there? What broke the cobbles up?

Anomalies 4 and 5

Clusters of bones were seemingly arranged. One cluster featured the "heads" of two mastodon femurs that were found paired up, together. The other "arrangement" looked similar to a collection of bones in a framed context.

As often happens in contract fieldwork, unexpected finds tend to eat up small budgets, and paleontologists live on scanty morsels to begin with. A northern Arizona paleontologist (also present at the 1968 meeting in Tucson where the 250,000y U-series dates were first discussed) helped the museum facilitate a $10,000 National Geographic Society emergency archaeology grant. You don't mess with the NGS until you are fairly sure of your claims, so the features must have looked pretty archaeological to the paleontologists. *Nothing else made sense.*

No natural agency or forces could selectively and collectively account for the anomalies turning up among the bones. They acknowledged that there was no absolute, direct evidence, but when all the anomalies were added together, it always spelled a-r-c-h-a-e-o-l-o-g-y. (To local archaeologists, not so much.) The paleontologists got the grant quickly.

It was not a kill site, but a butchering or processing site. By all counts, the mastodon was probably already dead, but still worth butchering; the tusks and bone would make for good tools plus all the other things such as high-protein marrow from bones, hide, and so on.

A cautious silence was the local *archaeological* reaction to the site by officials from San Diego's Museum of Man. They visited the site, looked, and listened, but did not say a word. The CDoT archaeologist merely scoffed. She didn't buy it for a second. One can only wonder: Had archaeologists been digging the site, would they have noticed anything strange? Most of us aren't trained to recognize an archaeology composed of a series of paleontological anomalies. *What the hell's a paleontological anomaly?*

That's not to say there wasn't a lot of head-shaking among the crew. Though dates would not be known for many months after they left the field, speculation on the site's antiquity was rife. The Arizona paleontologist, Larry D. Agenbroad, made a most ominous assessment to the museum crew: "If the site is less than 15,000 years old then it is probably cultural; if it is older, it is probably natural."

Had it stayed within the 15,000y maximum, you might have heard about the site on the evening news. There would have been a monument, and National Geographic would have scored another cover.

The U-Series dates said 180,000–300,000. What did the scientists say? Nothing. Silence. Tip-toe away. Maybe nobody will hear. More than a decade later, nobody has. From all accounts, no report was ever sent to *National Geographic*. One has to wonder what NGS thought about all this when they heard the dates. *Oh, no! Not another Calico! No thanks. Don't call us; we'll call you.*

So, instead of a world class archaeological discovery demanding its very own conference, published volume, TV show, and a national monument to commemorate the site...nothing. Nothing is known of this site outside a very small circle of participants. The report of the fieldwork was sent to CDoT and a couple other government agencies, and is not currently available for sale. What survives are some nagging memories among some of the professional geologists and paleontologists who worked and visited the site.

Robson Bonnichsen was one of a very small number of archaeologists who actually took the time to examine the materials in the lab and looked over the field notes and report. From a letter in the SDNHM files, he thought it was some of the most intriguing evidence he had seen regarding really early man in the New World.[43]

Whether or not the mastodon quarry is ever resuscitated, it should draw attention to the types of problems archaeologists should learn to expect in a pre-Clovis, pre-Modern world. It also calls to paleontologists to be on the lookout. After all, as Professor Krieger pointed out 40 years earlier, it was the paleontologists who first brought bone tools to the attention of archaeologists at the turn of the 20th century. This was how it was for me when Joaquin showed me the flattened rib fragment from his bone pit. In a pre-Mod world, a great burden of recognition will shift to paleontologists.

In the end, it was an archaeological call. If the museum paleontologists led the charge on this site, there is every chance they would not have faired too well. There is every chance they would have suffered a drop in credibility and respect, and a drop in grants and contract work. After all, this was southern California, and they all knew about what happened to archaeologists who claimed pre-Clovis sites.

And never forget the economics of great antiquity, and the budget increases that would now have a bona fide precedent. No developer in his right mind will welcome an extra couple of hundred thousand years of geology that will now have to be checked. Neither archaeologists nor paleontologists would have stood a chance in the academic nor economic climate of the day. They probably would still not stand a chance. The only chance will come from an informed public.

Again, it was an archaeological call. And again, it went unanswered. What can I say? Another case of truth defying reason and reason going to bed?

Pre-Mods, Unchained

Fagan's model of human technological evolution shows that the older we were, the ~~dumber~~ less-evolved and more intellectually challenged we were. Just look at those simpleton tools for those millions of years! That was "them." The spike is us! We are radiant! The world is our oyster. Kinda makes you proud to be a *sapien*.

Oops. It seems that everyone was way off base. In retrospect, maybe Fagan's chart means something else. Maybe it actually represents a psychological projection based on the diminishing returns of artifacts/information the further back we go. Maybe the chart actually represents the scope of our own knowledge, which dramatically lessens the further we go back in time. Just an idea. It certainly doesn't account for *erectus* sailors and javelin-makers, nor the traveling *ergasters*.

A decade ago, any talk about a Russian *habilis* or *erectus* sea travelers would have landed you in the academic rubber room and stripped of all credibility, an academic hell where nobody who was anybody would ever listen to you again. Speculation no longer, these fantasies are in our laps. It would appear that the intelligence reserved for the Upper Paleolithic needs to be shared with the erectus boatmakers and a million years earlier with the traveling ergastsers. The simplist Oldowan tools and a 4-foot body got us to the Silk Road. The next simplest, the Acheulean, took us to the islands. Yet, these stone tool types remained virtually the same for more than a million years. After years of brain sizes, tall foreheads, and tool traditions as official gauges of our pre-Mod intelligence (or lack thereof), that model, that template, that world view is gone. The model is no more. It has gone to meet its maker. It is a dead model.

These new discoveries are full of a host of new abilities and capacities that are so outrageous and unexpected that it will take some time to figure out all the ramifications so we can begin to construct better models. How teachable were pre-Mod babies? Maybe the exciting discovery of a 3.3ma-year-old baby skeleton in east Africa may give us answers in the near future. Time will tell.[44] Yet, do we really have that much time left? These are and will be unknown archeologies for us in the New World, and real estate is being developed at alarming rates.

It will take a dramatically different way of thinking, both with respect to northern adaptive demographics and seacoast living. We can only assume that much of the evidence is underwater. In the Old World, too, all discussions of early migrations were largely land routes, except for Australia. If you lived in Morocco and wanted to go to Gibralter, you had to walk all the way around the Mediterranean. Popeye *Erectus* should change all that.

In a Sane World

Thirty years ago, there should have been a mass stampede of trowel-bearers to Valsequillo and all other Pleistocene bone beds in the region. It should have been a gold rush! Careers are made on breakthroughs such as this, and they offer great renewals and excitement throughout the discipline and throughout society. The local economies around Puebla and Valsequillo would have been millions of dollars ahead with all the foreign crews and tourists being lodged down there. Heck, on beer sales alone! The amazing choice to avoid and forget these incredible sites exposed one of those fundamental differences between Old World and New World archaeology. In the New World, dates can kill.

The New Worlders might have had a point. Based solely on the evidence, some crazy questions emerge:

- Did pre-Mods migrate to the New World several hundred thousand years ago and evolve into Mods a couple hundred thousand years earlier than the Eurasian Mods?
- Were Upper Paleolithic techs independently invented in the New World 200,000 years earlier than the Old World?

❋ Did some of these New World Mods perhaps then migrate across the Atlantic around 50,000y and inspire the UP Revolution, only to return again to become the Clovis hunters?

❋ Can you pass me that worm in the bottle?

Questions alone should not have ended research, but it seems maybe they did. As such, Western Hemisphere archaeological communities have lost touch with some provocative archaeological discoveries in central Mexico. This account has only scratched the surface of what went on behind the scenes as the pathos of the discoveries grew and grew. Only one set of archives has been plundered (Dr. Cynthia Irwin-Williams). These were supplemented by direct help from members of the original crew: Malde, Steen-McIntyre, Naeser, Ray, Pichardo, Szabo. Along with Irwin-Williams and Armenta, the most significant loss was Roald Fryxell, the stratigrapher/archaeological geologist. It is precisely this element, stratigraphy, that represents the most recent carbuncle between archaeologists and geologists.

Some Mexican authorities argued that *some* of the artifacts were planted, and, as if rotten tomatoes, soiled the entire enterprise. End of discussion. Until now. There is a huge story sitting in boxes in central Mexico, be they artifacts or notes or local press archives. Tracking the stories behind the Pueblan headlines during the 1960s should be a rich chapter to explore. Pueblans were dancing and singing. Puebla was "The Eden of the Americas." It might have had something to do with the backing for the *African* outdoor zoo that opened there in the 1970s. As for the Eden of the Americas, it still is.

Profesor Juan Armenta Camacho deserves a statue, maybe several, for his incredible discovery, persistence, and dedication. The discoveries were top-of-the-morning kinds of things, and Armenta was at the vanguard, and then—bang—he was snuffed out and silenced.

How did the local papers carry *that* story? How did the good people of Puebla feel about being robbed of both their rightful legacy and their local hero?

Plenty of historical nuggets lie in wait for the burrower of archives belonging to Wormington, Brew, Krieger, Lorenzo, and others central to the original drama. One thing is guaranteed: a very exciting trip down a memory lane that inspired mass amnesia. Just remember to donate lavishly to the National Anthropological Archives of your choice, but donate.

In a perfect world, Valsequillo will become Ph.D. Central. Another 80-plus sites were found at Valsequillo back in the 1960s. Most of those may be underwater, but there are plenty of other exposures in the region, maybe even footprints. We need only look. The sandy silts of the Valsequillo Formation might be the perfect setting to try out new gizmos such as the subsurface radar or a proton magnetometer to help locate buried bone deposits.

It will save us a decade if someone finds Armenta's notes for the entire region. Irwin-Williams never published, and most of her personal field notes and photos are missing, both in the United States and whatever she was required to submit to INAH. Along with the artifacts and art, these archives are lost treasures in their own right. Nobody has seen Lorenzo's own records.

At one magic moment, the entire community was enjoying the mass titillation of a major discovery that drew everyone together like bugs to a light. Then, in the time it took to read the U-Series dates, everyone either stormed the exits or sat dumbfounded on the floor. A savage punchline. Legendary.

A complete and utter rejection of Valsequillo followed, forever stained with a black mark next to its name, the very same black mark that got it elected to NBC's archaeological chamber of horrors show about human origins.

Valsequillo has risen again, and archaeologists are faced once again with the question that drove some to drink. *What am I going to believe: The theory or my lying eyes?*

The poor geologists. All they knew was science, an evidence-driven enterprise. "Wrong" was okay but only if followed by an explanation and a demonstration of the error. In the stampede of archaeologists away from the discoveries, geological science simply vanished. Even after the 1981 article, it was as if the entire matter fell into a black hole. "Wrong" quickly evolved into "impossible" and "erroneous." And this is how things remained until George Carter asked Marshall Payn to stick his nose into it.

These were the most significant early sites in the New World, and no one was curious enough to ask Irwin-Williams about them. Neither the SAA nor any other official archaeological association—north or south of the border—expressed any interest in getting to the bottom of the Valsequillo mess. It was too controversial. It didn't make sense. It was impossible. It was an embarrassment. Take your choice. In the end, nothing was ever done to resolve the greatest geoarchaeological problem in modern archaeological history. It even had arrowheads. It even had art.

Perhaps they felt the way Marie Wormington felt: that Valsequillo destroyed Cynthia's brilliant career, and that maybe it would bite their own careers. It is difficult to fathom, but it had to be something strong enough to void out what could only have been an intense archaeological curiosity. Was it the little reminder from down deep: *Yeah, well, curiousity killed the cat, y'know.* If so, there is the other voice that should have reminded them: *So what? Cats have nine lives. Have some fun.*

Even if you reduce Valsequillo to its most recent dates, say, an extremely conservative 20–30,000y, the SAA community was still faced with buried Pleistocene sites, demonstrating at least two technological components, that were less sophisticated than Clovis assemblages, and potentially mirroring the Upper Paleolithic sequence via independent invention. This basic knowledge alone justified a paleoarchaeological stampede to Central Mexico. Instead, it became both a nonentity and taboo: Don't ask, don't tell, don't go there. And no one did. Professionals of both nations turned a blind eye to the artifacts, the art, the perfect matrix. They were so blind, the artifacts themselves are now missing and no one seems to care.

Valsequillo has now qualified for a place in the record books: There has never been a culturally fossiliferous region that fits the dream that this one fits, *and then been ignored.*

All the while, the 12,000y Clovis First bottom line was enforced by all U.S. academic, grant-giving and cultural resource management institutions. Even Caulapan's 20,000 year old dates were forgotten, as was the fact that it was a date reached by both C14 and U-Series methods. Thirty years have gone by.

Dates be damned. The sites, the artifacts, the art (!) were significant in, of, and by themselves, and remain so. Were the relations between archaeologists of the two nations so fragile that no one felt compelled to get to the bottom of it? This was, and remains, an awesome cache of sites and artifacts. International diplomacy is supposed to be what anthropologists are good at, especially with neighbors, and you would think that a discovery of this magnitude would over-ride "personalities." Just keep the angry dogs out of the room when you discuss it. It would have been that easy. Not then, not now—there is nobody who can deny that the artifacts were firmly trapped in Pleistocene sediments. That was reason enough to stifle the egos.

Lucky for us that the Valsequillo Reservoir didn't go anywhere except covered up by higher stands of water, and that the Mexican authorities have now placed the high stand perimeter under national protection. We can only hope that 21st-century archaeologists, and the institutions that support them, pay heed to Valsequillo, lest they rob another generation of what is one of the greatest and oldest *cultural regions* in the New World.

Closer to home, the next time you drive to Las Vegas, stop by and talk to Fred Budinger at the Calico Early Man Site. He'll line you up for a tour of Bassett Point and the Mojave Sink, another burning fuse that will soon blow the top off everything we thought. Calico's 40 year gamble is about to pay off. Louis Leakey did indeed reform the pre-Modern world in a single bound, Old World and New. This will disturb some and gratify the rest.

In the larger scheme of things, one of the great missing puzzle connectors is the unrecognized ambiguities of bipolar flaking, an entirely distinct and highly variable material language we have been all but blind to. Figuring out blades and bifaces is one thing. Figuring out the first 2 million years will take something more, and bipolar literacy will be required if we hope to get anywhere. As in every experimental endeavor, the more you do bipolar flaking, the more you begin to see it in the field and in collections. Thanks to Dr. Carter for telling us about it...50 years ago.

In the end, as a result of all this, there might actually be an answer to "there has to be a rational explanation." Maybe we don't know enough yet to know what is impossible from what is not, within reason. We are still students of our ancestors, not their teachers. Above all, we should be looking forward to some serious fun as the century unfolds.

As Ghandi said: "First they ignore you, then they ridicule you, then they fight you, and then you win."

What we win is a piece of the puzzle, a piece telling New World archaeologists they have a much larger stake in the Pleistocene pie than they probably imagined. Valsequillo is real. Materially present. Quantifiable. Mappable in time and space. Something priceless. Another dot to connect. A perceptible jump along the way. Historically a turning point, interrupted for sure, but hopefully back on track.

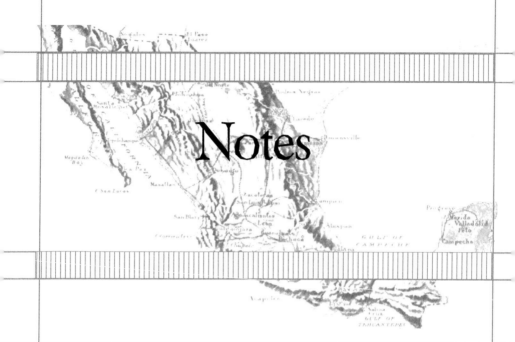

Notes

Part 1

Chapter 1.1

1. Leakey, "Finding."
2. *LIFE*, Aug. 15, 1960, p. 35.
3. Brandon, William. *The American Heritage Book of Indians*, 14.
4. Cote, *Mysterious Origins of Man*.

Chapter 1.2

5. Armenta, "Vestigios."
6. Malde, 1.
7. Cremo, Michael. *Forbidden Archaeology*, 354–366.

Chapter 1.3

8. Armenta, 11.
9. Ibid., 18.
10. Ibid.
11. Ibid., 13.

12. Ibid., 96.
13. Ibid., 97.
14. Wormington, 1.
15. Armenta, "Vestigios," 19; Coe, "Mexico."

Chapter 1.4

16. trans. Edith Mary Lowell, 1 .
17. Lorenzo, "Early Man."
18. Armenta, 10.
19. Cornwall and Mooser's field trip notes from Irwin-Williams's collection.
20. Ibid.
21. Ibid.
22. Ibid.
23. Ibid.
24. Armenta, "Vestigios.," 1–2

Chapter 1.5

25. Figgins, "The Antiquity."
26. Brew, 1.
27. Krieger, 1.
28. Ibid.
29. Ibid.

Chapter 1.6

30. Armenta, "Vestigios," 25.

Part II

Chapter 2.1

1. Irwin-Williams, "Preliminary," 1962.
2. Ibid.
3. Ibid.
4. Ibid.
5. Ibid.

6. Ibid.
7. Ibid.
8. Ibid.
9. Ibid.

Chapter 2.2

10. Irwin-Williams, "Preliminary," 1964.
11. Irwin-Williams, "Preliminary," 1966.
12. Ibid.

Chapter 2.3

13. Litvak King, 1996.
14. Armenta, "Vistigios," 1–2

Chapter 2.4

15. Steen-Mcintyre, 1.
16. Irwin-Williams, 1978: 10
17. Malde, 1.
18. Martin, 1.
19. Griffin, "The Origin," 45
20. Malde, 1–3.
21. Irwin-Williams, 1.
22. Malde, 1.
23. Malde, Irwin-Williams, 1–3.

Chapter 2.5

24. Compton, "The Interamerican," 1.
25. Lorenzo, "The Sobre," 1967.
26. Cote, *Mysterious*.
27. Paddock, 1–2.
28. Willey and Sablof, A *History*, 1.
29. Lorenzo, 1978, Lorenzo and Mirambell 1999
30. Malde, 1.
31. Irwin-Williams, "Associations.," 2–3
32. Turner, 1967.

Part III

Chapter 3.1

1. Orr 1968; Carter, "Evidence"; Carter, *Interglacial Artifacts*; Carter, "An Interglacial"; Carter, *Pleistocene*; Carter, "An American"; Carter, "Earlier Man."
2. Trueman et al 2005
3. Davis , 1969.
4. Dee, 1.
5. Josselyn, 1–2.
6. White, "Ethno Archaeology," 1968; Barnham, *The Bipolar*, 1987; Minshall, *Bipolar Flaking*; Honea, 1965; Hardaker, 1979.
7. Lee, "On Pebble.," 18.
8. Carter 1971, Johansen and Parker, "On Maizer," 1989; Sorenson and Raich, *Pre-Columbian*; .Riley, et. al., "Early Man," 1971.
9. Semaw et. al., "2.6-Million-Year-Old."
10. Schuiling, *Pleistocene* (1972); Schuiling, *Pleistocene* (1972); Leakey, "Archaeological"; Leakey, et. al. "Early Man."

Chapter 3.2

11. Fleisher, et. al. "Fission."
12. Renfrew, *Before*, 69; Stuiver, "Origins."
13. Griesemer, *The Fortnightly.*
14. Haynes , "The Calico."
15. Hurford, et. al., "Fission-Track"; Gleadow, "Fission track."
16. Szabo, et. al., "Dilemma."

Chapter 33

17. Szabo, et. al., "Dilemma."
18. Malde, geological map.
19. Ibid.
20. Malde, 1968.
21. Irwin-Williams, 1–2.
22. Wormington, 1–2.
23. Irwin-Williams, 1–2.
24. Ibid.

25. Szabo 1968
26. Irwin-Williams, 1–2.
27. Malde, 1.
28. Irwin-Williams, "Comments on the Associations," 1–2.

Chapter 3.4

29. Wormington correspondence to George Agogino, November 23, 1973, 1.
30. Fryxell, Wikipedia, 2006.
31. Email to author; April 2005, 1.
32. Email to author; May 2004
33. Bischoff, et. al., "Uranium Series," 33.
34. Willey and Sablof, "A History," 24.
35. Steen-Mcintyre, et. al., "Geologic."
36. Juan Armenta Camacho, translation by Caroline Malde.
37. National Anthropological Archives, 2005.
38. Martin, "Clovisia," 10.
39. E-Mail to author, October 2003.
40. Bordaz, 1971; Bordes, 1968.
41. Irwin-Williams, 1 –2.

PART IV

Chapter 4.1

1. Stengel, "The Diffusionists"; Guidon, "Las Unidades"; Guidon and Arnaud, "The Chronology"; Guidon, et. al, "Nature and Age"; Santos, et. al. , "A Revised."
2. Begley and Murr, "The First."
3. Steen-Macintyre, 1.
4. Menzies, 1421.
5. Xu, "Origin."
6. Meggars, et. al., "Early Formative."
7. Donelik, et. al., *Nearly concordant*." For a philosophy of science take on the Valsequillo discoveries, see Well and Clark, "Anatomy."

Chapter 4.2

8. Malde, 1.

Chapter 4.3

9. Steen-Mcintyre, 1.
10. Firestone, 1.
11. Reichelt, *Fossile.*
12. VanLandingham, "Diatom biostratigraphy," 1–2.
13. Ibid.
14. Ibid.
15. Kurten, "Preview of"; Guenther; Guenther, et. al., "Das Mexico"; Pichardo, "Redating".
16. Steen-Mcintyre, 1.
17. Repenning, 1.
18. Kurten and Anderson, *Pleistocene.*
19. Liddicoat, et. al., "Paleomagnetic."
20. Jefferson, 1.
21. Malde, 1.
22. Bell, et. al., 1.

Chapter 4.4

23. Ochoa, et. al., "New."

Chapter 4.5

24. Gruhn, "Linguistic"; Bonnichsen and Steele, *Method*; Bonnichsen and Turnmire, *Ice Age*; Bonnichsen, et. al., *Paleoamerican.*
25. Dillehay, *Monte*; Dillehay, *The Settlement*; McAvoy and McAvoy, "Archaeological"; Adovasio, et. al., "The Meadowcroft"; Adovasio, et. al. "Never"; Fiedel, "Older"; "Ice-full corridor," see Jackson and Duk-Rodkin; "Quarternary"; Mandryk, "Invented."
26. Ibid.
27. Lorenzo, "Early Man."
28. Waters, et. al., "Late"; Waters, et. al. "Evaluation"; Waters, et. al., "Diring."
29. Meltzer, et. al., "A Campaign."

Chapter 4.6

30. Marshall, 1.
31. Schwenninger, et. al.; Gonzalez, et. al., "Human"; Renne, et. al., "Age"; Huddart, et. al.; see also *www.mexicanfootprints.co.uk.*

32. Rice, "Debate"; Soloranzo, *Pleistocene*; Irish, et. al., "Prehistoric."
33. Guidon, "Pedra."
34. Largent, "Toluquilla," 17.

Part V

Chapter 5.1

1. Bradley and Stanford, "The North"; Petit, "Rediscovering."
2. Crabtree and Carey, "Ancient."
3. Firestone, et. al., *The Cycle*.
4. Fedje et al 2001:3
5. Stengel, "The Diffusionists"; Bowers, "Early," 212; Neves, et. al., "Early."
6. Reuters, "First."
7. Wilford, "Noble."
8. Learmonth, "First."

Chapter 5.2

9. McBrearty & Brooks, "The Revolution," 491–93; Bar-Yosef and Vandermeersch.
10. Fagan and Michaels, "Tools for Life."
11. Pavlov, et. al., *Pleiostene*.
12. Heeren, "Making"; Schuster, "Case."

Chapter 5.3

13. Pink Floyd, "Keep Talking."
14. CSFA, 2004.
15. Hall, *Mammoth*.
16. Dennell, "The World's," 767.
17. Bower, "German"; "Lower."
18. Gore, "The First."
19. Shipman, "Doubting."
20. Team Dmanisi, "Lithic"; "The Environmental."
21. Gore, "The First."
22. Dennell and Roebroeks, "An Asian."

Chapter 5.4

23. *Nature Australia*, "Ancient."
24 Ibid.
25. The World, "Fresh"; Moorwood, et. al., "Archaeological"; Moorewood, et. al., "Fission-track."
26. Handwerk, "New"; Moorwood, et. al., "Archaeology."
27.Bower, *Erectus*; Bednarik, "An experiment"; Bednarik, "Maritime"; Bednarik, "The Origins"; Bednarik, "Replicating."
28.Gee, "Beach"; Walter, et. al., "Early."
29. "Exaptations."
30. Ibid.
31. Shepard, "There's"; Rockets.
32. Morgan, *Aquatic.*

Chapter 5.5

33. McBrearty and Brooks, "The Revolution," 454–56
34. Stringer, "Evolution."
35. McDougall, "Fossil."
36. McBrearty and Brooks, "The Revolution," 495–96
37. Ibid.
38. Ibid., 496–97
39. "British," 2004.

Chapter 5.6

40. Caltech, 2001.
41. Weber, 2005.
42. Demere, et. al., *State.*
43. Robson Bonnichsen letter 2001 (on file at San Diego Natural History Museum).
44. Alemseged, et. al., "A Juvenile."

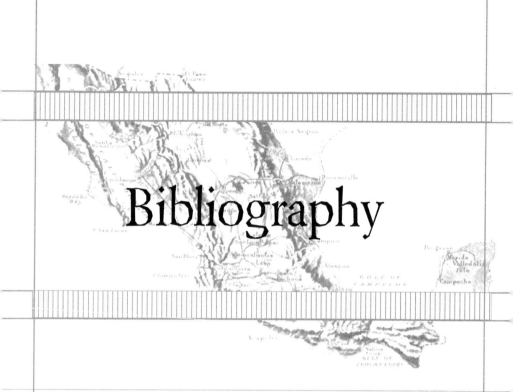

Bibliography

Adovasio, J. M., J. Donahue., and R. Stuckenrath. "The Meadowcroft Rockshelter radiocarbon chronology 1975–1990." *American Antiquity* 2 (1990): 348–354.

———. "Never say never again: Some thoughts on could haves and might have beens." *American Antiquity* 57(1992): 327–331.

Alemseged, Zeresenay, Fred Spoor, William H. Kimbel, René Bobe, Denis Geraads, Denné Reed, and Jonathan G. Wynn. "A juvenile early hominin skeleton from Dikika, Ethiopia." *Nature* 443(2006): 296–301.

Armenta Camacho, Juan. "Hallazgos Prehistóricos en el Valle de Puebla." *Centro de Est. His. de Puebla* 2 (1957).

———. "Hallazgo de un artefacto asociado con mamut en el Valle de Puebla." *Dirección Prehistoria Pub.* 7 (1959): 7–25.

———. *Vestigios de Labor Humana en Huesos de Animales Extintos de Valsequillo, Puebla, Mexico.* Published privately with aid from the American Philosophical Society and the Mary Street Jenkins Foundation, 1978.

Barham, John. "The Bipolar Technique in Southern Africa: A Replication Experiment." *South African Archaeological Bulletin* 42 (1987): 45–50.

Bednarik, R.G. "An experiment in Pleistocene seafaring." *International Journal of Nautical Archaeology* 27(1998): 139–49.

———. "Maritime navigation in the Lower and Middle Palaeolithic." *Comptes Rendus de l'Académie des Sciences Paris* 328 (1999): 559–63.

———. "The origins of Pleistocene navigation in the Mediterranean: initial replicative experimentation." *Journal of Iberian Archaeology* 3 (2001): 11–23.

———. "Replicating the first known sea travel by humans: the Lower Pleistocene crossing of Lombok Strait." *Human Evolution* 16 (2001): 229–42.

Begley, Sharon, and Andrew Murr. "The First Americans." *Newsweek*, April 26, 1999.

Beltrão, Maria da C. M. C. "Toca da Esperança: o sítio arqueológico mais antigo das Três Américas." *Carta Mensal.* 52(2006): 40–59.

Berger, R. 1972. "An Isotopic and Magnetic Study of the Calico Site." In *Pleistocene Man at Calico*, edited by W.C. Schuiling, pp. 65–69. San Bernardino County Museum Association, Bloomington, California.

Bischoff, J.L., R.J. Shlemon, T.L. Ku, R.D. Simpson, R.J. Rosenbauer, and F.E. Budinger, Jr. "Uranium-series and Soils-geomorphic Dating of the Calico Archaeological Site, California." *Geology* 9 (1981): 576–582.

Bonnichsen, Robson. 2000. "Mystery of the First Americans." *PBS: Nova.* *www.pbs.org/wgbh/nova/first/claim.html* (accessed 2002).

Bonnichsen, Robson and D. G. Steele, eds. *Method and Theory for Investigating the Peopling of the Americas.* Corvallis, Oregon: Oregon State University Press, 1994.

Bonnichsen, Robson, and Karen L. Turnmire, eds. *Ice Age People of North America: Environments, Origins, and Adaptations.* Corvallis, Oregon: Oregon State University Press, 1999.

Bonnichsen, Robson, Bradley T. Lepper, Dennis Stanford, and Michael R. Waters, eds. *Paleoamerican Origins: Beyond Clovis.* Dallas: Texas A&M University Press, 2006.

Bower, Bruce. 1997. "German mine yields ancient hunting spears." *Science News Online www.sciencenews.org/pages/sn_arc97/3_1_97/fob2.htm* (accessed 1999).

———. "Early Brazilians Unveil African Look." *Science News* 159 (2001): 212

———. "*Erectus* ahoy: prehistoric seafaring floats into view." *Science News* 164 (2003): 248 *www.sciencenews.org/articles/20031018/bob8.asp.* Accessed 2003.

Bradley, Bruce, and Dennis Stanford. "The North Atlantic ice-edge corridor: a possible Palaeolithic route to the New World." *World Archaeology* 36 (2004): 459–478.

Bryan, A. L., ed. *Early Man in America from a Circum-Pacific Perspective.* Archaeological Researches International: Edmonton, Alberta, Canada, 1978.

———. *New Evidence for the Pleistocene Peopling of the Americas.* Orono, Centre for the Study of the First Americans, 1986.

Budinger, F.E., Jr. "Evidence for Pleistocene Man in America: The Calico Early Man Site." *California Geology* 36 (1983): 75–82.

———. "A Search Strategy for Evidence of Early Man in America: A Preliminary Assessment of the Manix Type Section, Central Mojave Desert, California." *Proceedings of the Society of California Archaeology* 9 (1996): 113–119.

Budinger, F.E., Jr. and R.D. Simpson. Evidence for Middle and Late Pleistocene Man in the Central Mojave Desert of Southern California. In *Woman, Poet, Scientist: Essays in New World Anthropology Honoring Dr. Emma Louise Davis*, compiled and edited by the Great Basin Foundation, pp. 16–36. Ballena Press, Los Altos, California, 1985.

Caltech completes $111 million fundraising effort for the biological sciences, CalTech Media Releases. *http://pr.caltech.edu/media/Press_Releases/PR12180.html* (accessed 2006).

Carey, Bjorn. "Ancient People Followed 'Kelp Highway' to America, Researcher Says, LiveScience." February 19, 2006. *www.livescience.com. history060219_kelp_highway.html*. Accessed 2006.

Carter, George F. "Evidence for Pleistocene Man in Southern California." *Geographical Review* 11 (1950): 84–102.

———. "Interglacial Artifacts from the San Diego Area." *Southwestern Journal of Anthropology* 8 (1952): 444–456.

———. "An Interglacial Site from San Diego, California." *The Masterkey* 28 (1954): 165–174.

———. *Pleistocene Man at San Diego, California*. Baltimore: John Hopkins Univ. Press, 1957.

———. "An American Lower Paleolithic." *Anthropological Journal of Canada* 16 (1978): 2–38.

———. *Earlier than You Think: A Personal View of Man in America*. College Station, Tex: Texas A&M Univ. Press, 1980.

———. Early Man at San Diego: A Geomorphic-Archaeological View. *Proceedings of the Society for California Archaeology* 9 (1996): 104–112.

Chandler, J.M. Immigrants from the Other Side. *Mammoth Trumpet*. 17 (2001): 11–16.

Coe, Michael D. *Mexico*. New York: Praeger Press, 1962.

Compton, Carl B. *The Interamerican, Newsletter of the Instituto Interamericano*, Volume 14, No. 8, November 1967.

Cote, B. 1996. *Mysterious Origins of Man*. NBC network. Aired February 21, 1996.

Davis, Emma Lou. The Western Lithic Co-Tradition. In: *The Western Lithic Co-Tradition*, by E. L. Davis, C. W. Brott, and D. L. Weide, pp. 11–78. San Diego Museum Papers No. 6, 1969.

———. *The Ancient Californias: Rancholabrean Hunters of the Mojave Lakes Country*. Natural History Museum of Los Angeles County, Science Series 29 (1978): 1–193.

Deloria, Vine. *Red Earth, White Lies.* New York: Scribner, 1998.

Demere, T.A., R.A. Cerutti, and C. Paul Majors. *State Route 54 Paleontological Mitigation Program: Final Report.* Department of Paleontology, San Diego Natural History Museum, prepared for CalTrans, District 11. 1995.

Dennell, Robin. "The World's Oldest Spears," *Nature* 385, Feb. 27, 1997, p. 767; also *Science News Online*, March 1, 1997.

Dennell, Robin, and Wil Roebroeks. "An Asian perspective on early human dispersal from Africa." *Nature*, 438 (1995):1099–1004.

Dillehay, Thomas D., ed. *Monte Verde: A Late Pleistocene Settlement in Chile.* Seattle, Wash.: Smithsonian Institution Press, 1989.

————. *The Settlement of the Americas: A New Prehistory.* New York: Basic Books, 2001.

Dixon, E. James, *Bones, Boats, and Bison: Archeology and the First Colonization of Western North America.* Sante Fe, N.M.: University of New Mexico Press, 2002.

Donelick, R.A., K.A. Farley, and T.A. Dumitru. "Nearly concordant zircon fission-track and (U-Th)/He ages for Pleistocene-aged ash beds from the Hueyatlaco archeological site near Puebla, Mexico." Unpublished ms.

Fagan, Brian M., and G. H. Michaels. "Tools for Life." *www.mc.maricopa.edu/dept/ d10/asb/anthro2003/archy/lithictech/lithictech6.html (accessed 2006).*

Fedje, Daryl W., Quentin Mackie, E. James Dixon, and T. H. Heaton. "Late Wisconsin Environments and Archaeological Visibility on the Northern Northwest Coast," ms. p.3 *http://web.uvic.ca/~qxm/449/fedje2.pdf* (accessed 2004.)

Fiedel, Stuart J. "Older Than We Thought: Implications of Corrected Dates for Paleoindians." *American Antiquity*, Vol. 64, No. 1 (1999): 95–115.

Figgins, J. D. "The antiquity of man in America." *Natural History* 27 (1927):229–39.

Firestone, R., A. West, and S. Warwick-Smith, 2006, *The Cycle of Cosmic Catastrophes: Flood, Fire, and Famine in the History of Civilization.* Rochester, Vt.: Bear & Co., 2006.

Fladmark, Knut. "Routes: Alternate Migration Corridors for Early Man in North America." *American Antiquity* 44 (1979): 55–69.

Fleischer, R. L., P.B. Price, R.M. Walker, and L.S.B. Leakey. "Fission track dating of Bed I, Olduvai Gorge." *Science* 148 (1965) :72–74.

Gabunia, L., A. Vekua and D. Lordkipanidze. "The Environmental Context of Early Human Occupation in Georgia(Transcaucasia)." *Journal of Human Evolution.* 34/6 (2000): 785–802.

Gee, Henry. "Beach tools: The first things that humans did after they evolved was to head for the beach." *Nature Science Update* 2001. *www.nature.com/nsu/ 000504/000504-11.html* (accessed 2002).

Gleadow, A. J. W. "Fission track age of the KBS Tuff and associated himinid remains in northern Kenya." *Nature* 284 (1980): 225–230.

Gonzalez, S., D. Huddart, M.R. Bennett, A. Gonzalez-Huesca. "Human footprints in Central Mexico older than 40,000 years." *Quaternary Science Reviews* 25 (2006): 201–222.

Gonzalez, S., D. Huddart, and M. Bennett. 2006 Valsequillo Pleistocene archaeology and dating: ongoing controversy in Central Mexico, *World Archaeology* Vol. 38(4): 611–627

Goodyear Albert C. 2004 "Evidence of Pre-Clovis Sites in the Eastern United States. In *Paleoamerican Origins: Beyond Clovis*. Edited by R. Bonnichsen et al. Texas A&M University Press (in press).

Gore, Rick. The First Pioneer? *National Geographic Magazine* Aug. 2002, Vol 202, No. 2, 2002.

Greenberg, J. H., C. G. Turner II, and S. L. Zegura. "The Settlement of the Americas: A Comparison of Linguistic, Dental, and Genetic Evidence." *Current Anthropology* 27 (December 1986): 477–97.

Griesemer, Allan D. The Fortnightly Club of Redlands, California; *Meetings #1637 and #1640*. October 5, 2000 and November 16, 2000 *www.redlandsfortnightly.org/gries_00.htm* (accessed 2006).

Griffin, J.B. The origin and dispersion of American Indians in North America. In Laughlin, W.S. and Harper, A.B., eds., *The First Americans: Origins, Affinities, And Adaptations*, pp. 43–55. Gustav Fischer: New York

Gruhn, Ruth. The Pacific Coast route of initial entry: An overview. In *Method and Theory for Investigating the Peopling of the Americas*. Robson Bonnichsen and D. G. Steele, eds. Pp. 249–256. Corvallis, Oregon: Oregon State University, 1994.

———. "Linguistic Evidence in Support of the Coastal Route of Earliest Entry into the New World." *Man* XXIII/1, 1988.

Guenther, E.W., H. Bunde, and G. Nobis 1973 Das Mexiko-projekt der Deutschen Forschyungsgemeinschaft. VI [IV]. *Geologische und Paläontologische Untersuchungen im Valsequillo bei Puebla (Mexiko)*. Franz Steiner Verlag. Wiesbaden.Guidon, N. 1986.

Las Unidades Culturales de São Raimundo Nonato—Sudeste del Estado de Piaui, Brasil, In: Bryan, A. L. (ed.), *New Evidence for the Pleistocene Peopling of the Americas*. Orono, Centre for the Study of the First Americans, pp, 157-171

Guidon, N. Pedra Furada, a revision. II Simpósio Internacional "O Povoamento das Américas." December 16-21, 2006. Piaui, Brazil.

Guidon, N. and B. Arnaud. 1991 The chronology of the New World: Two faces of one reality. *World Archaeology* 23(2):167-178.

Guidon, N., A.M. Pessis, , F. Parenti, M. Fontugue, and C. Guerin. Nature and age of the deposits in Pedra Furada, Brazil: Reply to Meltzer, Adovasio, and Dillehay. *Antiquity* 70: 408–421.

Hall, Don Alan. *Mammoth Trumpet* Vol 11(1), 1996.

Hancock, Graham. *Fingerprints of the Gods.* New York: Crown Publishers, New York, 1995.

Handwerk, Brian. New "Hobbit" Human Bones Add to Evidence, Oddity, *National Geographic News,* 1995.

Hardaker, Chris. "Dynamics of the Bipolar Technique." *Flintknappers Exchange* 2 (1) 13–16.

Haynes, C. Vance. "The Earliest Americans." *Science* (1969): 709–715.

———. "The Calico Site: Artifacts or Geofacts?" *Science* 181 (1973): 305–310.

———. "The Clovis Culture." *Canadian Journal of Anthropology* 1 (1980): 115–121.

Heernen, Frederic. "Making love or making war? ; Caveful of Clues About Early Humans: Interbreeding With Neanderthals Among Theories Being Explored," *The Washington Post,* September 20, 2004.

Hoffman, L.V., R.S. Simpson, R.M. Higginbotham, and L.W. Patterson. "Lithic Flake Attributes: Calico Lithic Specimens and Experimental Knapping—A Comparison." *Current Research in the Pleistocene* 4 (1987): 56–57.

Honea, K. H. "The Bipolar Flaking Technique in Texas and New Mexico." *Bulletin of the Texas Archaeological Society,* 36 (1965): 259–267.

Hurford, A.J., A.J.W. Gleadow, and C.W. Naeser. "Fission-track dating of pumice form the KBS tuff, East Rulolf, Kenya." *Nature* 263 (1974): 728–744.

Irish, J.D., Stanley D. Davis, John (Jack) E. Lobdell, and Frederico A. Solórzano. "Prehistoric Human Remains from Jalisco, Mexico;" *Current Research in the Pleistocene* 17 (2000): 95–97.

Irwin-Williams, Cynthia. *Preliminary Report on Investigations in the Region of the Valsequillo Reservoir, 1962.* (Submitted to INAH, available at National Anthropological Archives, Md.)

———.1964. *Preliminary Report on Investigations in the Region of the Valsequillo Reservoir, 1964.* (Submitted to INAH, available at National Anthropological Archives, Md.)

———. *Preliminary Report on Investigations in the Region of the Valsequillo Reservoir, 1966.* (Submitted to INAH, available at National Anthropological Archives, Md.)

———. "Associations of Early Man with Horse, Camel, and Mastodon at Hueyatlaco, Valsequillo (Puebla, Mexico)." In *Pleistocene Extinctions: The Search For A Cause* (1967): 337–347.

———. 1967. "Comments on Allegations by J. L. Lorenzo Concerning Archaeological Research at Valsequillo, Puebla." In *Paleo-Indian Institute, Eastern New Mexico University Miscellaneous Publications, Number 1,* Portales.

————.1967. The Hoax Was A Hoax, *The INTERAMERICAN, Newsletter of the Instituto Interamericano,* Volume 14, No. 9, December 1967.

————. "Comments on the associations of archaeological materials and extinct fauna in the Valsequillo region, Puebla, Mexico." *American Antiquity* 34 (1969): 82–83.

————. "Commentary on geological evidence for age of deposits at Hueyatlaco archaeological site, Valsequillo, Mexico." *Quaternary Research* 16 (2000): 258.

Isaac, Glynn Llywelyn. *Olorgesailie : Archeological Studies of a Middle Pleistocene Lake Basin in Kenya.* Chicago: University of Chicago Press, 1977.

Jackson Jr., L.E., and A. Duk-Rodkin. 1996. "Quaternary geology of the ice-free corridor: glacial controls on the peopling of the New World." In Akazawa, T. and E.J.E. Szathmary. (eds.), *Prehistoric Mongoloid Dispersals,* pp. 214–227, Oxford, New York.

Johannessen, Carl L., and Anne Z. Parker. "Maize Ears Sculptured in 12th and 13th Century A.D. India as Indicators of Pre-Columbian Diffusion." *Economic Botany* 43 (1989): 164–80.

Kurtén, B. "Präriewolf und Säbelzahntiger aus dem Pleistozän des Valsequillo, Mexiko." *Quartär* 18 (1967): 173–178.

Kurtén, Björn, and Elaine Anderson. *Pleistocene Mammals of North America.* New York: Columbia University Press, 1980.

Largent, Jr. Floyd B. " Toluquilla, Mexico, American Laetoli." *Mammoth Trumpet* 21(2006): 17.

Leakey, Louis S.B. "Finding the World's Earliest Man." *National Geographic,* September 1960: 420–435.

————. "Pleistocene Man in America." In *Pleistocene Man at Calico,* edited by W.C. Schuiling, pp. 9–12. San Bernardino County Museum Association, Bloomington, California. 1972.

————. "The Problems of Calico: Some Background Thoughts. In *Pleistocene Man at Calico,* edited by W.C. Schuiling, pp. 13–16. San Bernardino County Museum Association, Bloomington, California, 1972.

Leakey, L.S.B., R.D. Simpson, and T. Clements. "Archaeological Excavations in the Calico Mountains, California: Preliminary Report." *Science* 160 (1968): 1022–1023.

————. 1970. "Early Man in America: The Calico Mountains Excavation." *Encyclopedia Britannica Yearbook of Science and the Future,* pp. 64–79. Encyclopedia Britannica, Chicago.

Learmonth, Blake 2003. "First Americans, Grave Robbers, Headhunters." *www.unm.edu/~abqteach/archeology_cus/02-01-02.htm* Accessed 2004.

Lee, Thomas E. "The First Sheguiandah Expedition, Manitoulin Island, Ontario." *American Antiquity* 20 (1954): 2, 101–111.

———. "The Second Sheguiandah Expedition, Manitoulin Island, Ontario." *American Antiquity* 21 (1955): 1, 63–71

———. "On Pebble Tools and Their Relatives in America." George F. Carter, *Anthropological Journal of Canada* 7 (1966): 18–19.

Liddicoat, J.C., R.S. Coe, P.W. Lambert, H.E. Malde, and V. Steen-McIntyre. "Paleomagnetic investigation of Quaternary sediment at Tlapacoya, Mexico, and at Valsequillo, Puebla, Mexico *Geofisica International*, 20 (1981): 3, 249–262

Lorenzo Bautista, J.L. 1967. "Sobre Metodo Arqueologico". *Boletin of the Instituto Nacional de Antropologia a Historia*, Junio, 1967. pp.48–51.

———. "Early Man Research in the American Hemisphere: Appraisal and Perspective." In, *Early Man in America from a Circum-Pacific Perspective*, edited by Alan Lyle Bryan, pp. 1–9, Archaeological Researches International: Edmonton, Alberta, Canada, 1978.

Malde, Harold E. "The Ecological Significance of Some Unfamiliar Geologic Processes." In *The Reconstruction of Past Environments*, assembled by James J. Hester and James Schoenwetter, pp. 7–13. Publication of the Fort Burgwin Research Center, No. 3. Taos, New Mexico, 1964.

———. Geologic map of Valsequillo area with unit descriptions. Unpublished Open File Map, several scales, Field Records Library, U.S. Geological Survey, Denver, Colorado, USA, 1968.

Mandryk, C. A. S. "Invented Traditions and the Ultimate American Origin Myth: In the beginning there was an ice free-corridor." In *Making the New World: Multidisciplinary Perspectives on the Peopling of the Americas*, Edited by C. Michael Barton and Geoffrey A. Clark, University of Arizona Press, 2002.

Mandryk, C. A. S. "The ice-free corridor (or not?): An inland route by any other name is not so sweet nor adequately considered." In *On Being First: Cultural and Environmental Consequences of First Peoplings*, C. deMille, J. Gillespie, and S. Tupakka, eds., Calgary, Alberta, 2002.

Martin, Paul S. 1987. "Clovisia the Beautiful!" *Natural History*, October, 96: 10

Martin, P.S., and H.E. Wright, eds. *Pleistocene Extinctions: The Search For A Cause*. New Haven: Yale University Press, 1967.

McAvoy, J.M. Radiocarbon age range and stratigraphic context of artifact clusters in pre-fluted point levels at Cactus Hill, Sussex Co., Virginia. Paper presented at the *65th Annual meeting of the Society for American Archaeology*, Philadelphia, 2002.

McAvoy, J.M., McAvoy, L. 1997. *Archaeological Investigations of Site 44SX202, Cactus Hill, Sussex County Virginia*. Virginia Department of Historic Resources, Research Report Series No. 8. Richmond.

McBrearty, S. and A. Brooks. "The revolution that wasn't: a new interpretation of the origin of modern human behaviour." *Journal of Human Evolution* 39(2000): 453–563.

McDougall, Ian, Francis H. Brown, John G. Fleagle. "Stratigraphic placement and age of modern humans from Kibish, Ethiopia." *Nature* 433 (2005): 733–736 (17 Feb 2005) Letters to Editor

Meggers, B.J., Clifford Evans, and Emilio Estrada. 1965. *Early Formative Period of Coastal Ecuador: The Valdivia and Machalilla Phases*. Smithsonian Contributions to Anthropology. Washington, D.C.: Smithsonian Institution.

Meltzer, David J., Ted Goebel, Vance T Holliday, Rolfe Mandel & Mike Waters. 2002 A Campaign to find the First Americans *Mammoth Trumpet* 18(1); cf. *www.centerfirstamericans.com/mt.php?a=101&h=cramer* Accessed 2004.

Meltzer, David J., J.M. Adovasio, and T.D. Dillehay. "On a Pleistocene human occupation at Pedra Furada, Brazil." *Antiquity* 68 (1994): 695–714.

Menzies, Gavin. *1421: The Year China Discovered America* New York: New York: William Morrow & Company, 2003.

Minshall, Herbert L. "Bipolar Flaking in Quartzite at Buchanan Canyon." *Anthropological Journal of Canada* 11 (1973): 20–24.

———. "A Lower Paleolithic Bipolar Flaking Complex in the San Diego Region: Technological Implications of Recent Finds." *Pacific Coast Archaeological Society Quarterly* 11(1975): 45–56.

———. *The Broken Stones*. San Diego, Calif.: Copley Books, 1976.

———. *Buchanan Canyon: Ancient Human Presence in the Americas*. San Marcos, Calif.: Slawson Communications, 1989.

Morgan, Elaine. *Aquatic Ape Hypothesis: Most Credible Theory of Human Evolution* London: Souvenir Press Ltd, 1999.

Morwood, Mike, and Penny van Oosterzee. *A New Human: The Startling Discovery and Strange Story of the "Hobbits" of Flores, Indonesia* New York: Harper Collins, 2007.

Morwood, M.J., F. Aziz, P. O'Sullivan, D.R. Nasruddin, and A. Raza. "Archaeological and palaeontological research in central Flores, east Indonesia: results of fieldwork 1997–98." *Antiquity* 73 (1999): 273–286.

Morwood, M.J., P.B. O'Sullivan, F. Aziz, and A. Raza. "Fission-track ages of stone tools and fossils on the east Indonesian island of Flores." *Nature* 392 (1998): 173–176.

Morwood M., R.P. Soejono, R.G. Roberts, T. Sutikna, C.S.M. Turney, K.E. Westaway, et al. "Archaeology and age of a new hominid from Flores in eastern Indonesia." *Nature* 431 (2004):1 087–91.

Peter Muello. "Find Puts Man in America at Least 300,000 Years Ago," *Dallas Times Herald*, June 16, 1987.

Nature Australia. 2001. "Ancient Mariners?" Thursday 6 September, 2001; p17–18; *www.amonline.net.au/archive.cfm?id=437* (access 2001).

News Hounds. 2005. The Mule Consented. *www.newshounds.us/2005/05/14 the_mule_consented.php* Accessed 2005.

Neves, Walter A., Mark Hubbe. "Cranial morphology of early Americans from Lagoa Santa, Brazil : Implications for the settlement of the New World." *Proceedings of the National Academy of Sciences of the United States of America* 102 (2005): 18,309–18,314

Neves, Walter Alves, André Prous, Rolando González-José, Renato Kipnis, and Joseph Powell. "Early Holocene human skeletal remains from Santana do Riacho, Brazil: implications for the settlement of the New World" *Journal of Human Evolution* 45 (2003): 759–782.

Ocean Rowing Society. 2004. "British pair becomes first mother and daughter team to cross Atlantic in rowboat." *www.oceanregatta.com/media_2004/ Cald_May6_Barbados.htm* Accessed 2004.

Ochoa-Castillo, Patricia, Mario Pérez-Campa, Ana Lillian Martín del Pozzo,and Joaquín Arroyo-Cabrales. New Excavations in Valsequillo, Puebla, México. *Current Research In The Pleistocene* 20 (2003): 61–63.

Orr, P.C. *Prehistory of Santa Rosa Island*. Santa Barbara Museum of Natural History, Santa Barbara, Calif. 2003.

Parenti, Fabio, Michel Fontugue, and Claude Guerin. "Pedra Furada in Brazil and its 'presumed' evidence: limitations and potential of the available data." *Antiquity* 704(1996): 16–421.

Pavlov, P., W. Roebroeks, and J. I. Svendsen. "The Pleistocene colonization of northeastern Europe: A report on recent research" *Journal of Human Evolution* 47 (2004): 3–17.

Petit, Charles W. 1998, Rediscovering America, *US News and World Report*, October 12, 1998: 56–64.

Pichardo, M. Valsequillo biostratigraphy II. Bison, tools, correlate with Tequixquiac: *Anthropologischer Anzeiger*. 57 (1999): 13–24.

———. "Redating Iztapan and Valsequillo, Mexico." *Radiocarbon*, vol. 42(2000): 305–310.

———. 2003, Overview of Central Mexican prehistory: Morphostratigraphy, chronostratigraphy, biostratigraphy: *Anthropologischer Anzeiger*. 61, no. 2, p. 141–174.

Pink Floyd 1994, "Keep Talking" (with Stephen Hawkings), *The Division Bell*. Sony

Reichelt, H., 1899 (1900), Fossile Bacillariaceen eines Kalktuffes aus Mexico, *Zeitschrift für angewandte Mikroskopie*, v. 5, no. 1, pp. 3–10.

Renfrew, Colin. *Before Civilization*, Alfred A. Knopf, New York: Alfred A. Knopf, 1973.

Renne, P., Feinberg, J. M., Waters, M. R., Arroyo-Cabrales, J., Ochoa-Castillo, P., Perez-Campa, M., Knight, K.B. "Age of Mexican ash with alleged 'footprints.'" *Nature* 438 (2005): E7–E8.

Reuters 1998. First Americans may have arrived 40,000 years ago. February 17, 1998 *www.cnn.com/TECH/9802/17/bering.strait.reut/* Accessed 2004.

Rice, John 2004. Debate Over Human Origins." In The Americas *http:// cnews.canoe.ca/CNEWS/Science/2004/10/03/654599-ap.html*; Accessed 2005.

Riley, C.L., J.C. Kelley, C.W. Pennington, R.L. Rands (eds.). *Man Across the Sea: Problems of Pre-Columbian Contacts*. Austin: University of Texas Press, 1971.

Rockets, Rusty 2005. Was The Missing Link A Tripping Chimp? *Science-a-Gogo*, 23 September 2005. *www.scienceagogo.com/news/food_for_thought.shtml* Accessed 2006.

Santos G. M., Bird M. I., Parenti F., Fifield L. K., Guidon N., Hausladen P. A. "A revised chronology of the lowest occupation layer of Pedra Furada Rock Shelter, Piauí, Brazil: the Pleistocene peopling of the Americas." *Quaternary Science Reviews* vol. 22 (2003): 2303–2310

Schuiling, W, ed. 1972. *Pleistocene Man at Calico*. San Bernardino County Museum Association, Bloomington, California.

———. 1979. *Pleistocene Man at Calico*. Second edition. San Bernardino County Museum, Redlands, California.

Schuster, Angela, 1999. Case of the Curious Cranium, Oct. 20, 1999, *Archaeological Institute of America www.archaeology.org/online/features/java/* Accessed 2003.

Scientific American Online, February 17, 2005. Fossil Reanalysis Pushes Back Origin of *Homo sapiens. www.sciam.com/article.cfm?articleID=00053DFE-C0B7-1213-80B783414B7F0000* Accessed 2005.

Semaw, S., M.J. Rogers, J. Quade, P.R. Renne, R.F. Butler, D. Stout, Dominguez-Rodrigo, W. Hart, T. Pickering, and S.W. Simpson. "2.6-Million-year-old stone tools and associated bones from OGS-6 and OGS-7, Gona, Afar, Ethiopia." *Journal of Human Evolution* 45 (2003): 169–177.

Shepard, Arnet. 2006. There's something fishy about human brain evolution. Natural Sciences and Engineering Research Council press release. *www.eurekalert.org/pub_releases/2006-02/nsae-tsf021706.php* Accessed 2006.

Shipman, Pat. "Doubting Dmanisi" *American Scientist*, November-December 2000 86(2000): 491ff; website, *www.americanscientist.org/template/AssetDetail/ assetid/23833* Accessed 2001.

Solórzano, Federico. A. 1989. "Pleistocene Artifacts from Jalisco, Mexico. A Comparison with Some Pre-Hispanic Artifacts." In: Bone Modification, ed. by. R. Bonnichsen and M.H. Sorg, pp. 499–514. *Orono: Peopling of the Americas Publications*, Center for the Study of the First Americans.

Sorenson, John and Martin H. Raich. *Pre-Columbian Contact with the Americas: An Annotated Bibliography*. Provo, Utah: Research Press, Provo, 1996.

Southern Poverty Law Center. 2002. The Propagandist 14 *Intelligence Report* Spring 2002 *www.splcenter.org/intel/intelreport/article.jsp?aid=136]* Accessed 2004.

Stanford, Dennis and Bruce Bradley. 2005. Constructing the Solutrean Solution. Clovis In The Southeast Conference: *Technology Time And Space*. October 26–29, 2005, Columbia, Metropolitan Convention Center, Columbia, South Carolina.

————.1977. *A Manual for Tephrochronology: Collection, Preparation, Petrographic Description and Approximate Dating of Tephra (Volcanic ash)*. Ph.D. thesis, University of Idaho, Moscow, printed privately by the author.

————. "Has man been in the New World for a quarter-million years?" *The Barnes Review*, IV(1998): 31–36.

————. 1998. "Suppressed evidence for ancient man in Mexico." *Nexus* August-September, 47–51.

Steen-McIntyre, Virginia, Roald Fryxell, and Harold E. Malde. "Geologic Evidence for Age of Deposits at Hueyatlaco Archeological Site, Valsequillo, Mexico." *Quaternary Research* 16 (1981): 1–17.

Stengel, Marc K. 2000. The Diffusionists Have Landed. *The Atlantic Monthly*, January 2000. *www.theatlantic.com/issues/2000/01/001stengel.htm* Accessed 2000.

Straus, Lawrence G. "Solutrean settlement of North America? A review of reality." *American Antiquity* 65 (2000): 2.

Stringer, C. Human Evolution: Out of Ethiopia. *Nature* 423 (2003): 692–695.

Stuiver, Minze. "Origins and extent of atmospheric 14C variations during the past 10,000 years," in *Radiocarbon Dating and Methods of Low Level Counting* (International Atomic Energy authority, Vienna, 1967: 27–42

Szabo, Barney J., Harold E. Malde, and Cynthia Irwin-Williams . "Dilemma Posed by Uranium-Series Dates on Archaeologically Significant Bones from Valsequillo, Puebla, Mexico" in *Earth and Planetary Science Letters* 6 (1969): 237–244.

Team Dmanisi. 2004. Lithic Assemblage. *www.dmanisi.org.ge/Lithics.htm* Accessed 2006.

Thieme, H. Lower Paleolithic hunting spears from Germany. *Nature* (1997): 385–807.

UC Berkeley. 2006 "Exaptations." *Understanding Evolution For Teachers* *http://evolution.berkeley.edu/evosite/evo101/IIIE5cExaptations.shtml* Accessed 2006.

VanLandingham, S. "Sangamonian Interglacial (Middle Pleistocene) Environments of Deposition of Artifacts at the Valsequillo Archeological Site, Puebla, Mexico." *Transactions of the 35th Regional Archeological Symposium for Southeastern New Mexico and Western Texas*, Southwest Federation of Archaeological Societies Annual meeting, April 9–11, 1999, Canyon, Texas, 81–98.

——. 2002 (abs) Sangamonian Age (80,000–220,000 B.P.) Artifacts at the Hueyatlaco Site, Puebla, Mexico. *Archaeological Society of New Mexico Annual Meeting*, May, 2002, Farmington, New Mexico.

——. 2003 (abs) Diatom biostratigraphy and paleoecology of Sangamonian Interglacial (sensu lato=80,000–ca. 330,000 yr BP) artifact bearing deposits in the Valsequillo region, Puebla, Mexico. *Third International Limnogeology Congress* Abstract Volume, Tucson, Arizona, 29 March–2 April, 2003.

——. "Diatom evidence for autochthonous artifact deposition in the Valsequillo region, Puebla, Mexico during the Sangamonian (sensu lato=80,000 to ca. 220,000 yr BP and Illinoian (220,000 to 430,000 yr BP)." *Journal of Paleolimnology* 36 (2006): 101–116.

Walter R.C., R.T. Buffler, J.H. Bruggemann, M.M. Guillaume, S.M. Berhe, B. Negassi, Y. Libsekal, H. Cheng, R.L. Edwards, R. von Cosel, D. Neraudeau, and M. Gagnon. "Early human occupation of the Red Sea coast of Eritrea during the last interglacial." *Nature* May 4, 405(2000): 24–5, 27

Waters, M.R., S. Forman, and J. Pierson. "Late Quaternary geology and geochronology of Diring Yuriakh: An Early Paleolithic site in central Siberia." *Quaternary Research* 51 (1999): 195–211

——. "Evaluation of the stratigraphy and age of Diring Yuriakh: a Lower Paleolithic site in central Siberia." *Current Research in the Pleistocene* 14 (1997): 87–89.

——. *Diring Yuriakh: A Lower Paleolithic site in central Siberia. Science* 275 (1997): 1281–1284

Webb, M.O., and Suzanne Clark. "Anatomy of an Anomaly." *Disputatio* 6 (1999): 3–8. *www.Disputatio.com/articles/006-1.pdf*

White, J.P. "Ethno-archaeology in New Guinea: Two examples." *Mankind* 6(1967): 409–414.

——. "Fabricators, Outils Ecaillès or Scalar Cores?" *Mankind* 6 (1968): 658–666.

Wikipedia 2006, "Roald H. Fryxell." *http://en.wikipedia.org/wiki/Roald_H._Fryxell* Accessed 2006.

Wilford, John. "Noble New Answers to an Old Question: Who Got Here First?" *New York Times* November 9, 1999.

Willey,Gordon G., Jeremy A. Sablof. A *History of American Archaeology*. San Francisco: W. H. Freeman, 1993.

World Today Archive Transcript Tuesday, 6 July, 1999; Fresh light shed on origins of man; *www.abc.net.au/worldtoday/stories/s33821.htm* Accessed 2006.

Xu, H. Mike 1996. *Origin of the Olmec Civilization*. University of Central Oklahoma Press. Cf. Mike's website *www.chinese.tcu.edu/www_chinese3_tcu_edu.htm* Accessed 2006.

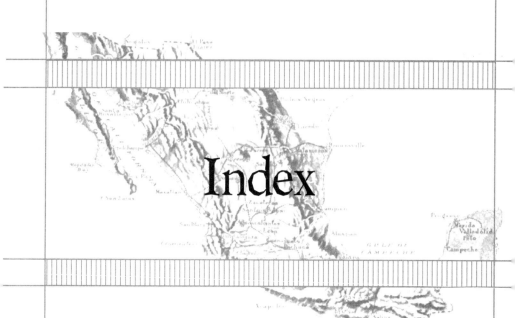

Index

A

Acheulean, 273, 283

Adovasio, James, 194, 228

Africa, 32, 147

Africa, human evolution and, 13

African Early Stone Age, 273

African Middle Stone Age, 271-276

Agenbroad, Larry D., 169, 282

Agogino, George, 186, 200-201

Aliens, 247-248

America Antiquity, 126, 128, 139, 161

American Heritage Book of Indians, The, 15

American Philosophical Society, 52, 60, 81, 117

Amomoloc, 67

Ancient Man in North America, 38

Anthropological Journal of Canada, 144

Aquatic Age Theory, 267

Archaeology, geology versus, 19, 88, 187

Archaeology, science vs., 156-173

Archeo-astronomy, 194

Argon, 147, 231, 236

Armenta Camacho, Juan, 14, 15-17, 18-22, 27-29, 30-40, 47-48, 52, 56, 60-86, 99, 100-104, 109, 130-131, 140, 143, 146, 158, 185, 189, 191, 212, 218, 221, 229, 284, 285

Armenta, Celine, 123, 195

Arroyo-Cabrales, Joaquin, 26, 203, 217-218, 223-226, 271, 283

Asia, 143

Asian tribes, 135

Atepitzingo, 153, 154, 157-158

Atlantic Monthly, 244

Australia, 137

Aveni, Anthony, 194
Aztec period, 36

B

Backfilling, 204
Baker, Adrian, 202, 203, 205, 209, 271
Baker, Larry, 189
Barnosky, Tony, 221
Barrance de Xochiac, 117-118
Bassett Point, 287
Becerra, 54
Bednarik, Robert, 263-264
Bell, R. E., 126, 161
Beringia, 249, 256
Berkeley Geochronology Lab, 231
Bernal, Ignacio, 43-44
Bhaktivedanta, 196
Bifacial thinning technology, 271
Bioturbation, 62
Bipolar flaking, 145, 255
Blackwater Draw, 41
Blade technology, 271-276
Blitzkrieg Scenario, 38
Boa Lesa, 261
Bonnichsen, Robson, 229, 230, 234, 239, 240, 282
Bopp, Monika, 43-44
Bordes, Francois, 51, 139, 177, 243, 279
Bradley, Bruce, 242-243
Brahmins, 144
Brain, human, 267
Brew, J. O., 25, 26, 108, 115, 126, 131, 188, 285
Brooks, Allison, 250, 272, 273-275
Brunet, Jean, 36, 153

Bryan, Alan, 227
Budinger, Fred, 287
Buena Vista lapilli, 179
Byers, Douglas S., 36

C

Calico Early Man Site, 138-139, 287
Calico, 149, 150, 167, 181, 200, 227, 249, 256, 262, 278, 279, 282
California Academy of Sciences, 211, 212
Calsequillo Reservoir, 287
Carbon 14, 16, 38, 39, 49, 82-83, 106, 110, 111, 112, 113-114, 138, 148, 151, 152, 153-155, 159, 173, 186, 226, 228, 286
Carter, George, 39, 137, 139, 144-146, 150, 157, 197-198, 200, 230, 239, 286, 287
Carterfacts, 144
Caulapan, Barranca de, 105-121, 127, 152, 153-155, 159, 173, 181, 186, 188, 201, 214, 217, 286
Chatters, R. M., 27
Climate, 66
Clovis culture, 9-11
Clovis First, 9-11, 16, 109, 110, 119, 142, 143, 144, 146, 155, 184, 188, 193, 194, 200, 227-229, 246, 271
Clovis technology, Solutrean technology and, 120
Clovis-Folsom techniques, 142
Clovisia, 186
Clovis-Solutrean connection, 243
Coe, Michael D., 36, 40
Colorado Scientific Society, 152
Columbus, Christopher, 198

Communism, 100, 101
Compton, Carl B., 122-123, 128
Cornwall, Ian, 36, 43-44, 45
Crabtree, Don, 243
Cramer, Joseph, 229, 230
Cramer, Ruth, 230
Creationists, 195-196
Cremo, Michael, 29, 195, 196, 197
Cruxent, J., 36
Cruz-Munoz, Valeria, 203, 223
Cudinger, Fred, 227
Cuicuilco Pyramid, 202
Cunnane, Stephen, 266-267
Current Research in the Pleistocene, 226

D

Darwin, Charles, 195
Dating shell, 113-114
De Anda, Luis Aveleyra Arroyo, 36
De Terra, Helmut, 36
Del Rio, D. Pablo Martinez, 35
Deloria, Vine, 195, 196
Dendrochronology, 148-149
Denver Museum of Natural History, 38, 49
Diatoms, 212, 231-236
Dillehay, Thomas, 228
Diring Yurick, 254, 255, 269
Disposable tools, 143
Dmanisi, 258, 267
DNA, 272-273
Donelik, Ray, 202
Dorenberh Skull, 210-214
Dumjitru, T. A., 202

E

E.T., 247-248
Earth And Planetary Science Letters, 170
El Horno, 67-71, 73, 79, 87, 99, 114, 115, 132, 152, 154, 157, 168,188, 201, 217, 240
El Mirador, 64-66, 73, 79, 114, 188, 201
Erlandson, Jon, 245
Evolution, 148, 195
Evolution, Africa and human, 13
Exaptation, 266

F

Fagan, Brian, 194, 251, 252, 256, 273
Fangs, 258-259
Farias, Sabrina, 203, 205, 207
Farley, Ken, 202
Feature blocks, 81-83
Fedje, Daryl, 245
Fedoseva, Svetlana, 254-255
Figgins, J.D., 49, 51, 82, 83, 131
Fingerprints of the Gods, 195
Firestone, Richard, 211, 243
Firing, 267
First International Symposium for Early Man in American, 227-228
Fission Track dating, 151, 180-184
Fladmark, Knut, 245
Flannery, Kent V., 36
Flooding, 62, 79
Flores Island, 260-261, 263, 265, 267, 276
Folsom techniques, 142
Forbidden Archaeology, 29, 195, 196, 197, 213

Foreheads, 251-252
Forman, Steve, 255
1421, 198
Friends of the Pleistocene, 168
Fryxell, Roald, 27, 176, 177, 184-185, 197, 207, 217, 236, 279-280, 285

G

Garcia, Princiliano, 203
Geology, archaeology versus, 19, 88, 187
Geology, Valsequillo and, 270-271
Georgia (Russia), 257-259
Glaciers, 151
Glass Fission Track dating, 151
Goebel, Ted, 230
Goles, Gordon, 27
Gomphothere, 15
Gonzalez, Alberto Rex, 36
Gonzalez, Silvia, 237-238
Goodyear, Al, 239, 243
Graham, Russ, 220
Great Journey, The, 194
Griesemer, Allan D., 149
Griffin, James, 110, 119
Gruhn, Ruth, 227
Guidon, Niede, 239
Guimpera, D. Pedro Bosh, 36

H

Hancock, Graham, 195, 196
Hayden, Julian, 229
Haynes, C. Vance, 41, 101, 127, 150, 169, 200, 229
Heston, Charleton, 195
Heyerdalh, Thor, 243

Hills, 134-137
Hindu orthodox, 196
Hiser, David, 46
Hobbit, 260, 262
Holliday, Vance T., 230
Holocene interglacial, 212
Hrdlicka, Ales, 82, 183
Hueyatlaco Ash, 10, 105, 174, 207, 209, 220, 226, 231, 237, 271
Hueyatlaco, 16, 22, 24, 26, 74-78, 79, 80, 85, 86, 87-99, 113, 119, 124, 152, 154, 157, 168, 174, 180, 188, 201, 202-209, 217, 222, 224, 227, 230, 240
Human brain, 267
Hustedt, F., 213

I

Ice Age, 14, 15, 25, 32, 38, 54, 82, 115, 243, 245
Ice-free corridor, 193, 228
Illinoian ice age 212
INAH *Boletin*, 122, 127
Irwin, Cora, 51
Irwin, Cynthia, 38, 48, 49-55
Irwin, Henry, 53
Irwin-Williams, Cynthia, 10, 18-22, 26, 58, 60-86, 87-89, 101-104, 106, 107, 108, 109, 112, 113, 122-130, 139, 141, 146, 153, 155,158, 160-168, 169, 170-173, 174, 177, 181, 184, 186, 187-189, 200-201, 204, 205, 207, 209, 217, 220, 226, 229, 240, 242, 243, 251, 271, 284, 285, 286
Isolationism, 198, 199, 244, 246

J

Javelins, 256-257
Jefferson, George, 220
Jomon, 199-200
Josselyn, Dave, 141-142
Journal of Human Evolution, 271, 272
Journal of Quarternary Research, 184, 185
Jurgens Cody site, 186

K

K/Ar technique, 147, 151, 180
Kapthurin Formation, 273-274
Kelle, Sally, 276
Kettle, Sarah, 276
Krieger, Alex D., 36, 41, 51, 52, 53, 54, 55, 84, 140, 143, 146, 282, 285

L

La Malinche, 47, 98, 105, 106
Lake Manix, 279
Law of Superposition, 66
Lawrence Berkeley National Laboratroy, 211
Leakey, Louis, 13, 15, 79, 81, 134-137, 138-139, 146, 147, 149, 150, 156-157, 181, 256, 272
Leakey, Mary, 13, 139, 147, 279
Leakey, Richard, 272
Learmonth, Blake, 247, 264, 265
Lee, Thomas (Tom), 144, 150
Lena Basin, 255
Levant, the, 273
Libby, 113
Liddicoat, Joseph C., 27, 220, 237
Lindenmeier Paleoindian site, 153
Lithic analysis, 145

Lorenzo, Jose Luis, 24-25, 28, 29, 42, 47-48, 54-55, 58, 98, 99, 100-104, 122-132, 163-164, 173, 174, 179, 204-207, 209, 214, 285

M

MacNeish, Richard S., 36, 84
Malde, Harold (Hal), 10, 27, 28, 47, 87, 88, 99, 105-114, 127, 151-152, 153, 157-163, 164, 168, 170-173, 174, 177, 181, 184-185, 188, 197, 207, 214, 220-221, 231, 237-238, 284
Maldonado-Koerdell, Manuel, 36, 54
Male, 179
Mandel, Rolfe, 230
Mandryk, Carole, 245
Martin del Pozzo, Ana Lillian, 19, 186, 200, 203, 226, 229, 237
Martin, Paul, 27, 109-110, 112, 113, 115
Mata Menge, 261
McAvoy, Joseph, 228
McBrearty, Sally, 250, 272, 273-275
McDougall, Ian, 272
McKinney, Bob, 24-26, 107, 207
Meggars, Betty, 199-200, 245
Mehringer, Peter H., 169
Meltzer, J. David, 230
Menzies, Gavin, 198
Mesoamerican archaeology, 122
Mexico, 40
Microencephaly, 262
Middle Stone Age, 272-276
Minckley, William, 112
Mirambell, Lorena, 24, 127
Mochanox, Yuri, 254-255
Mods, 252, 266
Mojave Desert, 134

Mojave Sink, 287

Montiel, Hector, 64-65

Mooser, Federico, 43-44, 45-46

Morocco, 263

Morwood, Mike, 261, 262

Muller-Beck, Hans Jurgen, 36, 140

Mysterious Origins of Man, The, 29, 195, 200

N

Naeser, Barney, 27

Naeser, Charles, 19, 177, 180, 182, 187, 197, 217, 284

National Anthropoligical Archives, 123

National Geographic Society, 138, 139, 281

National Geographic, 46

National Science Foundation, 22, 108, 117, 195

Native Americans, 143

Natural History, 186

Nature, 162, 169

NBC, 195, 200, 285

Neanderthals, 16, 25, 157, 187, 249, 250, 251, 252-253

Nebot, Edgar, 203

O

Occam's Razor, 11

Ochoa-Castillo, Patricia (Pati), 24, 203, 205, 226, 229, 231, 237, 271

Olduvai Gorge, 13, 14, 15, 19, 79, 81, 147-148, 149, 150, 151, 156-157, 180, 258

Olio-Pleistocene boundary, 44, 46

Olmec Civilization, 199

Onnichsen, Robson, 226, 227, 228

Orr, Phil, 137

P

Pacheco, Arturo Romano, 36

Paddock, John, 124-126

Paleoindian, 71

Paleolithic sites, 51, 157

Paleontology, 30-31, 159

Payn, Marshall, 22, 197-202, 229, 236-237, 286

Peabody excavations (1962), 60-86

Peabody Museum, 51, 117, 124

Pearson, Jr., P. J., 113

Pedra Furada, 234

Perez-Campa, Mario Antonio, 24, 202, 203, 204-205, 229

Peterson, Frederick, 36

PGAA, 211, 212

Pichardo del Barrio, Mario, 27, 103, 153, 214, 217, 218-219, 222, 274

Plate tectonics, 184

Pleistocene Age, 15, 43, 46-47, 54, 66, 73, 76, 109, 114, 127, 151, 213, 218, 243, 246, 258, 270, 284, 286

Pleistocene Formation, 79

Pleistocene Lake Manix, 124, 127

Pleistocene-Holocene boundary, 88

Popocatepetl, 47, 179

Porter, Steve, 185

Post-Genome Porject, 278

Potassium-Argon technique, 147, 151, 180, 231

Pre-Clovis, 9, 11, 54, 108, 109, 127, 146, 173, 200, 222, 229-230, 239, 244-245, 278, 282, 283

Prehistory, 277-278

Pre-Mod, 267, 268-269, 282, 283-284

Primary reduction techniques, 255
Protactinium, 153-154
Puebla Valley, 98, 99
Puebla, 24, 26, 30, 38, 39, 67, 87, 117, 212, 250, 284, 285
Punta de Furada, 193, 239

R

Radiocarbon, 110, 112, 117
Rancholabrean, 220
Ray, Clayton E., 27, 87, 88, 99, 103, 108, 113, 124, 158, 214, 284
Ray, Richard G., 108
Red Earth, White Lies, 195
Redeposition, 61-62, 75, 79, 214
Reduction techniques, primary, 255
Renne, Paul, 231, 236, 240, 271
Repenning, Charles, 218, 219-220
Rhodesia Man, 250
Richtmire, Philip, 259
Rio Alseseca, 56, 106
Rio Atepetzingo, 106, 117
Rio Atoyoc, 42, 85, 86
Roberts, Frank H. H., 52, 183, 257
Romano, Arturo, 43-44
Rosaire, Charles E., 36, 140
Rubin, Meyer, 27, 106, 108, 112, 118, 159

S

Sagan, Cark, 246
Salas, Guillermo, 127
San Bernardino County Museum, 137, 149
San Diego Museum of Man, 144, 282
Sangamon interglacial, 212
Schoningen, 256, 267
Schuster, Carl, 36, 140

Science, 150, 151, 162, 169, 255
Science, archaeology vs., 156-173
Seafaring, 193, 197, 263-265
Shang Dynasty, 199
Sheguindah, 144, 150, 256, 278
Shell, dating, 113-114
Siberia, 194, 195, 254-256, 269
Silk Road, 259, 283
Simpson, Ruth DeEtte (Dee), 36, 137-140, 149, 150
Smithsonian, 15, 52, 100, 199
Society for America Archaeology, 115, 128, 177, 201, 286
Solorzano, Federico, 238
Solutrean Solution, 243
Solutrean technology, Clovis technology and, 120
Solutrean-Clovis connection, 243
Southwestern Anthropological Association, 184
Spanish Civil War, 100
Stanford, Dennis, 25, 195, 200-201, 242-243, 245
Statigraphy, 66
Steen, Virginia, 99, 108
Steen-McIntyre, Virginia, 10-11, 27, 29, 105-114, 123, 177, 179-180, 184-185, 186, 195, 197, 200, 201, 202, 203-204, 210, 213, 214, 220, 227, 228, 231, 237, 284
Stengel, Marc, 244
Sterling, Rod, 264
Stone Age, 110, 264
Stone technology, 269
Stratigraphy, 147
Stringer, Christopher B., 257
Stuiver, Minze, 148

Sumbawa, 261

Sun King, 100-104

Szabo, Barney, 9, 27, 151-152, 157-158, 159, 160, 162, 164-168, 170-173, 181, 217, 236, 284

T

Tamers, M. A., 113

Tantavel Man, 238

Taphonomy, 279

Taylor, Dwight W., 27, 108

Tecacaxco, 45, 71-73, 79, 103, 114, 188, 201, 203

Technology, Clovis vs. Solutrean, 120

Teotihuacan, 202

Tephras, 10

Tetela Brown Mud, 177, 179, 180, 182

Tetela Peninsula, 32, 45, 81, 203

Tetela, 14, 16, 45, 66-78, 114, 117, 151, 152, 153, 189, 214

Texas Christian University, 199

Texas Street site, 146, 150

Thieme, Hartmut, 256-257

Thompson, Richard, 29, 195, 196, 213

Thorium, 153-154

Thorium-Uraniun dating, 132

Timreck, Theodore (Ted), 200

Tlapacoya, 26, 127, 131, 179-180

Toca de Esperanca, 193, 276

Toluquillo Tuff, 66

Tools, disposable, 143

Topper Site, 243

Tostado, D. Denen Sanchez, 37

Tree ring analysis, 148-149

Turner, George, 131-132

U

U.S. Geological Survey, 25, 118

UFOs, 264, 269

Upper Paleolithic, 236, 250-251, 252-253, 254, 271, 272, 276, 283

Uranium Series (U-Series), 16, 71, 152-155, 159-161, 163-167, 170-173, 180, 181, 217, 240, 281, 282, 285, 286

Uranium, 10

Usewear, 237

V

Valsequillo Formation, 44, 66-67, 72, 75, 85, 86, 99, 203, 222

Valsequillo Formation, fauna from the, 218-219

Valsequillo Gravels, 16, 33, 36, 46-47, 61, 66, 74, 79, 111, 117-118, 179, 209

Valsequillo project personnel, 26-27

Valsequillo Reservoir, 9, 27, 30,60, 64, 98, 117

Valsequillo, 9-11, 15, 17, 19, 56-58, 110, 127, 146, 147-155, 156, 163, 184, 185, 186, 187, 197, 199, 200, 214, 218, 221, 222, 239, 242, 248, 249, 251, 261, 267, 276, 279, 284, 285, 286

Valsequillo, geology and, 270-271

VanLandingham, Sam, 209, 210-214, 226, 231-236

Vestigios De Labor Humana En Huesos De Animales Extintos De Valsequilli, Puebla, 28

Villafranchian state, 44

W

Waters, Michael (Mike), 227, 228-229, 230, 231, 236, 237, 240, 255

Watts, James, 196

Wheat, Joe Ben, 186

Wild Horse Arroyo, 82

Willey, Gordon, 126, 183

Williams, David, 87

Wilson, Chuck, 24

Wisconsin ice age, 88, 144, 212, 238

Wormington, Hanna Marie, 18, 27, 35, 37-39, 41, 47, 51, 52, 53, 54, 55, 56, 84, 131, 132, 139, 146, 160-161, 163, 169, 174, 186, 188, 226, 229, 285, 286

Xalnene Tuff, 64, 66-67, 84, 203

Xu, Michael, 199, 245

Yellowstone National Park, 180

Zacachimalpa, 118

Zalnene Ash, 237-238

Zinj, 13, 14, 81, 149, 151, 258, 269, 272

About the Author

Christopher Hardaker earned an MA in anthropology from the University of Arizona and began working as a field archaeologist 30 years ago, dividing his research between the nature of stone tools and developing simple geometry into an archaeological tool to explore architectural traditions ranging from Chaco Canyon, New Mexico, to Washington, D.C. He first learned of the "professionally forbidden" older horizons of New World prehistory in 1977 on a visit to the Mojave Desert's Calico Early Man Site, established by the legendary Louis S. B. Leakey. It was there that he first heard the name Valsequillo. He is currently analyzing the astonishing 60,000-plus artifacts from Calico.